FADING CORPORATISM

Fading Corporatism

*Israel's Labor Law
and Industrial Relations
in Transition*

GUY MUNDLAK

ILR Press

AN IMPRINT OF
CORNELL UNIVERSITY PRESS
ITHACA AND LONDON

First published 2007 by Cornell University Press

Printed in the United States of America

Library of Congress Cataloging-in-Publication Data

Mundlak, Gai.
  Fading corporatism : Israel's labor law and industrial relations in transition / Guy
Mundlak.
    p. cm.
  Includes bibliographical references and index.
  ISBN 978-0-8014-4600-9 (cloth : alk. paper)
  1. Labor laws and legislation—Israel.   2. Industrial relations—Israel.   3. Corporate state—
Israel.   I. Title.
  KMK1220.M86 2007
  344.569401—dc22
2007018958

Cornell University Press strives to use environmentally responsible suppliers and materials to the fullest extent possible in the
publishing of its books. Such materials include vegetable-based,
low-VOC inks and acid-free papers that are recycled, totally
chlorine-free, or partly composed of nonwood fibers. For further
information, visit our website at www.cornellpress.cornell.edu.

Cloth printing   10 9 8 7 6 5 4 3 2 1

To Yaffa and Yair

Contents

Preface

This book surveys Israeli labor law from 1920 to the present. The process of writing and publishing a book does not always conform to the pace of events, particularly when the subject matter is contemporary history. The book is therefore updated until the end of 2005. References to court cases and events that began before 2005 were updated at the end of 2006. However, no developments since that time have been integrated into the text. In my opinion, no such event undermines the central argument of the book; several reinforce it.

Presenting a book in English that focuses on Israel's labor law presents many editorial dilemmas. Moreover, the book's claim is that Israeli law developed on the basis of continental European systems and is now adopting features of American law. Hence it is difficult to determine how to translate the law and how to convey a "feel" of the Israeli story. While providing a consistent method was the most important goal, I have also attempted to keep the book as simple and user-friendly as possible.

Generally, translation of legislation draws on State of Israel—Ministry of Labor and Social Affairs, *Labour Laws* (2000)—an unofficial publication of Israeli labor legislation, translated into English. This translation is also used by the International Labor Organization (ILO) in its NATLEX database. For reasons of consistency, I have usually adhered to the terminology of the law unless I found its terms to be exceptionally undesirable (in which case it is mentioned in a footnote). Where necessary there are explanations of the terminology in footnotes. For the most part, the terms chosen are based on internationally shared perceptions about the basic elements of labor law. However, the readers must bear in mind that there are always important differences among legal health law but also implied a considerable rewriting of labor law at the same time. The current state of affairs indicates that most legal references from more than ten years ago have become outdated.

The types of changes that can be deciphered upon a close reading of the Israeli legal system are more commonly apparent in transitional political regimes. Yet in Israel there was no political revolution. Although in 1977 the right-wing Likud Party ended the hegemony of the Labor Party, which had been in political control from the founding of the state in 1948, the transition was democratic and did not alter the basic political foundations of the state. Israel did not go through the processes of transition that have been characteristic of, for example, Eastern Europe. The political transformation also predated changes in labor law by at least a decade. Moreover, much of the newly protective labor law has been legislated during the years in which the right-wing party has ruled. It is therefore not possible to directly link changes in law with the left-right changes in the Israeli political map. A relationship exists, but there are too many gaps to be filled.

How, then, do we explain the extensive legal transition in Israel? There are two common ways of doing this. The first is to account for law's transition by drawing on legal reasoning. This type of explanation suggests, for example, that the changes in labor law are a result of changing jurisprudence. The Supreme Court has developed a jurisprudence that draws on values, purposes, and balancing-of-rights tests. Consequently, the law is more commonly phrased in terms of good faith, human dignity, reasonableness, public policy, and the like. Two basic laws on human rights were passed in 1992 and have been acknowledged to comprise a constitution in a state traditionally thought of as having none. The Supreme Court has extended the protection of human rights to the private sphere. All of these general changes affected labor law. This type of explanation, however, is not sufficient. It does not explain why many branches of the law have generally remained intact while labor law has changed. Moreover, the explanations fail because they are self-referential. They do not explain why the general principles changed as well. At a higher level of abstraction, these explanations conceive of all changes in law as being derived from within the legal system itself. They assume that the legal system is closed and that it develops its own rhetoric, logic, and structures. Changes may have taken place because some rules simply didn't work. Others rules were needed instead. These explanations assume that there are benchmarks by which to measure the outcomes of the legal system and decide when they should be replaced. These benchmarks may include consistency, clarity, preference for judicial discretion over rules, and the like. Yet this legalistic explanation is not really satisfying either. It does not explain why the previous regime of labor law no longer performed well enough? Where did it fail? Moreover, problems of consistency and clarity require only relatively technical adjustments in the law. Such changes hardly account for the scope of the change in labor law.

There are, of course, variations to this first type of explanation. For example, popular discourse tends to place emphasis on personalities. Many changes in labor law are often explained as a result of the changing composition of the Labor Court. The president of the National Labor Court resigned in 1997 and was replaced by one with different views and a different temperament. More sophisticated explanations explain changes in labor law by reference to changes in the general jurisprudence of Israel and point to the importance of Chief Justice Barak, the president of the Supreme Court in Israel, in inducing change. These explanations can probably account for one change or another, but they hardly succeed in capturing the complexity of transformation and the multiple agents involved in the process. They assume that the law is a one-person show. They don't explain, and in fact lack the tools to explain, whether these unique personalities could have achieved the same changes under differ-ent circumstances. They can't account for changes that take place outside the courtroom, and they ignore the role of the legislature. They are not satisfac-tory because they assume, just like the previous type of explanation, that the legal system can be explained by reference to the legal system itself. They are even more disconcerting than those previous explanations because they cannot be rigorously tested and are often more dependent on anecdote than on fact.

Unlike the law-centered explanation, there is an alternative type of explana-tion to the rapid rewriting of labor law, which is characterized by disregard, lack of interest, and even hostility toward the legal reasoning itself. These views are more difficult to characterize because in their external appearance they are usually silent about the law. There are books about transformation, books about society, and books about labor, in all of which the analysis hardly touches upon the legal rule. When law is mentioned, it is deemed to be exoge-nous to the study of economic, social, and political systems. It's not that any-one suggests that laws do not exist but only that law doesn't really matter. Law is held to be a passive reflection of market pressures, the electorate's power, and social processes. To understand law it is therefore necessary to study other systems. But once the study of other systems is undertaken, the study of law actually becomes no longer interesting in itself and is relegated to the lawyers, who can deal with law's internal logic and rhetoric in their quint-essential professional manner.

The two views of legal transformation are not really in tension with one an-other. They actually share a fundamental assumption. Both views relegate law to a separate sphere of inquiry. Gouging a strict divide between the legal and other social systems may be methodologically convenient but not convincing. To overcome this imposed division of labor, the fundamental premise of this book is that law is not simply a mirror of other processes, for it has also taken part in constituting them. Law and industrial relations are autonomous sys-tems, each with its own agents, institutions, modes of strategic interaction, and communications. The political and social systems have used law to strate-gically affect the nature of the industrial relations system that was being incre-mentally constructed. But law also reflected the range of strategic interactions among the agents of other systems, particularly the industrial relations sys-tem. The proposed explanation for the new labor law is therefore based on the *interaction* between the legal and the industrial relations systems, without assuming that one is exogenous to the other.

Juxtaposing law and industrial relations side by side allows another kind of explanation for the transformation that has taken place in both systems. The argument made in this book is that the rapid disintegration and current rewriting of labor law are a response to the collapse of what was (roughly) a corporatist regime. At the same time law also constituted the corporatist regime and took an active role in constituting the new system.

The original web of rules constructing Israeli labor law was developed for several decades from the foundation of a corporatist industrial relations system in pre-statehood Palestine until after the foundation of the Israeli state. At the peak of what is designated here as "corporatist labor law," sometime in the 1980s, the legal rules were intended to minimize legal intervention and entrench the autonomy of the social partners (i.e., trade unions and employers' associations). Law further supported and protected a unique system of interests representation that was characterized by centralization, concentration of interests, and the delegation of power from the state to the active associations in the industrial relations system. The corporatist model was therefore to construct "a law without law"—that is, a law based on the autonomous making of norms and not by means of state-authored instruments (laws and adjudication).

A second phase of labor law began in the late 1980s; this book takes the year 1987 to be the pivotal year, although any single date is probably artificial and oversimplified. In 1987 the Minimum Wage Law was passed after more than ten years of political deliberations, expropriating the determination of a national minimum wage from collective bargaining. Soon thereafter other legal developments followed. The second phase of labor law came in tandem with the gradual decline of the Israeli corporatist system, and a mismatch became apparent. The corporatist nature of the Israeli system faded. Membership rates in trade unions and the coverage of collective agreements declined. Collective bargaining became decentralized, and the concentration of interests representation that prevailed in the past was no longer sustained. The declining role of collective agreements was compensated for by a growing use of regulation and by the lively intervention of nongovernmental organizations in the struggle over regulation. The corporatist system was gradually replaced by a pluralist alternative.

The labor law that was devised to entrench the corporatist system was no longer adaptable and did not respond to the problems that arose once the centralized and autonomous making of norms was no longer regularly negotiated. At this stage, the state-centered authors of labor law—most notably the legislature, courts and executive branch—as well as new agents in civil society, started an intensive phase of rewriting labor law. It was quite clear that the decline of the corporatist system not only rendered labor law at that time inappropriate but also made planned reform impossible. To compensate for the decline of corporatism, legal arrangements were expected to provide a new set of agreed-upon, acceptable, and suitable norms. Yet the same causes underlying the decline of the corporatist agreement also prevented negotiations over a general social pact to guide reform. Labor law was therefore rewritten piecemeal, without a unified agenda and by numerous agents.

Unlike the first phase of labor law, which sought to *entrench* corporatism, the second phase sought to *construct* a new system. In this process, the objectives of labor law have changed. What seems to be a dense web of incremental developments is actually more than just a quantitative change. The second phase of labor law is qualitatively different because it provides a different concept of law and its relation to other social systems, most notably the industrial relations system. The previous legal regime sought to a great extent to isolate industrial relations from legal rules and entitlements and to leave the definition of rights and duties to the social partners. The current system is based on stricter, far-reaching, and intrusive legal rules that govern individuals as well as the social partners. Law was transformed from a *facilitative* into a *governing* instrument.

The decline of the Israeli corporatist structure was relatively rapid. The current system is transitory in nature and therefore defies simple classifications, and it certainly contradicts any simple thesis regarding the convergence of labor regulation in the global village. It is, however, a fascinating laboratory for transformation, as the relatively rapid pace and nature of decline highlight differences between systems. From a legal system that was based on instruments and premises characteristic of corporatist and semicorporatist regimes that prevail in continental Europe, Israeli labor law has turned to rapidly adopting institutions molded in American law. The Israeli laboratory allows a comparison that is usually difficult to make. The cleavage between the American and Swedish systems, for example, allows only a limited scope of comparison, unlike extensive comparisons that can be made between similarly designed systems such as those of the United States and Canada or the Netherlands and Belgium. However, the comparison between the polarized corporatist and pluralist models of labor law in Israel is feasible because the changes took place in the same country over a relatively short period of time.

While the case study of Israel has comparative implications that extend beyond Israel's borders, it is also strongly rooted in local history, society, and the political economy. The discussion of labor law in this book is not intended to be a comprehensive treatise on the subject. It follows a selective approach that seeks to highlight particular features that are instructive even for those who are not interested in law per se. It chooses various cases, statutes, and other legal instruments that can shed light on society.

Labor law serves multiple roles in this scholarly analysis of transformation. First, labor law is akin to a variable that is being explained. As argued at the outset, labor law did not change because of changes in the legal system but because of changes in the industrial relations system. Second, labor law is studied as an important instrument for mobilizing change. The study of how corporatism was replaced cannot ignore the changing structure of law. Third, labor law is also a social text. It substantiates nonlegal claims that are often difficult to demonstrate. For example, when scholars and participants in popular debates refer to the growing individualism that has taken hold in Israel, such statements are often supported by very impressionistic accounts. Some of these statements sound like a longing for better days. Yet a careful reading of the law provides a rich text from which social values can be deciphered. All three references to "the law" are developed throughout this book.

The Functions of Labor Law

To serve the multiple references to law, "labor law" here is defined broadly to include all legal instruments that affect the labor market. It can be argued that such a broad definition is overinclusive, as many legal rules have a direct or indirect impact on the labor market. A change in the general law of contracts, constitutional law, or tax policy can have a significant effect on the contractual component of labor law. However, because this book does not provide a comprehensive discussion of all labor law, the expansive scope is valid as it does not limit the discussion a priori to any particular, potentially underinclusive classifications of labor law. Labor law is not defined on the basis of a particular ideological justification ("all laws that protect workers"; "laws that remedy market failures"), nor is it defined technically as drawing only on legal instruments that are explicitly intended to reform the rules applying to the labor market ("statutory labor standards"). Instead I include within labor law any kind of regulation that is instrumental to its functions. At a high level of generality, labor law has three functions. These are independent of the type of industrial relations system and are in my view applicable to labor law in all regimes. They are therefore used here as an organizing (but not explanatory) device that helps to unfold and present the many tiers of transformation.

The first function of labor law is to define where the regulation of labor takes place: in the private or public spheres or in civil society. This is labor law's metalevel. It determines which system of norms prevails when several systems compete. Law determines whether collective agreements prevail over individual contracts and how statutes apply to both. It can also determine the relationship between norms that are negotiated at the sector level and those determined at the workplace level. The substantive content of collective agreements, contracts, and statutes is of lesser importance for this preliminary task of labor law. What matters most for the metalevel is who decides the norms, how they are decided, and how norms and agents interrelate. The second function is to mark the borders of power in the relationship between workers, whether as individuals or as organized groups, and employers (again—individuals and associations). This is often deemed to be the central role of labor law. The third function of labor law is to mark the borders of power between workers and other workers, be they individuals or groups—whether they are working at present, have worked in the past (pensioners), or are unemployed. The third function is often presented as an insiders-outsiders problem but is generally not placed on the same level as the second. In this book all three tasks are viewed as equally important for the study of labor both in itself and as an explanatory framework for transition in other systems, and for reading labor law as a social text. The only caveat is that a methodological reading requires starting with the first task, as it lexically precedes the other two. Unless one understands the legal choices made at the metalevel, it is difficult to identify the relevant sources of law used to fulfill the other two functions.

The general functions are not addressed in the same manner in all countries. A legal regime defines more particular objectives to fulfill the three functions, and these serve as a guideline for the development of the particular institutions. These objectives are at the center of this discussion. For example, in the corporatist phase the first function was designed to ensure the supremacy of the collectively negotiated norm over all other norms (markets and statutory standards). After the decline of the corporatist regime, the objective of labor law was to strengthen both contractual and statutory norms over the collectively negotiated norms. Some legal instruments were found to be conducive to accomplishing these objectives in the corporatist system (e.g., extension orders and derogation arrangements) while others were tailored to the pluralist system (e.g., greater statutory and adjudicative intervention by means of flexible legal terms, such as "good faith").

It is argued that the different objectives and legal institutions used in the corporatist and pluralist phases of labor law are more than a coincidental conjuncture of legal rules. In both phases, the objectives and the institutions used to fulfill them displayed a very clear and coherent logic. In the corporatist phase, labor law's objectives addressed the first function by granting autonomy to the social partners to negotiate social affairs at the level of civil society. This required a number of supportive legal institutions. First of these was the minimal intervention of law by means of mandatory employment standards in law. The initiative for the few laws that were passed usually came from the social partners, who viewed the statutory formalization of norms, which had already been established in collective bargaining, as beneficial to their own interests. At the same time, the law ensured that collectively bargained standards superseded individual negotiations, rendering individual contract law less important. Given the objective of labor law regarding its first function, there was little need for law to fulfill the other two functions. The social partners were given the power to determine for themselves the legitimate use of power within the industrial relations system, and matters of inclusion and exclusion were determined by means of collective agreements. It was therefore the first function, with its preference for leaving the governance of the labor market to autonomous self-regulation, that explains the almost total absence of law in the fulfillment of the other two functions. This is the notion of corporatist labor law—to construct law that minimizes the role of law itself.

In the second phase, roughly from 1987 onward, the corporatist objectives that facilitated negotiations on the basis of class at the level of civil society were no longer appropriate. Labor law was designed to entrench centralized of the state in collective bargaining, and the gradual writing of an employees' bill of rights. Chapter 7 describes the transition in labor law with regard to the third function—that is, the relationship between workers, as individuals and groups, and other workers. The discussion of this often neglected function of labor law draws on two major examples—the legal treatment of foreign workers and the debate on the legal regulation of temporary work agencies.

Although the book tells a local story of change, its implications extend beyond the Israeli experience. Part 4 of this book seeks to generalize on a comparative and theoretical level. Chapter 8 draws on the findings of the Israeli experience to contrast the different objectives of corporatist and pluralist labor law in other countries. Chapter 9 further attempts to abstract from the Israeli situation by observing more broadly the relationship between law and industrial relations. Instead of focusing on one or the other, as was demonstrated at the outset to be the more common approach, it emphasizes the relationship between the two. This provides a possibility of bridging legal and industrial-relations scholarship and avoiding mutual assumptions of exogeneity.

Part I

CORPORATISM

and/or attitude representation, a particular modal or ideal type institutional arrangement for linking associationally organized interests of civil society with the decisional structures of the state" (Schmitter 1974, 86). The main hallmark of corporatism in the governance of the labor market in particular and the broader social and economic spheres in general is extensive negotiations between well-organized groups of labor and capital (employers), with the state actively involved (Teulings and Hartog 1998; Streeck and Schmitter 1985; Katzenstein 1984; Schmitter 1974). These negotiations are conducted by means of collective bargaining agreements that are set at levels higher than the single enterprise, usually at the industry, regional, and state levels. Some agreements are elevated to the level of social pacts among the three agents representing labor, employers, and the state. Their coverage is broad, and they commonly have a mandatory effect that makes them more powerful mechanisms than merely voluntary guidelines and recommendations. The power of corporatism therefore derives from the construction of social consensus based on the principle of bipartite and tripartite negotiations. Corporatism is viewed as a midlevel governance system to be distinguished from the hierarchical power of the state and from private ordering, that is, individual-based market transactions.

To understand the unique features of corporatism as a system of interests representation, it is useful to identify its "other." The alternative to corporatism posed in the literature is "pluralism" (Schmitter 1977, 1989). Pluralism is strongly associated with private ordering but need not imply an unfettered market environment. A pluralist system displays rules that govern the labor market, but these emerge from a different system of interests representation. Trade unions are assimilated to other interest groups, and while employers' associations are rare, they are viewed as other organizations of business. The pluralist system recognizes collective bargaining but does little in terms of promoting it, treating it as a voluntary exchange between associations. Corporatism's emphasis on concentration and centralization in representing interests is not on the pluralist state's agenda. This does not deny the associations the possibility to advance coordination, but without the state's support such an objective is difficult to attain. As a result, collective negotiations are for the most part decentralized and conducted at the enterprise level. Thus the pluralist system is a system that strongly preserves the nature of free exchange and admits collective bargaining to the extent that it is desired by the workers and employers as individuals. Pluralism acknowledges the importance of legislation and the setting of substantive labor standards, but regulation is based on the relative power of political parties and the power of interest groups. Regulating labor does not assume any uniquely designed scheme.

Pluralism is presented as corporatism's "other" because it is easier to administer. It is based on liberties (such as the liberty of workers to associate and the liberty to vote) and not on the state's positive endorsement of rights and powers to specially designated social partners. When corporatist institutions fade, pluralism remains as the default. Corporatism is a project that requires construction, while pluralism is a project that already exists. Hence, corporatism is often measured and studied, but pluralism is merely assumed. By comparison with the "normality" of pluralism, the logic and institutional design of corporatism seems particularly complex.

It has been argued that the distinction between pluralism and corporatism is overstated and, at most, a caricature or an "ideal type" of two positions situated on a continuum, neither appearing in reality in its pure form (Bobacka 2001, 20–24; Cox 1988). Indeed, when posing corporatism and pluralism as two sides that frame this project, it is clearly impossible to assign to each of the two terms a precise set of definitions and institutional examples. Instead, they should be treated as push-and-pull forces that mold the choice of institutions for governing the labor market. Assuming the more general view of corporatism, it is necessary to identify its core components (and by reversing them, the core components of pluralism as well). There are two ways to characterize corporatism. The dominant method is to identify it on the basis of its institutions. A secondary approach is to observe corporatism's substantive outputs. This chapter surveys the fundamental institutions and norms associated with corporatism, with an emphasis on the former. With regard to both, the description is not intended to resolve methodological or theoretical questions but to illustrate the fundamental dilemmas associated with the corporatist design of governance. As will be demonstrated later, the institutional response to these dilemmas was at the core of the corporatist labor law that developed in Israel. The fading of the corporatist system in Israel awoke the dormant pluralist alternative.

The Institutional Design of Corporatism

On the basis of the general description of corporatism, it is possible to outline a number of fundamental features that comprise the corporatist structure. These features can be grouped into three interrelated categories: corporatist associations and the principle of state recognition, the internal organization of the associations ("internal characteristics"), and the interaction between them ("relational characteristics").

Associations

At the core of the corporatist system are associations situated between the private and the public spheres, which are also distinguished from other voluntary communities and groups that function in civil society. Streeck and Schmitter (1985) propose that corporatism is based on associations that, in their more perfect form, can be characterized as "private interest governments," "agencies of regulated self-regulation," or "the public use of private organized interests." The prominent associations that comprise the corporatist system represent the that corporatism would prefer to silence.[10] It has therefore been suggested that corporatism does not necessarily make strikes unnecessary but merely changes their nature and objectives.

The second relational feature of corporatist institutions is the requirement that collective agreements will be mandatory, binding on all parties, and extended to regulate broad segments of the population. This requirement distinguishes corporatism from the view that collective relations are merely voluntary and nonenforceable (as was the case in the United Kingdom). Corporatism views the negotiations' outcomes as a substitute for legislation. Hence, the outcomes of negotiations must be binding in order to avoid individual derogations from the agreements that are shaped by the relative market power of the parties in individual transactions. Such derogations undermine the collective nature of arrangements and their role in the decommodification of an individual's status and well-being. This is a feature that generally appears in most systems of industrial relations, but its importance in corporatism is augmented because of the central role of bargaining, the comprehensive scope of issues relegated to the sphere of social negotiations, and the distance between the bargaining agents and individuals. Consequently, the negotiations' outcomes appear as binding as state laws to individual workers and firms. This application deviates from the law of contract, which holds obligations to be the product of individual consent.

Various measures may be employed to achieve comprehensive coverage by collective agreements. It is possible to distinguish between measures that seek to ensure comprehensive coverage within the unit of bargaining and those that seek to extend coverage beyond the natural bargaining sphere (EIRO 2002). The former include, for example, laws that mandate the application of agreements to members of the signatory union, as well as to members of other unions and nonmembers. A similar outcome can be reached by the signatories' consent to compulsion as a means of inducing the employer to extend agreements to all the employees, or by employers' voluntary application of the agreements to all employees regardless of membership status. By contrast, extension orders, whether issued by the legislature or the executive branch, apply the agreements to employers who are not members of an employers' association and to their employees.[11] Consequently, such employers lose the advantage of opting out of the representative organizations taking part in

10. The Israeli case demonstrates this trend well. There are, however, other examples, such as Italy, where wildcat strikes emerged to contest the abolition of the *scala mobile* (Baccaro 2003, 12).

11. The common practice of issuing "awards" that characterized the unique nature of industrial relations in Australia and New Zealand in the past was also consistent with the objective of extending collective agreements beyond the domain of bargaining. The logic of extension can also be identified in the method of wage setting in the United Kingdom, through wage councils. While none of the three countries mentioned here can be classified as corporatist per se, it has been acknowledged that they sustained elements of centralized bargaining of a corporatist nature.

corporatist negotiations. It should be noted that corporatist extension of coverage results from the external (to the social partners) extension of a particular collective agreement, rather than the voluntarily use of one agreement as a model for others, as is the case in pluralist pattern bargaining (Katz 1993).[12]

The relatively rigid requirement that agreements should be broadly applicable, mandatory, and binding, can be contrasted to the less rigid framework constructed for negotiations. A comprehensive ordering of the labor market through collective negotiations can be achieved if there is a very broad voluntary membership (e.g., when membership is motivated by the Ghent system) and a lesser level of intervention by the state in extending coverage of agreements beyond the voluntary unit. Alternatively, a low level of membership requires a high degree of external intervention to ensure a corporatist level of coverage. Broad voluntary membership is deemed more desirable because it attenuates the state's need to use power (i.e., law) to intervene in the ordering of the labor market. A high level of state intervention to ensure broad coverage may undermine the premises of corporatism. This is best demonstrated by the case of France, where fewer than 10 percent of the workers are trade union members but the coverage of collective agreements extends to over 90 percent (Flanagen 1999). This is but one of many phenomena, on account of which France has been deemed an example of statism rather than corporatism.

The Outcomes of Corporatist Systems

The general definition of corporatism, thus far, has been procedural or structural in nature. Corporatism implies governance by means of negotiations and consensus building among singular, centralized, state-recognized associations representing labor and employers. This structural definition omits the substantive outcomes resulting from negotiations. However, corporatism has also been associated with various substantive norms, such as wage compression, wage restraint, low levels of unemployment, and lower levels of inequality.

Must corporatism be defined on the basis of these outcomes (Cox 1988)? One answer holds that corporatism need not be associated with any one substantive outcome. One of the premises of the corporatist system is that associations negotiate their own norms. There is no one particular norm that can serve as a benchmark for the corporatist system. An alternative response suggests that the nature of corporatist negotiations necessarily requires the prevalence of low unemployment because high levels of unemployment imply a

---

12. Pattern bargaining designates a situation in which the trade union selects one employer with whom negotiations are conducted, followed by an attempt to replicate the collective agreement to other employers in consecutive bargaining rounds. The distinction between corporatist arrangements for broad application of agreements and pluralist pattern bargaining is not clearcut. The German IG Metall's prominent role in wage bargaining for many years can be viewed as a hybrid of pluralist pattern bargaining and a nonformal method of corporatist wage coordination.

dualist market and a failure of corporatist associations to advance broad interests, rather than the narrow interests of the associations' members. Consequently, failure to achieve this particular outcome is indicative of a systemic failure in the structural design of the corporatist system. This latter response suggests a type of reflective equilibrium between the characteristics of the process and its substantive outcomes.

What is the range of norms associated with corporatism? There has been a surge of theoretical and empirical literature on corporatism, starting in the early 1980s, pointing to corporatism's strengths and weaknesses. Although the literature is sometimes inconclusive and the empirical studies are open to criticism for their choice of typology in identifying corporatist regimes (Flanagan 1999, 1150–75; Leertouwer and de Haan 2002), it is nevertheless instructive for assessing the range of substantive norms associated with corporatism.

Corporatism and Wage Restraint

One line of studies ties corporatism and the centralization of collective bargaining with wage restraint. When unions act collectively, they accept greater wage restraint than they would otherwise concede if acting independently (Moene, Wallerstein, and Hoel 1993). It is assumed that the bargaining agents, especially when conducting negotiations in coordination with the state, are better informed about the macroeconomic conditions and are more capable of assessing the consequences of various policy options. It is further argued that corporatist institutions enable wage setters to avoid the various negative externalities driven by wage bargaining on behalf of small groups (Crouch 1985; Bruno and Sachs 1985; Calmfors and Driffil 1988; Soskice 1990). Lars Calmfors (1993, 161) summarizes various types of negative externalities that have been proposed in the literature. The externalities are derived from the rising labor costs for employers in collective negotiations and are consequently distinguished by the agents who bear the rising costs: consumers, other producers, the economy, investors, and other employers competing for the same labor force. Of special significance is the externality that is imposed on other workers. This may take the form of increased unemployment or an "envy externality" resulting from workers' intersubjective assessment of wages, or from the need to restructure efficiency-wage arrangements. Consequently, centralized bargaining avoids raising wages for one group without considering the effects on other groups, such as consumers or workers.

Both explanations for the alleged relationship between corporatist structures and wage restraint have been contested. A critique of these arguments can take one of two forms. The stronger version is that corporatist negotiations do not provide the benefits attributed to corporatism. The weaker version holds that these benefits are related to corporatist systems but to other systems as well. The first critique holds that while corporatist associations have better information regarding macroeconomic performance, they suffer from the same problem that governments have regarding the absence of information on preferences at lower levels. Thus, information advantage on one level may be offset by information disadvantage at another. To demonstrate the second type of critique, Calmfors and Driffil (1988) make the argument that both highly centralized and decentralized systems fare well in terms of wage restraint, as opposed to systems in which wage bargaining is conducted at the midlevel (namely, the industry level). This type of critique is less detrimental to the values associated with corporatism because it only holds that with regard to this specific norm (wage restraint) corporatism is not the only system to yield such results. Generally, the relationship between the centralization of bargaining and wage restraint has been empirically demonstrated in either its strong (exclusive relationship) or weak (corporatism is one of the systems associated with wage restraint) versions (Calmfors 1993, 179–80).

Corporatism and Full Employment

Wage restraint is not only an end in itself; it is also correlated with the objective of full employment (Flanagen, Soskice, and Ulman 1983). This is merely an extension of the externalities problems noted above, yet it has been asserted to be one of the most important outcomes of corporatist bargaining. Given that a rise in wages can have adverse effects on employment levels, centralized bargaining is constrained by employment targets. On one side of the bargaining table, centralized unions continue to represent the unemployed and therefore internalize their interests as well. On the other side of the table, employers opt for wage restraint and higher employment levels, especially when raising wages would require them to initiate layoffs. The internalization of the negative externality caused by unemployment therefore helps to overcome the "insiders-outsiders" problem, which pervades labor market governance by institutions (Lindbeck and Snower 1988). The evidence regarding the relationship between the centralization of wage setting and unemployment demonstrates the weaker thesis, according to which the centralization of wage setting is one way of promoting low levels of unemployment. As in the general discussion of wage restraint, the alternative method is highly decentralized bargaining—shaped for the most part by market forces with little institutional interference—or (less effectively) enterprise-based bargaining (Layard, Nickell, and Jackman 1991; Moene and Wallerstein 1995).

Corporatism and Equality

The association of corporatist systems with equality has also been demonstrated. This stems from several factors. First, wage equality derives from the higher levels of wage compression (or lower levels of wage dispersion) that have been demonstrated to be correlated with corporatist arrangements (cf. Freeman 1988; Agell and Lommerud 1992; Rowthorn 1992). Unlike the ambiguous evidence regarding wage restraint, the data consistently indicate that

2   The Israeli Variant of Corporatism

The study of Israeli law and industrial relations, which is presented in detail in the following chapters, advances the proposition that law and industrial relations were situated in a corporatist equilibrium, which gradually disintegrated, giving way to an emerging pluralist equilibrium. Labor law initially was designed to uphold, stabilize, and entrench the corporatist regime that developed in Israel from the pre-statehood period until the 1980s. Later, when the corporatist system started to disintegrate, labor law had to be rewritten to construct a new industrial relations system. The many changes in labor law are therefore embedded in social and economic institutions. Moreover, law played a role in constructing these institutions to begin with. While this book focuses mostly on the law, the explanatory framework for the discussion is the distinction between corporatism and pluralism The particular developments in law and industrial relations presented here have been chosen to illustrate this dichotomy.

The legal and industrial relations systems are embedded in the historical, cultural, and economic features of Israel. It is therefore important to adapt the general and rather theoretical distinction between corporatism and pluralism to the Israeli reality. Arguably it is also necessary to justify the relevance of the distinction to Israel, as some have argued that Israel's system in the past was never strictly corporatist (Shalev 1992; Grinberg 1991; Chermesh 1993), and it seems that any account of the present state of affairs, whether corporatist or pluralist, is likely to be even more controversial. This chapter is intended to provide a brief overview of the rise and fall of the Israeli corporatist regime.[1]

---

1. The task of presenting an industrial relations system is a difficult one, and it has been confronted in different ways by various textbooks and monographs, particularly those that present comparative overviews of systems (cf. Ferner and Hyman 1998; Visser and Russeveldt 1996).

The analysis corresponds to some of the salient features of the corporatist/pluralist distinction that were presented in the previous chapter. It seeks to justify the relevance of the corporatist/pluralist framework and to describe the transition from corporatism to pluralism in the industrial relations system. However, as the presentation confirms, the Israeli case was not a paradigmatic example of corporatism, and at present it is not a classic representation of pluralism either.

Like the discussion in chapter 1, the presentation here is split into two types of characteristics. In the first part I observe the institutions of the industrial relations system, with particular emphasis on the General Histadrut, around which the system as a whole evolved. In the second part I observe three salient areas in which corporatist partners are assumed to produce distinct policies—centralized collective bargaining at the national level with (almost) universal applicability, limited use of industrial action, and efforts to promote full employment and equality. In both parts, I show how the eradication of corporatist characteristics, warped as they were to begin with, led to the decline of the corporatist system. In the third part of this chapter I engage directly with the argument that the Israeli system was not corporatist, and while I agree with the critics, I still read their work and arguments as an affirmation of the chosen framework and as a guideline for the discussion that follows. The chapter concludes with a short summary of the explanations for the transition from corporatism to pluralism in Israel, opening the door to a broader discussion of the role of law in the transformation.

From Corporatist to Pluralist Agents

In Israel the industrial relations system represents the interests of three groups: labor, employers, and the state.

Labor: To unfold the particularities of the Israeli variant of corporatism, it is necessary to start with the labor side of the triangle. Perhaps the most important and idiosyncratic feature of the Israeli system of industrial relations was the dominance of the General Histadrut. Commonly described as a federation of trade unions, the General Histadrut was actually constituted and later recognized by law as a primary organization from which trade unions evolved. However, the General Histadrut was much more than just a trade union—it was also the provider of many social services as well as an important political player. Although it was not the sole representative of labor, it was the dominant player in the past and remains so in the present, albeit to a lesser extent. Besides the General Histadrut, only a handful of trade unions participated in the industrial relations system.

Employers: Employers' associations were extremely weak before statehood and only at a relatively late stage did they grow into meaningful agents in the

---

For the sake of manageability, the description in this chapter does not seek to encompass an encyclopedic survey of the Israeli system (cf. Ben-Israel 2002b).

industrial relations system. During the first two decades after statehood their weakness and fragmentation were partially a result of the fact that the largest employer, other than the state, was the General Histadrut itself. The Histadrut therefore affected both labor's and the employers' sides. However, over time the private-sector employers succeeded in coordinating their activities, and in 1967 they established the Federation of Israeli Economic Organizations (FIEO). This is a federation of approximately fifteen employers' associations, including all the major employers' associations in Israel.

The state: The State of Israel was founded in 1948. However, organized industrial relations predated statehood. The discussion in the following chapter begins with the establishment of the General Histadrut in 1920. During the years 1920–1948 the British Mandate ruled in Palestine and was designated as the government. In addition, there were organizations on both the Arab and Jewish sides that governed their respective communities. Since 1948, the state has been limited to the formal governmental structure. However, even since statehood, the state is hardly a unified agent. As will be demonstrated, its various branches (legislature, executive, and the judiciary) play different, and sometimes conflicting, roles. Moreover, the state is entrusted with multiple tasks—the regulator, the largest employer, and an active partner in bargaining rounds.

Whether labor or employers carry more weight in industrial relations is a controversial question in the industrial relations literature. It seems that while at first the emphasis was on the trade unions, over time there has been a shift toward an emphasis on the role of business (Hall and Soskice 2001). However, undoubtedly the key to understanding Israeli industrial relations in the past—as well as their present condition—lies in the position of the General Histadrut.

Labor

MAPPING LABOR'S REPRESENTATIVES

In the past, Israel evinced an almost anomalous, extremely high level of concentration. The central organization representing labor's interests is the General Histadrut.[2] It is difficult to characterize the Histadrut. Any description is likely to be controversial and embedded within a broader controversy over the early days of the labor movement in Palestine and Israel and over the substance behind the concept of constructive socialism, state building, and nationalism (cf. Sternhell 1995; Shapira 1997). Clearly it is more than just a federation of trade unions. For simplicity's sake, it can be regarded as a trade union itself, but for many years it was also a social and national movement and has even been characterized as a "state within a state." Most trade unions

---

2. The name of the General Histadrut has changed several times over the years since its foundation. I will therefore use the term "General Histadrut" consistently throughout this book, regardless of the period of time in reference. The word "Histadrut" standing alone refers to the General Histadrut. Other trade unions (such as the National Histadrut—the General Histadrut's rival—or the Engineers' Histadrut—an organ within the General Histadrut) will be referred to by their specific names.

in Israel, as well as other entities representing labor such as regional councils, were all organs of the mammoth General Histadrut. At its peak it organized more than 80 percent of Israel's workers, and over 90 percent of the organized workers in Israel (Cohen et al. 2004).

Unlike the difficult task of cutting through the many layers of the Histadrut, the mapping of labor's representatives outside it is a simple one. Until the 1940s there were various local trade unions that were under the auspices of the General Histadrut, but some actually predated it. From the 1940s, most trade unions were organs of the Histadrut, with few exceptions. The external trade unions can be divided into two groups. The first included unions affiliated with political and social movements but whose role in the industrial relations system (i.e., engaging in collective bargaining) was marginal: the National Histadrut, which organized workers from the right wing of the Israeli political map, and the Mizrachy Histadrut, which organized religious-Zionist workers. A third, very small histadrut was that of the ultraorthodox, non-Zionist workers (Pagi). Of the three, only the National Histadrut remained a relevant agent.[3] A second group of external unions was the trade unions that represented small groups of professional workers, with no ambition to expand to other occupations and no pretension of being a social movement. These included the High School Teachers Union, the Physicians Union, the Journalists Union, and the University Academics Unions. The primary school teachers were sometimes partially outside the General Histadrut, sometimes partially inside, and left the General Histadrut altogether in 1997. In the 1990s several small unions were established, including the Researchers in the Ministry of Security Union and the Junior Academic Staff Unions in the public universities.[4]

THE GENERAL HISTADRUT

Describing the General Histadrut is a daunting task. From its name, which has changed over the years, through its institutional structure, which is complex and changing as well, and finally to its history and ideology, almost any statement that seems to be merely "descriptive" often masks a political or ideological stance.

Historical Background   The General Histadrut was established in 1920. At the time, social and political life in Palestine was organized by the political parties. The two dominant, albeit very small, parties were the Zion Laborer (socialist) and Young Laborer (nonsocialist) parties. In 1919 the Labor's Unity Party was founded, which united the Zion Laborer Party with the agricultural organizations throughout Palestine. The political structure of the Jewish

3. The National Histadrut's role in the industrial relations system can be compared by observing its marginal, or marginalized, role in the corporatist phase (chapter 3) with its growing (yet strongly contested) role in the postcorporatist phase (chapter 7).

4. On the background to the newly formed unions, particularly those that were formed in the process of legal disputes, see chapter 5.

stage (cf. Chermesh 1993; Harel, Tzafrir, and Bamberger 2000; Cohen et al. 2003).

Cohen et al. (2003) further note that while most of the trade union members were members of the General Histadrut during the 1970s, by 2000 the Histadrut organized only two-thirds of the total membership. This was due to the increase in membership in the rival National Histadrut and the separation of the large Primary School Teachers Union from the General Histadrut.[6]

WHEN the data on membership are viewed together with qualitative findings on the gradual decentralization within the Histadrut and the withdrawal of public functions and support from the Histadrut, a clear picture emerges in which all the fundamental characteristics of corporatist associations have gradually faded with the rise of a pluralist industrial relations system. Internal centralization and concentration of workers' interests no longer prevail to the same extent as in the past. It is noteworthy, however, that membership rates are still relatively high in comparison with those of most pluralist regimes. Moreover, despite many challenges from within, the Histadrut remains a primary organization, which, unlike a federation, has more control over its organs.

Employers

Employers in Israel were sorted in the past into three distinct groups: public employers (the state, local municipalities, state-owned companies, and public organizations—such as the National Insurance Institute and the Employment Bureaus); the Histadrut-owned sector (organized as the Cooperative Association of Labor—Chevrat Ovdim, which included a major bank, insurance company, retail and wholesale outlets, the largest industrial concern, agricultural holdings, a construction company, and more); and private employers.

Clearly the anomalous feature of the Israeli system was the large Histadrut-owned sector. This concentration of ownership in the hands of what was, inter alia, a trade union distinguishes the Israeli case from capitalist, socialist, and worker-owned (e.g., the former Yugoslavia until the late 1970s) economies. With the decline of the corporatist framework, much of the Histadrut-owned sector was sold off and in a sense "privatized" away from the Histadrut, hence eliminating the anomaly of the General Histadrut being the second largest employer in the state.

Employers' associations are relevant only to private-sector employers.[7] Many employers' associations were established before the state was founded

6. The increase in membership in the National Histadrut is mostly due to the controversial collective agreements signed with temporary work agencies. See chapter 7 for an extensive discussion of these agreements and the rivalry between the General and National histadruts.

7. There were attempts to design a public employers' association. The only outcome of these attempts was the establishment of the Center for Local Government, which has been treated as an employers' association under case law because it serves as a coordinating body for most local governments (except for the three largest municipalities).

(farmers, craftsmen, industrialists, the diamond industry, and more). From the outset they were for the most part industrial associations (organizing on the basis of industries). However, their role in employment or industrial relations was at first very weak. Only during World War II did they become more active, and in the 1940s the first collective agreements of relatively general applicability were signed by employers' associations (on cost-of-living adjustments). The strong position of the Histadrut in the industrial relations system, the fact that it was the second largest employer in Israel, the strong alliance between the Histadrut and the state and relatively small private sector, and conflicts of interests among the employers all cast a long shadow over the employers' associations and attenuated their strength (Shirom and Jacobson 1975; Shalev 1992). In light of this institutionally embedded weakness, the employers' associations sought to concentrate their power and in 1967 established a federation of most employers' associations—the FIEO (Dror and Shirom 1983). To date, the employers' associations have usually remained neutral with regard to competing political parties.

Unlike the data on membership of workers in trade unions, that on membership in employers associations is scarce. Shirom (1983) cites figures that suggest the rate of membership in the larger associations ranged from 70 to 95 percent (in 1978). These figures are usually cited throughout the corporatist period. In the only detailed study available for the postcorporatist period (Cohen et al. 2005), only 38 percent of the private employers sampled reported that they were members of, or otherwise affiliated with, an employers' association. This figure includes a group of employers (approximately a quarter of the 38 percent) who reported that they were not members but affiliates (Amitim) of the association. The status of an affiliate was devised in the mid-1990s in the larger associations, most notably the Industrialists Association. It allows all privileges of membership and requires the payment of dues, but collective agreements signed by the association do not cover or bind the affiliates. Clearly, this undermines the effort to achieve concentrated representation.

State

The state is heavily implicated in the industrial relations system. It is the largest employer, and it also directly affects the employment policies of other employers who rely on the state budget. It is the policymaker in the economic and social spheres. It is also implicated and involved in broad collective agreements. As will be discussed in chapter 9, there is a strong relationship between the study of the *state* and the study of *law* that is developed throughout the remainder of this book. The following chapters will therefore extensively explore the role of the state as a legislature (chapters 3, 5, 6), the problems created by the state's being the largest employer (chapters 6, 7), and the difference between the legislature and the courts (chapters 4, 5) and between the legislature and the executive branch (chapters 6, 7).

As background, however, it is necessary to note several relevant characteristics of the Israeli state. First and foremost, it is important to observe the political relationship between the General Histadrut and the hegemonic political party. A notable characteristic of Israeli politics was the hegemonic position of the Labor Party from the pre-statehood period until 1977. Although the labor movement was amoebic, with splits and mergers between the center and the left throughout this period (Shalev 1992, app. 4), it is crudely justified to state that the Labor Party dominated the political map.[8]

It was noted earlier in this chapter that the Histadrut's relationship with the Labor Party was in fact one of the pillars of its strength. The Labor Party's involvement in the Histadrut manifested itself in, among other things, the decisions regarding appointments and candidates to head the Histadrut and fill its senior roles. At the same time, it will be demonstrated in the following chapter that the Histadrut also had a strong influence on the legislature and government. This was highly evident in the process of legislation. It would therefore be wrong to emphasize only one direction of influence and more accurate to observe the relationship as symbiotic (Shalev 1992, chaps. 3, 5,7). The Labor Party needed the Histadrut just as much as the Histadrut needed the party. Both were not really autonomous agents, although at the same time neither was really the other's servant.

In 1977, four years after the 1973 war, the right-wing Likud Party became dominant for the first time. From 1977 to the present, the Likud has been the party that formed a coalition following most elections. In the following twenty-seven years the Labor Party formed a coalition only during 1992–1996 and 1999–2001 (approximately six years altogether). Between 1984 and 1990 there were also joint unity governments that were based on a broad coalition of the Likud and the Labor Party (national unity governments). Thus, for fifteen of the twenty-seven years since the Likud first succeeded in claiming a majority, the Labor Party has been in the opposition.

Beyond the shift of power from the Labor Party to the Likud, it is also important to note the fragmented nature of coalitions and party politics in Israel. The number of parties has grown considerably since the early days of statehood. In most instances, religious and ultrareligious parties have taken part in the parliamentary coalition and hence in government. The need to assemble coalitions that are based on multiple parties has led to compromising coalition agreements and, over time, to weak governments, of which several did not succeed in completing their four years in power as provided by law.

It is also important to note which party members were assigned the responsibility of acting as the ministers of labor, welfare, and finance. This is instructive for understanding the relationship between the finance and spending sides of the state, which are symptomatic of its different and sometimes conflicting

---

8. Shalev's analysis of left-wing parties in Israel goes only to the end of the 1980s. Further developments are of somewhat lesser importance as the overall position of the labor parties has declined and the strong alliance between the Labor Party and the General Histadrut is no longer maintained.

roles. Between 1948 and 1977, all ministers of finance were affiliated with parts of the labor movement. Since the Likud became the stronger political party, it has dominated economic policy in most of the governments. A different pattern evolved with regard to the ministries of labor and welfare.[9] At the outset the Ministry of Labor, too, was considered an important ministry to be staffed by leading figures from within the Labor Party, such as Golda Meir (1949–1956) and later—Yigal Alon and Yitzhak Rabin. By contrast, the Ministry of Welfare was chaired, with some exceptions, by representatives of the religious parties. After 1977, the ministries of labor and welfare were merged. While at first the new Ministry of Labor and Welfare was chaired by an external professional, it was later gradually moved to coalition partners, especially from the ultraorthodox parties. In the few years during which the Labor Party returned to power, it was viewed again as a party bastion.[10] However, the ministry lost much of its political glory. This was part of the growing split between the finance and spending branches of government.

Moreover, both the finance and labor ministers from 1977 onward (again, with some exceptions) rapidly became detached from the corporatist system of social and political governance. The ministers were influenced by a different political climate, and they no longer viewed the corporatist system as an end in itself or as a particularly important instrument of governance. Especially in the spending branches of labor and welfare, the ministers viewed their ministries as a means to promote factional interests in favor of their political constituencies. This process has been designated by some as part of a general factionalization of Israeli politics (Gutwein 2004).

The fall of the Labor Party in 1977 and its very partial recovery since are symptomatic of the move away from the background conditions that are typical of or necessary to corporatism. The rise of political factionalism and the growing divide between the financing and spending branches of government are further consistent with the evolution of a pluralist regime.

From Corporatist to Pluralist Norms and Practices

As was noted in the previous chapter, several practices and norms are associated with corporatism: collective bargaining at the national level and broad applicability of collective agreements, a low level of industrial action (strikes and lockouts), and policy objectives (as well as outcomes) of full employment and a low level of social inequality. Each of these will be examined in the Israeli context. The description indicates that the corporatist system that prevailed in the past wasn't a perfect case study of corporatism. However, it also

9. The ministries of labor and welfare were separate until 1977, at which time they were united into one. In 2003 labor was split from welfare again and merged with the Ministry of Commerce and Industry.

10. See the introduction to part 3 of this book, which describes the prominent role of Labor Minister Ora Namir.

indicates the extent of similarity between the Israeli and corporatist models, as well as the relationship between the pluralist model and the industrial relations system that has evolved since the early 1980s.

Collective Bargaining

Neither centralization nor decentralization in collective bargaining has ever been a unidirectional process. In the early years of the Histadrut, collective agreements were local and generally uncoordinated. Only toward the end of the British Mandate did collective agreements proliferate and emerge beyond the local (enterprise or municipal) level (Shalev 1992). After the establishment of the state there was a growing tendency to centralize, particularly in the area of wage policy. But in the mid-1960s, some decentralization appeared again, and broad agreements for the most part prescribed the contours for sector-level bargaining (Sussman 1969). In 1970 yet another shift took place, and for the first time the state became involved directly in negotiations with the FIEO and the Histadrut, leading to the first of several broad social pacts (Galin and Tab 1971; Shirom 1983; Margalit 1994). By the early 1980s collective bargaining was becoming more centralized as more agreements were being bargained at the national and sector levels (Shirom 1983).

The most important agreements at the national level were the so-called package deals. These were perhaps the most corporatist-like agreements in the evolution of the Israeli system. They included wage restraints on behalf of the Histadrut, employers' agreements to price stability, and the government's assurance of stability in regulated prices and taxes. Shortly after the package deals became part of the repertoire, they started to include the determination of minimum wage and cost-of-living adjustments. As described in the previous chapter, like other corporatist arrangements, the national agreements were complemented by agreements at lower levels that eased the pressure of concentrated representation.

However, even at the time of the periodic package deals and national collective agreements, it has been found that there was a strong wage drift that undermined the attempts of the corporatist pact to achieve wage restraint. Brauer (1990) noted that the extent of the wage drift indicated that Israel had a potential for being corporatist but that this potential was only partially realized. Moreover, Kristal (2004) and Kristal and Cohen (2007) found that despite the practice of peak-level bargaining that emerged from 1970 onward, a parallel process of decentralization was taking place. As figure 2.2. shows, by the 1970s local (enterprise-based) agreements and craft-based agreements had begun to replace the more comprehensive and centralized industrial agreements. In later stages the authors also point to the declining use of extension orders as a method of making industrial agreements applicable to broad segments of the relevant industries.[11]

11. On the nature of extension orders and their impact, see infra chapters 3 and 8.

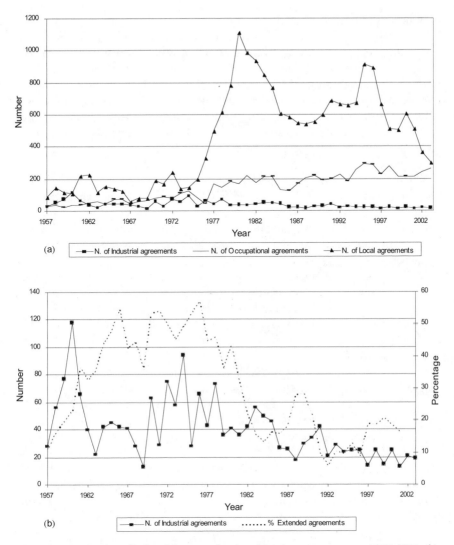

Figure 2.2 (a) Number of industrial, occupational, and local wage agreements, 1957–2003. (b) Number of industrial agreements and percentage of agreements for which an extension order was issued. Sources: Data collected by Tali Kristal from the Registry of Collective Agreements. Kristal (2004), Kristal and Cohen (2007).

Other studies have reached similar conclusions with regard to the private sector (Brauer 1990) and public sector (Sussman and Zakai 1996). Yet it is important to note that a further divide emerged between agreements that regulated wages in the public sector and those that were limited to the private sector (Grinberg 1991), a point to which I will return shortly in the general assessment of Israel's corporatism.

One of the most important national agreements was signed in 1986 in an effort to halt the process of hyperinflation (Grinberg 1991). Despite what seemed to be a strengthening of the corporatist system, it was perhaps the last significant national pact, and the one that presaged the system's end. Since then there has been a gradual decentralization as well as a general decline in the coverage of collective agreements (Sussman 1995; Kristal and Cohen 2007). While peak-level bargaining has continued since then, mostly for the public sector and to a lesser extent covering the private sector as well, the content of negotiations has been limited, and gradually the regulation of wages disappeared from the bargaining table, with the exception of cost-of-living adjustments. Minimum wage, which was an important part of the national bargaining agenda, was also removed from the sphere of collective bargaining to legislation in 1987, further reducing the interest and incentives for the parties to engage in peak-level bargaining. The use of extension orders has become almost marginal in the system as a whole, although it has not disappeared altogether.

To summarize, despite the establishment of institutions that were geared toward centralized tripartite negotiations, there was hardly any period of time that could be characterized by strictly centralized bargaining. When industrial agreements proliferated, nationwide bargaining was weak. When nationwide bargaining developed, after the federalization of the employers' associations, then local and craft-based bargaining undermined centralized agreements and the wage drift grew. However, it is clear that whatever centralized components prevailed in the system gradually disappeared from the mid-1980s to the present. Nevertheless, traditions and historical institutions do not tend to disappear altogether, and even at present there are some examples of centralized agreements that would not appear in pluralist regimes such as the American system. Among the issues that are not consistent with total decentralization are cost-of-living adjustments (often rendered unnecessary because of low inflation), regulation of pensions and the reform in the pension system, regulation of the temporary work industry, and fringe benefits of marginal economic cost (e.g., paid leave for bereavement).

Strikes and Industrial Action

Another important feature of the Israeli system that does not easily conform to the theoretical description of corporatism is the consistently high rate of industrial action (strikes). The effects of industrial action in the pre-statehood period were extensively discussed by both the British Mandatory government and the leadership of the Jewish population in Palestine (De-Vries 1999). While industrial action fluctuated, and actually declined during war, it continued persistently throughout the period 1948–1965. As shown in figure 2.3, during the corporatist years strikes were frequent. As we move away from the corporatist phase, well into the 1990s, the number of strikes remains stable, but workdays lost as a result of strikes are generally on the rise. These trends

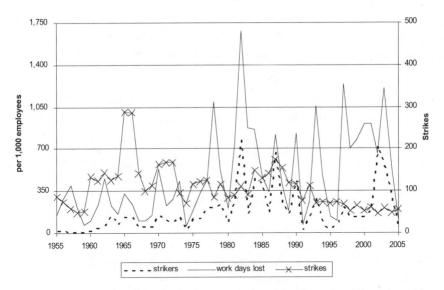

Figure 2.3 Strikes, strikers (per 1,000 employees), and workdays lost (per 1,000 employees), 1955–2005. Source: Israeli Central Bureau of Statistics (various years), Kristal (2007).

are even more extreme for strikes in the public sector, where most of the strike activity is concentrated (Bar-Tsuri 1995; Mundlak 2004).

Comparing the strike rate in Israel with that of other countries also helps uncover emerging trends. Shirom (1983) demonstrated that although the strike rate (measured in number of workdays lost per thousand workers) in Israel was higher than that of some corporatist countries—Switzerland, Sweden, Germany, and the Netherlands—it was lower that that of other countries—including Italy, Canada, the United States, Australia, the United Kingdom, Denmark, Belgium, and France. Israel was therefore situated at the high end of the corporatist cluster. Two decades later, a similar comparison (Mundlak 2004) found that Israel's strike rate is higher than those of all the above-mentioned countries—corporatist and pluralist alike. Despite some methodological caveats about this comparison, Israel's location at the high of end of states with a high propensity for strikes remains.

Another characteristic of strikes in Israel is that a high proportion are wildcat strikes—that is, strikes that are unauthorized by trade union officials (Shirom 1983; Chermesh 1993; Mundlak and Harpaz 2002). These are almost never spontaneous reactions by the workforce but rather strikes initiated by the workers' committees. As was noted earlier, workers' committees are denied the power to declare a lawful strike by the trade union bylaws. The rate of wildcat strikes is therefore symptomatic of the gap between formal powers and the locus of power in fact.

How do these findings comport with the theory of corporatism? Korpi and Shalev (1979) explain that access to the political arena allows workers to find more effective ways to improve their position than by conducting strikes. At the national level, social pacts and broad collective bargaining that includes concessions by all three parties also contain an obligation of the parties to re-frain from unilateral action on the one hand and from industrial action on the other.

Overall the relatively high rate of strikes continued persistently throughout the corporatist period and therefore does not conform to the typical correla-tion between corporatism and industrial peace. A common explanation of these strike patterns holds that there were no legal restrictions on strikes. This explanation is weak because, as will be demonstrated throughout the follow-ing chapters, there were several attempts to restrict industrial action by law, but they generally had little effect on the number of strikes. A different expla-nation holds that the high rate of strikes is reflective of a weak system for me-diating conflicts—that is, that institutional dispute resolution may have been too weak (Mundlak 2004). Clearly, this explanation only opens further ques-tions as to why corporatist institutions for interests mediation failed. These questions will be addressed in the following chapters.

Despite these quandaries, some of the features of strikes in Israel strengthen the image of transition from corporatism to pluralism. Strikes have become more intense and volatile with the decline of the political backing that the cor-poratist pact enjoyed. The high proportion of wildcat strikes also evolved from intrinsic difficulties in the design of the corporatist pact in Israel, which was very far-reaching in its exclusion of workers' committees from formalized active participation.

Full Employment and Equality

Corporatism is associated with various outcomes—namely, wage restraint, full employment, and equality. As in the discussion of the previous character-istics, a comparison of the corporatist phase with the more pluralist phase that replaced it strengthens the general findings regarding these outcomes. Full em-ployment was clearly a policy objective during a large part of the corporatist phase but has not been since then. Similarly, rising inequality in Israel has been found to be associated with the decline of corporatist features, such as centralized bargaining.

During the first years after statehood, unemployment remained relatively high because the state had to cope with massive waves of immigration. How-ever, the employment of the newly arrived immigrants was a high priority for the state as part of the prevailing ideology of constructive socialism. To that extent, benefits substituting for employment that characterized welfare states at that time were very slow to be introduced. By contrast, the state sought to encourage employment growth by public employment absorption plans and public investment in private industry (Gal 2002).

In the mid-1960s, unemployment increased during a period of economic depression. Shalev (1992) notes this as one of the anomalies of the Israeli

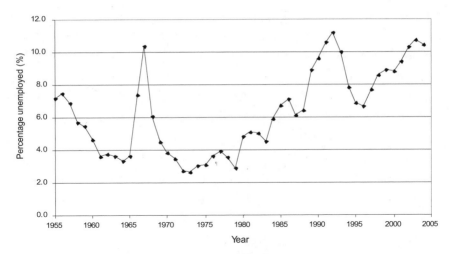

Figure 2.4 Percentage of unemployed in civilian labor force, 1955–2004. Source: Israeli Central Bureau of Statistics (various years).

variant of corporatism because unemployment was used as a policy and strategy to control labor. This was also one of the reasons for admitting Palestinian workers from the occupied territories following the Six Day War in 1967 (see chapter 7). These strategies are not consistent with the corporatist model, which offers alternative modes of social and economic control that are based on agreement and not on the threat of unemployment. However, rapid economic growth, together with the continuing importance of full employment, brought the unemployment rate down to 2–5 percent throughout the 1970s. Figure 2.4 describes the changes in the unemployment rate from 1955 onward.

Curbing unemployment during the 1970s had its price, as the public sector increased significantly and heavy taxation was necessary to fund these expenditures. The full employment policy of the 1970s is often described as having had a horrendous effect on the Israeli economy. Again, this happened despite the theoretical strength of corporatism, which is assumed to complement full employment with other restraining measures to avoid such outcomes.

Starting in the 1980s, partially as a result of the economic outcomes of the full-employment policy of the past and partially as a result of the changing political regime, full employment gradually came to be avoided as a policy objective. During the 1980s unemployment levels gradually rose to more than 6 percent in 1985 and almost 10 percent toward the end of the decade and thereafter.

Similar trends can be seen with regard to inequality. Patterns of inequality generally match those of unemployment. Figures 2.5. shows the level of inequality among wage earners during the period 1970–2003. These trends are highly correlated with the general inequality among the Israeli population.

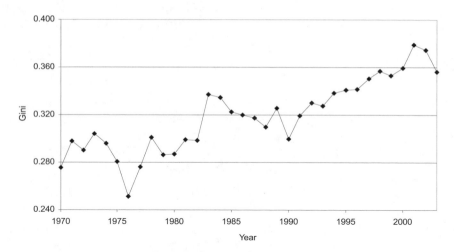

Figure 2.5 Hourly wage inequality (Gini coefficient) among salaried workers aged 25–64, 1970–2003. Source: Israeli Central Bureau of Statistics (various years).

A high level of inequality in the first years of statehood was moderated by a full-employment policy and the gradual structuring of welfare state institutions. A comparison of the level of inequality in the heyday of the corporatist regime with that of later years, as corporatism declined, reveals that inequality is constantly on the rise. Inequality in the population generally is also matched by growing inequality in the labor market itself. Kristal and Cohen (2007) demonstrate a rise in inequality from the 1980s onward among wage earners and that the decline is partially attributed to the decline in union membership and the decentralization of collective agreements. Otherwise stated, the evidence confirms that inequality has been on the rise with the fading of corporatist institutions.

On the face of it, both unemployment and inequality confirm the transition from a corporatist to a more pluralist regime in Israel. It is, however, important to insert a caveat into this neat image of transition because unemployment and inequality did not spring up spontaneously from the more pluralist mode of governance. It would in fact be surprising if they had, because the transition was gradual and, as noted, has yet to be completed. The seeds of the current inequality, labor market participation, and unemployment are to be found in the corporatist phase. Vulnerable groups in Israel—most notably the Arabs (who are residents of Israel) but also the Mizrachim (the Jewish population that emigrated mostly from the Muslim countries)—were relegated to the lower levels of a segmented labor market in the corporatist phase. To attribute their relative situations in the labor market and the economy only to the rising pluralist system would be to ignore the effects of past corporatist segmentation. This critique of the seemingly neat transition from corporatism to pluralism, discussed in the following section, is the most fundamental argu-

ment made against the application of the corporatist/pluralist divide to the
Israeli experience.

The Corporatist Nature of the Israeli System

Split Corporatism

Was the Israeli system corporatist at all? The thrust of the argument in this
book assumes a corporatist structure in the past. However, some of the data
presented throughout this chapter questions this assumption: collective bargaining was never wholly centralized; for many years employers' associations
were weak; and industrial action, unemployment, and inequality were high.
Moreover, two of the most important books on industrial relations in Israel,
written by Shalev (1992) and Grinberg (1991), contest the argument that Israel ever really had a corporatist system.

In a nutshell, both Shalev and Grinberg point out that the basic premises of
comprehensive representation of interests typical of a corporatist system were
undermined by a strong tendency toward dualism. Shalev demonstrates the fusion of corporatism with dualism, a marriage that theoretically seems to contain a strong internal contradiction, from the British Mandate until the late
1970s. Grinberg follows up on the same theme until the pact of 1986.

Shalev's argument is that the fundamental motives and bargaining chips in
the political exchange between the Histadrut and the state were significantly
different from those of "normal" labor movements; the Histadrut, corporatism, full employment, and the welfare state were all rooted in national
interests. To this extent, he emphasizes the Histadrut's treatment of the Palestinians residing in Israel on the basis of exclusion. Other groups were subor-
dinated by this dualist policy, including the Mizrachim (Jewish migrants
from the Arab countries) and later the Palestinians from the occupied territories (Grinberg 1993) and migrant workers (see chapter 7). Grinberg sustains
the seeming contradiction between corporatism and dualism but also points
to the evolution of two separate (and hence "split") systems of industrial
relations—one for the public sector and another for the private (and Histadrut-
owned) sector. While in the private sector the Histadrut performed in a manner that corresponded to the corporatist prescription of wage restraint and a
relative degree of industrial peace, the public sector experienced a severe
wage drift initiated by the stronger organs within the Histadrut. These organs also account for the relatively high proportion of strikes in the public
sector.

It seems to me that the faults both authors find with the corporatist characterization of Israel are warranted, but they do not undermine the fundamental
claim presented here. Corporatism, we learn from both authors, can coexist
with dualist tendencies. In my view dualism is neither the stark opposite of
corporatism nor the fundamental characteristic of American industrial relations and labor market governance. When corporatism is contrasted with plu-

ralism, as suggested by the classical corporatist structure, then dualism can probably coexist with both. This is in fact the major argument presented in chapter 7, which compares current (more pluralist) methods of dualism with those that prevailed in the corporatist phase from a legal perspective.

Both Shalev and Grinberg can be read as rejecting the corporatist characterization of Israel. I read them as rejecting simple classifications and too narrow a reading of the corporatist literature. In my understanding, what they suggest is that any simple and convenient pigeonholing of the Israeli case should be avoided in favor of attending to history and peculiar events that do not fit the abstract definition of corporatism. With these clarifications in mind, I do not find the general framework that is used here to be much in tension with the critique of the political sociologists.

A Decline of Corporatist Institutions

The discussion of the various features of the industrial relations system in this chapter clearly indicates that the system at present is very different from that of the past. Membership rates in employers' associations and trade unions have declined dramatically, as has the coverage of collective agreements; collective negotiations have been decentralized and brought close to the shop floor; the state has become independent of the "social partners"; the importance of the Labor Party and of social-democratic politics has been eroded; the Ministry of Labor has been neglected; industrial action has become more volatile; inequality and unemployment have been on the rise. What are the explanations for all these changes?

Some explanations suggest that Israel has experienced pressures and effects similar to those of other developed countries. On the demand side, there has been a considerable change in the structure of the Israeli economy. On the one hand, traditional labor-intensive industries have shrunk and moved across the borders to other countries in which production costs are lower. On the other hand, new high-tech industries have developed wholly outside the corporatist pact. Globalization has therefore played an important role, underlining the differences between the old and new economies, increasing labor market disparities, and weakening the solidarity basis of the corporatist pact. Moreover, the influx of foreign capital and labor into the Israeli labor market has affected the nationalist bond that kept the system intact and its agents committed during the corporatist phase. Technological changes have rendered traditional production processes obsolete in some workplaces (particularly in the stronger organizations), leading to more individualized forms of compensation. On the supply side, it is possible to point to the growing heterogeneity of the workforce, which renders centralized representation of interests more difficult (Harel, Tzafrir, and Bamberger 2000). Social and individual values in Israel have also affected the legitimacy of solidarity-based arrangements, as more workers are seeking instrumental and individualistic values at work (Sharabi and Harpaz 2002).

Other explanations for the transformation are more particular to Israel. First of all, the political transformation in 1977 had an impact on the corporatist triangle. Although the impact was not immediate, its effects were not postponed for long (Reshef 1986). However, the decline in the Histadrut's power was not only a symptom of a broader political process but also a cause of further disintegration. What was once designated as "a state within a state," the cornerstone of the corporatist triangle, has become a meager and struggling organization. This became most evident when the other pillars of the Histadrut began to collapse. Disintegration spiraled and snowballed because the very peculiar logic of the corporatist triangle was torn apart. The Histadrut was no longer the second largest employer, a factor that in the past heavily affected its inclination toward wage restraint. It became politically weak, which affected its power to discipline its organs. It was stripped of its social advantages, most notably by the National Health Insurance Law, and thereby lost important advantages it had previously offered to its membership (Haberfeld 1995).

It is difficult to distinguish the "universal" effects from the local ones. They interacted. Internal problems affected the capacity of the system to adapt to the rules dictated by globalization. At the same time, changing cultural values, globalization, and technology strongly impacted the capacity of the corporatist system to sustain broad pacts and agreements. Yet in this book it is less important to distinguish the universal from the local. Instead, I seek to assess what role law has played in this transition.

Some have argued that legal rules exacerbated the decline of the corporatist pact (Raday 2002). The following chapters will seek an extensive answer to this question. They will assess the extent to which legal rules brought about the decline of corporatist bargaining. They will further note the advantage of taking law seriously on the one hand while realizing its limited explanatory power on the other. However, now that the corporatist/pluralist distinction has been spelled out in detail, a more thorough explanation of the role of law can be attempted. The following two parts of this book look at the development of labor law from 1920 to 2005.

Part II

CONSTRUCTING CORPORATIST LABOR LAW, 1920–1987

On the basis of the questions presented at the end of the first chapter, part 2 describes the enabling legal conditions of the Israeli corporatist system and how they came about.

It is difficult to establish the starting point for a study of corporatism and labor law in Israel. An evident starting point could be the foundation of the state in 1948. The theory of corporatism accentuates the role of the state in industrial relations, and the notion of state was too ambiguous and fragmented in the pre-statehood period of Israel for this concept to apply. At the same time, the creation of labor law after 1948 is rooted in norms and social institutions that were established during the British Mandate over Palestine (Likhovski 1998).[1] The pre-statehood period is therefore described in the first part of chapter 3 to the extent it is necessary to decipher the developments that started in 1948.

Yet not only is it necessary to trace the origins of Israeli labor law back into the pre-statehood years, but it is also important to distinguish between two stages after statehood: the period until 1969 when the labor courts system was established and the years thereafter. The period 1948–1969 was characterized by intensive legislation of statutes governing both individual and collective labor law. This period is discussed in detail in chapter 3. The legislative period ended in the mid-1960s as further attempts to legislate began reaching an impasse. In 1969, the venue of lawmaking moved from the legislature to the

---

1. Arguably, a historical view might actually require the assumption of an even earlier starting date in the period of Ottoman rule, prior to the British Mandate. Yet the Ottoman labor law was so general and dull that its "legacy" to the developing labor law in subsequent periods bears only passing mention.

labor courts. Chapter 4 shifts the emphasis from the legislature to the labor courts system, because once this special tribunal was established, it assumed the role of securing the corporatist system from potential threats and mediating opposing positions to relieve some of the tensions inherent in the corporatist system.

Together the three periods distinguished here had an enormous impact on the development of labor law, which is on the one hand connected and dependent on the general law of the state and at the same time based on a separate system of corporatist communications. They must be viewed as three components of a single ongoing legal project. Each phase developed the "law," broadly defined, in a different venue. Consequently, labor law is polycentric; it is not rooted in a single normative source. It is as much in statutes as it is in collective agreements and individual contracts.

The closing date for this part of the book is equally difficult to establish. As shown in the second chapter, the decline of the corporatist system began in the 1980s and perhaps should be traced back to the political elections of 1977. At the same time, the dramatic fall in membership and coverage of collective agreements did not appear until the mid-1990s, once health-care reform was launched. When did corporatism cease? When did labor law change in a qualitative manner, rather than merely a slight change of degree? The data suggest that it may not have disappeared altogether, and therefore any one particular date might seem to be arbitrary. My choice of 1987, then, is conveniently functional. This was the year in which the Minimum Wage Law was legislated. In retrospect, I find this law to be the most significant representation of the changing relationship between law and the industrial relations system. In the following chapters, I will demonstrate that at the same time changes emerged in the Labor Court. Both the statute and the case law will be discussed in the introduction to part 3.

3 Legislating for Corporatism, 1920–1968

This chapter focuses on the period of corporatist legislation in Israel. The discussion points out that while corporatism is based on autonomous norm making by the social partners with the state's intervention (as a negotiating partner and not as a legislature), lawmaking need not necessarily be considered inimical to corporatism's principle of autonomy. Legislative processes in the period described here evolved from within the corporatist industrial relations system, and law was viewed as a means to accommodate the system's needs. In part 3 of the book, later legislative processes will be contrasted with those described in this chapter and shown to be a threat to corporatism and a result of its collapse. Consequently, the description provided in this chapter and in part 3 suggests that law and corporatist institutions are neither allies nor foes. Some types of law and some legislative processes are part of the "enabling conditions" of corporatism, while others undermine it.

What makes legislation an enabling condition of corporatism is a combination of process and content. In terms of process, the discussion emphasizes that laws in the corporatist phase emerged by the initiative of the social partners, were legislated after the social partners reached an agreement on the content, and were later implemented by means of further negotiations. In terms of content, the laws are divided into two groups. Some laws, which provided the substantive norms, codified common practices that already prevailed in collective agreements. In these laws, the norms were intended to have universal application throughout the labor market to avoid undercutting of the corporatist pact. At the same time the social partners sought to maintain the corporatist advantage and hence avoided regulation of wages and protection from dismissals. To preserve the superiority of the collectively negotiated norm, the social partners and the legislature included particular measures,

61

such as derogation clauses that allowed deviation from the statute by means of collective bargaining. Other laws prescribed the rules for collective bargaining. In these laws the social partners sought to secure the appropriate rules for the corporatist system, the assurance of centralization and concentration of interests representation, the autonomy of the associations (the social partners), and the extension of the collective norm within and outside the bargaining domain.

For the most part the chapter deals with the years after statehood, but as will be demonstrated, it is necessary to commence earlier with the pre-statehood years to understand the legislative agenda and its rapid implementation within a few years thereafter. The first part of this chapter describes the development of collective norms and their relationship with law in the pre-statehood period. In the second part I argue that the social partners, and most notably the General Histadrut, were prepared with a legislative agenda even before the Israeli state was founded. Together with the employers' associations they strongly influenced the legislature throughout the period of lawmaking in the 1950s. In some fields, most notably the making of a constitution, legislation failed for reasons unrelated to labor. Yet in the core of labor law, the legislative project was dominated by the interests and needs of the social partners. The following analysis demonstrates this with regard to both statutory labor standards and the law of collective bargaining. All the laws were promulgated only on the basis of drafts submitted by the social partners and were not accepted unless supported by them. Moreover, the content of the laws included mechanisms to ensure the ongoing control of the social partners over future legislation. The role of the leading party in the Knesset and the executive branch was to identify compromises and solutions against political objections to this legislative agenda in a manner that would not undermine the corporatist partners' quest for autonomy and recognition.

Autonomy and Independence: Labor Law and Labor Norms until 1948

At the time Palestine was a part of the Ottoman Empire, labor law was governed by the Magella, the Ottoman legal code, to which two particular laws were added in later stages.[1] The Ottoman law dealt only with individual employment relations, treating the employment contract as yet another example of a rental contract. It provided no statutory minimum standards and was generally adapted to the characteristics of an agrarian society in which the employment relationship was the exception rather than the rule. Only with the

---

1. The Ottoman Law of Strikes (1909), later canceled by the Israeli Settlement of Labor Disputes Law (1957), and the Law of Professional Guilds (1912), which was never formally canceled but also had never been implemented and can therefore be assumed to have been voided by the rules of transition to statehood in the Law and Administration Ordinance (1948).

British Mandate over Palestine following World War I did the development of labor law begin to receive more particular attention.

While small associations resembling trade unions had appeared by the end of the nineteenth century, it was only in 1920, when the General Histadrut was established, that the presence of collective action also made it necessary to consider how this action should be regulated under the law. The Histadrut itself was founded on the basis of the Ottoman Associations Law (1909), which remained on the books until 1980, when abolished by the Israeli Associations Law. The Ottoman law, however, was general in nature, dealing with various types of nongovernmental associations, and merely provided the organizational shell for the Histadrut's activity and its legal standing. It had no impact on the association's objectives and the nature of its action as a trade union. In this respect, its noninterventionist stance was considered an advantage, and from the Histadrut's perspective it served as the benchmark of convenience with which later efforts to regulate and monitor trade unions were compared.

The British Mandate over Palestine was engaged at one way or another in an effort to regulate the labor market in Palestine, or abstain from regulation, for almost thirty years.[2] The presiding governors tended to apply British conceptions of labor law to their colonies, but Palestine was somewhat of an exception. The vast differences, economically and politically, between the Arabs and the Jews in Palestine made the task of standardization more difficult to apply (Lewinthal 1954; Horovitz and Lissak 1977). The British government also held that labor law at that time was not necessary because the development of industry in Palestine was still in its infancy (Likhovski 1998, 698). Furthermore, the British Mandate applied the political attitude prevalent in Great Britain at that time, namely, an attitude of nonintervention in labor relations.

Initial attempts to legislate labor standards on the basis of an ordinance that was enacted in Egypt were rejected by the colonial Office because of the costs involved in its enforcement (Likhovski 1998, 699). Later attempts to introduce labor legislation into Palestine dealt for the most part with the issues of occupational health and safety and compensation for injuries suffered at work. Special protections for women and children were also legislated, but were merely the residue of the failed effort to enact a more comprehensive ordinance regarding labor standards.[3] Except for the protection of women and minors, these issues are generally considered marginal in the field of labor law, and the core labor standards that had already been developed in Great Britain and in the International Labor Organization (ILO) conventions were not

2. For a general description of labor law's development at the time of the British Mandate, see Zamir (1966) and Doron (2003).

3. In the area of occupational health and safety the following ordinances were enacted: the Steam Boiler Ordinance (1925), the Mining Ordinance (1925), the Matches Prohibition Ordinance (1925), and the Machinery (Fencing) Ordinance (1928). In the area of workers' compensation, the Workmen's Compensation Ordinance (1927) was enacted, and in the area of labor standards the only ordinance was the Industrial Employment of Women and Children Ordinance (1927).

introduced. Moreover, the standards applied to Palestine in the British ordinances were generally low, both objectively and in comparison with the British standards. All other issues that were placed on the legislative agenda were abandoned, as the general view was that unless absolutely necessary legislation was best avoided.

The scanty labor regulation introduced by the Mandate seemed to be a token of appeasement for the benefit of the Histadrut. Together with the minimal ordinances on occupational health and safety, the British ruler also passed the Prevention of Intimidation Ordinance (1927), which sought to restrict violence in the process of industrial disputes and picketing.[4] This ordinance did not abolish the Ottoman law that permitted strikes, but it restricted any activity other than the cessation of work, as well as any strike activity in the public services, broadly defined.[5] The Ottoman law also held that any violation of these provisions was a criminal offense. The British ordinance merely added criminal offenses regarding any threat or act of intimidation that might be used in a strike (Bar-Shira 1929, 187–90). Despite the effort of the British Mandate to market this ordinance together with the occupational health and safety ordinances as a single package, the restrictions imposed on industrial action were taken by the Histadrut to outweigh all the minimal rights provided by the other ordinances. It also signaled to the Histadrut the danger of far-reaching labor legislation, which could potentially curtail its activity rather than abet it.

Only at a much later stage, starting in 1943 with the establishment of the British Mandate's Department of Labor and Department of Social Welfare, did the regulation of the Palestinian labor market increase, and initial attempts were made to start a government-supervised welfare system.[6] In addition, the British Mandate Department of Labor sought to address the slack enforcement of labor standards, often infringed by the British government itself and disregarded by private employers except when enforced by means of collective bargaining. However, the scope of issues regulated was still limited to occupational health and safety and to the extension of special protections to women and minors.[7] Generally, despite the establishment of the Labor Department, the formal law governing labor relations was still regarded as standing in the margin of labor market regulation and had little impact on either individual or collective employment relations. New legislative attempts were described by a

4. On the trade-off, see Likhovski (1998, 700). The rules regarding the prevention of intimidation were later incorporated into the Penal Law Ordinance (1934), sections 210–11.

5. The Ottoman Law on Strikes (1909).

6. The Department of Labor was established by the Department of Labor Ordinance (1943).

7. In the area of occupational health and safety, the most important development was the enactment of the comprehensive Factories Ordinance (1946), the Industrial Accidents and Occupational Diseases (Notification) Ordinance (1945), and the Workmen's Compensation Ordinance (1947). In the area of labor standards, the new ordinances were still restricted to the regulation of women and minors—the Employment of Children and Young Persons Ordinance (1945) and the Employment of Women Ordinance (1945).

leading Jewish labor lawyer of the time as a "good move . . . but not a coherent labor protection scheme designed to compile a labor codex" (Bar-Shira 1948, 61).[8]

The minor role of law in the period 1917–1948 should be contrasted with the very significant developments in autonomous collective regulation as it applied to the Jewish labor market. The relationship between these developments and law was twofold: they were not directed by law, but they were also not prohibited by the it. They were developed voluntarily, based on the economic and social incentives for the Jewish labor force to organize as a means of gaining leverage in the labor market, as described in the previous chapter. The collective agreements signed at that time were perceived as socially binding, but they were not justiciable (and hence in the nature of a gentlemen's agreement), and they did not entitle the workers, as individuals, to any enforceable rights. In such a lawless regime, where no ordinance prescribed the status of collective agreements, their status in fact matched the status accorded to collective agreements in Great Britain at the time.

The extensive use of collective agreements provided all the norms not legislated by the British Mandate. There are estimates, although probably exaggerated, that 71 percent of Jewish-owned enterprises were governed by collective bargaining agreements, and that 82 percent of the Jewish workforce was covered by such agreements.[9] However, the norms developed in these agreements had an impact that exceeded even the broad coverage of the agreements, as they were viewed as embodying the basic employment norms of the Jewish labor market.[10] These norms included, inter alia, the actual right to organize in trade unions, the right to cease work on May 1, the right to limit the workday to eight hours, the right to prior notice before dismissals, protections against unjust dismissals, severance pay, cost-of-living adjustments, seniority wage premiums, sick-days pay, and even maternity benefits (Bar-Shira 1929, 11).[11] As will be demonstrated in the following section, regarding the debate on the desirability of statutory standards after the Israeli state was founded, it may be argued that the passive approach the British Mandate adopted with regard to

8. Also see the editorial that was published in volume 1 of *Chikrei Avodah* (Labor Research), a journal that was published by the General Histadrut's research department, pages 7–8 (1947).

9. Bar-Shira (1948); also see ibid.

10. The significance of extending these norms to Jewish employees and employers, above and beyond the direct coverage of collective agreements, was realized by the Supreme Court of Israel in 1954, in CA 25/50 S. Wolfson v. Spanis Ltd., PDI 5(1):265. The majority of the court was unwilling to extend these norms as binding law to employees employed by foreign enterprises, as was the case in the particular lawsuit, but they did acknowledge that they were applicable to the Jewish sector. The dissenting opinion was willing to extend these norms to the Jewish sector, based on geographical criteria, i.e., acknowledging the norms to be binding even on foreign employers in cities and neighborhoods where Jews formed a majority of the workforce.

11. The limited set of rights that appear in collective agreements in Bar-Shira's book in 1929 becomes much more extensive by the end of the Mandate period, as can be seen in Bar-Shira (1948).

the regulation of the labor market actually created an incentive for individual workers to organize and support trade union activity. There was no substitute for the achievements of the Histadrut in the area of employment rights and also in the broader social sphere (i.e., social security or health care—Kanev 1942).

The importance of autonomous collective bargaining over the formal writing of labor law at the time can be demonstrated by the British Mandate's unsuccessful effort to extend the scope of labor legislation. During the last few years of the British mandate, three important ordinances were enacted. The most important of the three was the Trade Union Ordinance (1947), which was based on the British Trade Union Act of 1871, as later amended and developed in 1876 and 1913.[12] This model of legislation, which was exported by the British ruler to its various colonies, encountered stiff resistance from the agents of the already developed autonomous system of collective bargaining. The ordinance required a declaration of the High Commissioner for it to come into effect, but given the objections of the General Histadrut to the ordinance, such a declaration was not forthcoming and the ordinance was rendered moot by the founding of the Israeli state.

The Histadrut's objection to the Trade Union Ordinance was first and foremost to the requirement that the trade unions be supervised and monitored by a governmental agency. The ordinance also required prior registration and held that registration could be annulled by the government. Severe restrictions would have been placed on the collection of union dues, and personal responsibility placed on the union leaders at the same time for compliance with collective agreements and the law. The Histadrut's demand that collective agreements be recognized and enforced was not incorporated into the ordinance. The Histadrut was therefore concerned that such supervision would undermine the autonomy of the agents to collective bargaining and only harm the already established, dense net of collective agreements (Zamir 1970, 61). Two other ordinances, one seeking to establish trade boards and the other to establish industrial courts, both following patterns of industrial relations in the United Kingdom at that time, suffered the same fate and were never implemented.[13]

The pursuit of autonomous lawmaking was accomplished not only by refuting the British ordinances and placing restrictions on their governing power but also by further developing autonomous norms and alternative modes of dispute resolution. Most significantly, the autonomous sphere carved out by the Histadrut developed its own internal adjudicative facilities—the Comrades Tribunal (De-Vries 2000; Shamir 2000, 75–99). Although this tribunal was

---

12. The normative origins of the Trade Union Ordinance were in the British Trade Union Act (1871) and subsequent amendments. Yet the British Mandate's ordinance did not adopt the British acts precisely. Most notably, the ordinance added various regulatory measures that could enhance the government's power to oversee and control trade union activity.

13. Trade Boards Ordinance (1945); Industrial Courts Ordinance (1947). For the Histadrut's position on the latter, see the editorial, "The Industrial Courts Proposal," *Chikrei Avodah* 1 (1947):3–6.

not designed to address employment disputes, the fusion of the Histadrut's alleged trade union ideology, socialist ideology, and internal modes of dispute resolution can be later identified in the many varied forms of dispute resolution systems that developed in industrial relations after nationhood. Many of the observations on the early Comrades Tribunal are applicable to later forms of dispute resolution, including the strong tilt toward collective and institutional interests over individual ones (Shamir 2002) and the ambivalent relationship between the quest for autonomy and legalization (Bar-On and De-Vries 2002).

The objection of the Histadrut, as well as of the employers' associations, to the regulation of collective bargaining in Palestine had been argued on the basis of a need for autonomy in the industrial relations system. Consequently, at the time the Israeli state was founded, most of the formal provisions of labor law (i.e., statutes) were accepted into Israeli law until changed or developed by Israeli legislation. But this legacy of the British Mandate's legislation was in reality insignificant and its lasting contribution was only in the area of occupational health and safety, with regard to standard setting, enforcement, and compensation.[14] The more important inheritance, which served as the real basis of the corporatist paradigm of law, was the existence of a system for collective bargaining and social provisions, characterized by autonomy (lack of interference by the state) and voluntary independence (lack of recognition and aid from the state).

To conclude, the initial development of the legal and industrial relations system dates back to the pre-statehood period. Most notably, the centrality of collective agreements for the regulation of the labor market meshes well with the corporatist theory. At the same time, the dualism within the labor market, nationalist separation, and other features of the warped Israeli variant of corporatism also had their start in the pre-statehood period. However, from a legal perspective, one of the major features of the this period is that collective bargaining and the state were relatively detached from each other. Unlike corporatist regimes, including Israel after statehood, where collective bargaining is integrated into the state's governance scheme, the industrial relations system in the pre-statehood period can be better characterized as a side-by-side model, rather than the interactive exchange between the state and the social partners that serves as the major trademark of corporatist systems. Perhaps theories of consociational governance and interests representation, colonialism, and migration may contribute more to understanding these early processes (Shafir and Peled 2002). At the same time, in retrospect these processes were crucial to the construction of a more typical model of corporatism after statehood.

---

14. This is also one of the last areas in Israeli law that is still governed by ordinances of the British Mandate, although these have been amended numerous times. The Accidents and Occupational Diseases (Notification) Ordinance of 1945 and the Factories Ordinance of 1946 are still in effect (although the latter has been renamed the Work Safety Ordinance).

Autonomy and Recognition: The Years of Legislation 1948–1969

With the establishment of the state, and even a few months prior to independence, the Histadrut had already prepared an agenda for drafting Israel's labor law (Bar-Shira 1948, 62–78). This, however, was not an "interest group" agenda. The deliberations on the new agenda were conducted by individuals within the Histadrut who also had an impact in the dominant political party and in the Jewish Agency, and the agenda had an overall nationalist perspective. This agenda was echoed almost word for word in the first sitting of the Knesset, when the government announced its plans to commence with extensive legislation in matters of labor and social security.[15]

In the emerging consensus over the need for renewed labor legislation in the Israeli state, a number of basic principles were established. First, there was agreement that workers' rights must be made constitutional. Not only should they be put into law, but they also had to be made the founding principles of the Israeli state. Second, there was a demand to strengthen the position of autonomous lawmaking through collective bargaining. The Histadrut's position was not against all legislation in the area of collective labor law. In this sense, its approach was somewhat different from that of the British trade unions. What it sought in legislation was to secure its autonomy on the one hand but at the same time to receive legal recognition of collective agreements and their enforceability. The third and fourth components of the agenda derived from the second. The Histadrut sought to preserve its dominant role in providing social services. Thus, despite its support for devising a comprehensive social security scheme, it demanded that such a scheme not interfere with its administration of health care, pensions, and other social services. In the same spirit, the Histadrut was in favor of developing statutory minimum standards but held that these must be limited so as not to make collective bargaining redundant.

The Histadrut's broad agenda for the writing of Israel's labor law could be characterized as continuing the trend of the pre-statehood years and breaking away from it at the same time. The Histadrut sought to maintain the autonomy of the collective bargaining process, but by contrast with the British Mandate years, it also asked for the formal recognition of collective agreements and for the state's intervention in enforcing and encouraging collective bargaining. In this sense, the Histadrut's position was different from that of the previous period, when it viewed the optimal state of affairs as consisting of a side-by-side model. In this model, law and collective bargaining are parallel avenues that do not interact with each other. In the absence of any significant influence over Mandate rule, the Histadrut viewed interactions between law and collective bargaining as a threat to its autonomy. By contrast, after the foundation of the state, the newly elected government was no longer an ad-

15. *The Knesset Protocols* D.K. vol. 1:56 (1948).

versary. It was democratically accountable to the electorate, but, more important, it was dependent on the Histadrut as one of its major sources of power. Law was no longer a potential threat but rather a potential instrument for strengthening and securing the autonomous sphere of bargaining.

Except for the constitutionalization of labor's rights, all the other goals defined by the Histadrut at the time the state was founded were achieved (relatively) shortly thereafter. The constitutional objective failed only because the writing of a constitution failed as a whole. The major barrier to a constitution was the controversy over the relationship between the Israeli state and the Jewish religion. By the time the process of writing a bill of rights was renewed (1990), the postcorporatist phase of labor law was already well developed, accounting for the neglect of labor rights as constitutional rights (Mundlak 1999c). This problem will be discussed in greater detail in chapter 6.

By contrast, the objective of maintaining social services within the control of the Histadrut succeeded. This was one of the strong corporatist trademarks in the Israeli system. Like the Ghent system, in which unemployment funds are administered by the trade unions, the Histadrut realized that prior to labor law, its hegemonic position relied on the public's actual reliance on the Histadrut. Adopting the Ghent model at the time was not an option because of the government's general objection to including unemployment benefits in the Israeli social security system (Gal 1994, 1997, 2002). Yet the Histadrut had even stronger cards to play than unemployment funds because during the British Mandate it assumed the responsibility for building and managing social provisions and services. Upon the foundation of the state, the government appointed a national commission that was headed by Kanev (Kanevski) (State of Israel 1950; Lotan 1964; Doron 2002), a leading member of the Histadrut's research and policy-setting group. In the recommendations of the commission—and even more in their implementation—there was an objection to taking away services already provided by the Histadrut on the grounds that it was necessary to preserve institutional continuity. Doron and Kramer (1991, 11) note that "the political leadership that prescribed the views and positions of the Histadrut leadership at the time refused to let go of its existing social and welfare institutions, that were considered to be one of the major achievements of the labor movement." Consequently, until the mid-1990s both health care coverage and pensions were for the most part provided by the Histadrut. This was found to be the most important reason for membership in the Histadrut (Haberfeld 1995).

The failure of the constitutional project on the one hand (for reasons not related to social or economic issues) and, on the other, the relative ease with which the Histadrut's social role was accepted in the domain of social security legislation brought labor legislation to the forefront. The core of the corporatist paradigm of labor law was rooted in the careful design of labor legislation, as will be described for the remainder of this chapter.

The following sections outline the two central domains of law that constituted the corporatist project in Israel—the legislation of statutory standards (the substantive norms) and the law of collective bargaining (the procedural norms. Following the discussion of the developments in each of these areas, an additional section will describe what was missing from the developments in labor law during the initial phase of statehood, leading to the adjudicative stage from 1969 onward. However, even in the adjudicative phase the basics that were planted in the early years remained. Law continued to evolve from the social partners, geared to their interests and continuing the project of autonomy and recognition.

Legislating Labor Standards

The corporatist nature of legislation can be identified both in the legislative process itself and in the substantive norms it provides. The legislative process was characterized by agreements between the social partners prior to the legislation itself. The end norms sought to ensure more than just protective standards. They provided an ongoing role for the social partners and collective agreements in the implementation of the laws themselves. The legislative process and its outcomes sought to diminish the threat to corporatist governance posed by legislation.

THE LEGISLATIVE PROCESS

The most striking legal development in the area of labor law during the years 1948–1969 was the adaptation of norms that were established in collective agreements during the pre-statehood years to statutory standards. On this matter the Histadrut held an ambivalent position. On the one hand, it represented broad segments of the population and was therefore interested in promoting a statutory safety net for all workers. Even putting ideology aside, the Histadrut was concerned with wage undercutting by workers who are not covered by collective agreements and the potential disincentive for employers to negotiate agreements. At the same time, the Histadrut sought to maintain its position as the sole negotiator for rights at work, and the greater the gap between individually negotiated and collectively negotiated agreements, the greater the incentive for individuals to join the union. There was therefore a need to craft a distinction between norms that had to be incorporated into collective agreements and norms that had to be ensured to all the workers. In compromising these conflicting interests, the Histadrut devised a list of issues it thought suitable for legislation—namely, working hours, annual leave, prior notice before dismissals, protection of wages, and the establishment of a state-run Employment Exchange (Bar-Shira 1948, 75–78). By contrast, the determination of wages and the norms of unjust dismissals were deemed to be matters that should remain in the sphere of collective bargaining. These are usually the two areas deemed to stand at the heart of corporatist self-regulation.

To prepare the labor laws for the Knesset, an advisory body was established, consisting of prominent representatives of the Histadrut, the major employers' associations (the Industrialists Association and the Chamber of Commerce representing small businesses), and the Ministry of Labor and Social Security (Zamir 1966, 316). The debates in the advisory committee to the Minister of Labor and Social Security dealt with one law after another, were short and very pragmatic, and focused mostly on small details. There were few principled objections. The consensus-building process in the advisory committee extended beyond the deliberations of the committee itself. The drafts prepared by the advisory committee were submitted by the government to the Knesset and were accepted almost without amendment.

More than a dozen statutes were legislated from 1949 to 1964. The first laws provided minimum standards in traditional areas, most notably including annual vacations, overtime, weekly rest, and special protections to women and minors in the labor market. These issues were quickly dealt with and their legislation was completed by 1954.[16] The second set of laws was intended to provide the regulatory infrastructure for autonomy and recognition of collective bargaining, as explained in the following subsection. This set of laws was concluded by 1959 and included related statutes, such as those dealing with the establishment of the Employment Bureau.[17] The next attempt to legislate on employment matters—the Employment Contract Law in 1968—failed. This was the first time a law on employment-related issues failed to pass, and it also marked the termination of the legislative period in building the corporatist model of labor law. The next wave of legislation, starting in 1987, will be discussed in the following chapters and contrasted with the 1948–1964 wave.

THE SUBSTANTIVE NORMS

The substantive norms in the labor laws of the first years were based on two premises. First and foremost, the laws reflected the prevailing norms that had been established previously in collective agreements. For example, overtime pay, severance pay, and maternity leave were all based on preexisting negotiated norms. Second, the norms were sometimes improved, at other times reduced, on the basis of the international and comparative standards.

Setting statutory norms that provided less than collective agreements did was not deemed to be a problem because statutory norms were explicitly held to establish minimum standards that did not constrain more advantageous conditions in collective bargaining.[18] At the same time, raising norms over and

16. The more important laws that belong to this group, include Discharged Soldiers (Reinstatement in Employment) Law (1949), Annual Leave Law (1950–51), Hours of Work and Rest Law (1951), Night Baking (Prohibition) Law (1951) (repealed 1998), Women's Equal Rights Law (1951), Apprenticeship Law (1953), National Insurance Law (1954), Youth Labour Law (1953), Employment of Women Law (1954), and Labour Inspection (Organization) Law (1954).

Later legislation that belongs to this category includes Severance Pay Law (1963) and Male and Female Workers (Equal Pay) Law (1964).

17. Collective Agreements Law (1957), Settlement of Labor Disputes Law (1957), Wage Protection Law (1958), and Employment Service Law (1959).

18. For example, Annual Leave Law (1951), sec. 38; Hours of Work and Rest Law (1951), sec. 35; Employment of Women Law (1954), sec. 23; Severance Pay Law (1963), sec. 31.

above what was acceptable in collective agreements was only resorted to when the prevailing agreements varied in their standards. Furthermore, several laws included derogation clauses in the statutes, making it possible to preserve the negotiated norms despite the higher level established by the statute. Derogation clauses are characterized by the permission they grant to the bargaining partners to reduce the safety net protection determined by the legislature. Derogation clauses appear in several countries that are generally heavily regulated and have an extensive collective bargaining system. The importance of derogation clauses lies in allowing flexibility, despite the overall rigidity of statutory standards. The advantage to the bargaining partners is that they have broad leeway to negotiate their own norms, treating legislation as neither a floor nor a ceiling of rights. Moreover, if derogation is allowed only by means of collective bargaining, then the advantage to the trade union remains. From the employers' point of view, derogation clauses create an incentive to negotiate with the union, especially when statutes are rigid and establish a relatively high level of minimum standards.

Derogation clauses in the statutes were not open-ended. They usually required not only a collective agreement but also the Minister of Labor's approval. The risk was that a blanket provision granting derogation rights to the bargaining partners might undermine the significance of the statutory minimum standards. This was especially true with regard to the potential of rival unions outside the Histadrut to negotiate derogatory agreements. Most notably, the National Histadrut was viewed to be a threat as it consistently took a pro-employers' position against excessive regulation. Thus, to maintain the efficacy of the statutory standards, derogation was allowed only in limited circumstances. For example, the Hours of Work and Rest Law (1951) held that the Minister of Labor could approve a collective agreement prescribing a workday or a workweek longer than those prescribed by the statute.[19] Similar constraints appeared in other laws.[20] However, derogation arrangements were considered inappropriate for laws dealing with vulnerable groups, such as women and minors.

Despite the limited use of derogation clauses in the statutes, their significance, in both theory and practice, should not be understated. They were used by the social partners as a means of inserting some flexibility into the rigid

19. Hours of Work and Rest Law (1951), sec. 5.
20. Section 5 of the Wage Protection Law (1958) prohibits "inclusive wage" arrangements in employment contracts. "Inclusive wage" is the inclusion in wages of overtime remuneration for work during the weekly rest or annual leave pay according to the basic wage. The result of inclusive wage agreements is usually a considerable extension of the workday and workweek.

Section 14 of the Severance Pay Law (1963) allows replacing severance pay with contributions to a provident fund law. This is a partial derogation clause because the employee is entitled to full severance pay, but instead of being paid out upon dismissal, the sums for severance pay are accumulated on a monthly basis in a provident fund.

Also see section 6(b1)(1) of the Night Baking (Prohibition) Law (1951; repealed 1998), which permitted the Minister of Labor to approve a collective agreement that allowed baking to begin at 4 a.m. instead of 6 a.m.

standards prescribed by the law and as a means of "taking over" the regulation of the labor market from the state. One of the more striking uses of the derogation clauses was in the transition from a six-day to a five-day workweek. The transition, which required an extension of each workday beyond eight hours, was not accomplished by legislation. Instead, a collective agreement derogated from the maximum workday of eight hours prescribed by the Hours of Work and Rest Law, holding that a workday could be prolonged up to nine hours. The collective agreement that derogated the statutory standards received the approval of the Minister of Labor and was later extended to cover most of the employers in the state.[21] Derogation on the one hand and the use of extension orders on the other created a dynamic and dialogic interaction among the legislature, the social partners, and the executive branch.

A more common method of amending statutory standards is secondary legislation. Labor legislation, in Israel and elsewhere, is usually complemented by regulations that are drafted by the executive branch. These include exceptions, improvements, expansions, and detailed provisions necessary for the execution of the law. The common requirement that was introduced into the labor legislation of the first phase was that the Minister of Labor, who is in charge of writing the secondary legislation, "shall not exercise his powers, except after consultation with the national workers' organization representing the largest number of workers and representative national organizations of employers who, in the opinion of the Minister, have an interest in the matter."[22]

The consultation requirement ensured that the social partners would remain involved in the legislation process. This assuaged their fear that once a matter was legislated it would remain outside their control. As demonstrated by the example of the transition to the five-day workweek, the social partners viewed their position as *partners* (to the legislature) in the establishment of

21. The instruments used for the transition were therefore the General Collective Agreement signed by the Histadrut and the Federation of Economic Organizations (the Registry of Collective Agreements (1988), 7037/88), approved by the Minister of Labor (Government Records—Yalkut HaPirsumim 3586 (1988), 91), and extended by the Minister of Labor (Government Records—Yalkut HaPirsumim 3799 (1990) 3858).

22. Cited from section 33 of the Hours of Work and Rest Law (1951). Similar provisions appear in the Annual Leave Law (1951), sec. 37; Employment of Women Law (1954), sec. 21; Collective Agreements Law (1957), sec. 34; Employment Service Law (1959), sec. 90; Severance Pay Law (1963), sec. 32; Acquisition of Undertakings by Employers (Special Cases) Law (1987), sec. 11; and Minimum Wage Law (1987), sec. 18(c).

Section 42 of The Employment of Youth Law (1953) requires consultation with the Council for Working Youth Affairs, which is based on tripartite representation and therefore does not deviate from the general scheme of consultation described here. Similarly, section 43 of the Settlement of Labor Disputes Law (1957) requires consultation with the tripartite-based Labor Relations Council, and section 43 of the Labor Inspection (Organization) Law (1954) requires consultation with the tripartite Institute for Safety and Hygiene.

Ordinances inherited from the British Mandate do not include such consultation provisions (Accidents and Occupational Diseases (Notification) Ordinance 1945; Work Safety Ordinance (New Version) 1970). Legislation after 1987 does not include them either.

work-related norms and not as passive recipients of the laws enacted. More interesting, however, is the identity of the consulting agents. The consultation clauses require consultation with all relevant employers' associations but only with the *most representative* union, or the union representing the largest number of workers. This was clearly intended to ensure that the only consultation that took place would be with the Histadrut. As noted in the previous chapter, at the time the Histadrut represented most of the workers, while rival unions were considerably smaller. Although suggestions were put forward in various legislative processes to design a consultation clause covering all relevant unions, similar to the one with employers' associations, these ideas were always rejected.[23]

The explicitly asymmetric consultation clauses are indicative of the Histadrut's determination to preserve its monopolistic role in the implementation and development of the statutes. There were other, more subtle examples in the newly enacted statues. Such, for example, was the case of the leave funds that were established by the Annual Leave Law.[24] The purpose of the funds was to allow for workers with a high degree of mobility between jobs to "hoard" their leave rights in a fund to which every employer who employed them would contribute, and thus accumulate their rights according to their seniority in the labor market rather than in a particular workplace. The statute authorized the Minister of Labor to establish state-owned funds or to certify nonstate funds.[25] The only limitations were that there should be only one fund in each industry (or sector) and that the funds were to be governed by employees. Soon after the law was passed, the National Histadrut, the General Histadrut's most vocal rival, petitioned the Supreme Court to void the Minister of Labor's authorization of the General Histadrut's leave funds.[26] The Court upheld the minister's authorization, but it indicated in its decision that the three funds belonging to the General Histadrut were merely branches of the Histadrut's pension plans and were managed by the General Histadrut. The idea of the leave funds' self-management by employees was substituted by the General Histadrut's centralized management. Consequently, the General Histadrut achieved recognition as the provider of services even to temporary workers, often not covered by collective agreements.

To summarize thus far, the Histadrut's position in the legislative process and in the implementation of the law was a cardinal feature of the first wave

23. For example, in the meetings of the advisory committee regarding the preparation of the Annual Leave Law (1951). The proposal appears in the summary report of the committee from February 2, 1950 and was discussed by the committee on April 10, 1950 (voted 4–2 against the duty to consult with all unions). The committee protocols are on file with the author.

24. This discussion is of purely historical value. Although the legal arrangements still exist in the law books, the funds were used for only a short period of time and then terminated. They have not been reestablished since.

25. Annual Leave Law (1951), sec. 18.

26. Supreme Court HCJ 282/51 National Histadrut and Others v. Minister of Labor and Others, PDI 6(1):237.

of standards setting in Israeli legislation. The Histadrut shaped the agenda, wrote the drafts of the laws, and took an active part in the advisory committee to the Minister of Labor. The norms that were legislated relieved the Histadrut of its ambivalent position on legislation. They gave it the power to negotiate standards over and above the statutory minimum but also the power to derogate from the minimum in certain circumstances. The laws further provided the Histadrut with a monopolistic position in the consultation clauses, as well as an advantage in the administration of norms, as demonstrated by the litigation over the Histadrut's leave funds. Thus, from conception to implementation, the statutory standards were stamped with the Histadrut's trademark.

The legislation of substantive norms was concluded rapidly. Subsequent attempts to legislate such norms were rare. Because of the extensive coverage of collective agreements, they were usually deemed unnecessary. Some legislative attempts succeeded and were legislated on the basis of the aforementioned model.[27] Other legislative attempts failed because the bargaining partners did not succeed in forging a prior agreement on the norms. Absent an agreement, the status quo remained. This was most evident with regard to the Employment Contract Law, which was to serve as the basic legal codex for employment contracts. The proposals for the law reached an impasse—once in 1968 and then again in 1985.[28] Not surprisingly, both proposals diverged from the list of standards to which the Histadrut had conceded in 1948. Generally, both infringed on the Histadrut's principle that wages and dismissals should be regulated by collective bargaining and not by law. The point of controversy in 1968 was on the right of striking workers to receive their wages, and in 1985 it was the norm governing unfair dismissals.[29] Hence, the corporatist system did not imply consensus. However, it did consistently indicate that law must be a product of prior agreement.

Preserving Autonomy and Advancing Recognition: The Law of Collective Bargaining

Outside the sphere of employment standards (the substantive norms), the Histadrut sought a formal recognition of the freedom of association in law. However, it emphasized that freedom of association has multiple meanings

27. The only significant law that was legislated after 1969 was the Sick Pay Law (1973), and although it is chronologically outside the period of time surveyed here, it structurally and thematically belongs in it.

28. Proposal: The Employment Contract Law 8 (1968 *Legislative Proposals* 384).

29. I thank Ruth Ben-Israel, who served as the legal adviser of the special committee that devised the draft of the law, for her explanations of the processes that led to the proposal's annulment. The indications for the controversy can be found in the committees' protocols, from February 18, 1986 and May 27, 1986. Also see letters submitted to the committee by the Industrialists' Association on November 15, 1985, by the Federation of Contractors and Builders in Israel on November 8, 1985, and by the Association of Independent Employers in Israel from January 12, 1986. Documents are on file with the author.

and that the desired recognition must be tailored to the nature of existing institutions in Israel. The Histadrut took the British Mandate's Trade Union Ordinance of 1947 as the model to be avoided (Bar-Shira 1948, 65–66). The distinction between its own model and the British was twofold. First, instead of advancing freedom of association by registration and governance of the bargaining partners, the Histadrut insisted that freedom of association must advance the autonomy and immunity of the bargaining process from state intervention. Second, instead of leaving the collective bargaining unenforceable, the state must use its power to enforce the collective agreements. Together, these two distinctions provided the principle of autonomy and recognition.

Passage of procedural laws on collective bargaining was completed in a very short time. The two important laws—the Collective Agreements Law and the Settlement of Labor Disputes Law—were enacted in 1957, and the ancillary Employment Service Law and Wage Protection Law followed in 1959. The sequence of laws is important in itself. The Collective Agreements Law was the Histadrut's top priority, while the Dispute Resolution Law was something the Histadrut was aware it would have to accept in return but toward which it reacted with a commonsense strategy of damage control. The Employment Service Law followed at a later stage because it took away from the Histadrut one of its most important functions in the labor market—placement services. The acceptance of the law was made possible once the Histadrut achieved a secured legal regime in its favor in the 1957 legislation.

The discussion here will briefly describe the salient features of the Collective Agreements Law, which to date remains the most important law in the sphere of collective labor relations. Several features of the other laws will be mentioned in brief: the rejection of compulsory mandatory arbitration, the nationalization of the employment bureau, the introduction of agency fees to the trade union by nonmembers, and the constitution of tripartite governing bodies. These are some of the more important examples of how collective labor law was devised to promote the principles of autonomy and recognition.

THE COLLECTIVE AGREEMENTS LAW

As was the case with regard to the substantive norms, the Histadrut's agenda for autonomy and recognition in the area of collective bargaining was already structured at a detailed level at the stage of transition into statehood.[30] All of these components of the Histadrut's agenda were accepted into the Collective Agreements Law (1957).[31] Corresponding to the corporatist nature of the industrial relations system and to the system's needs, the law advanced three major objectives. First, concentration and centralization required that the state, the employers, and labor would each present the concerns of its side of the trilateral negotiations in a uniform voice. As noted in the first chapter, this goal is most difficult to achieve with the representation of labor, owing to the

---

30. Bar-Shira (1948, 68).
31. For a thorough exposition of the Collective Agreements Law, see Ben-Israel (1977).

unique nature of labor organization (Offe 1985, 170–220). Thus, the central objectives of the Collective Agreements Law were to act as a gatekeeper denying representation to associations that could undermine centralized bargaining and to secure the centralized application of the negotiations' outcomes to all workers. Second, it was important to establish the centralization of bargaining in the sense of comprehensive coverage of agreements. This required the structuring of rules that would ensure the application of the agreements to the broadest category of workers possible. Third, the legislative guarantee of the freedom of association was also aimed at ensuring the autonomy of the bargaining partners. I will expand on the institutional design of these objectives.

Gatekeeping   At first glance the law might seem to have failed in the task of positing stringent entry requirements. It provided no definition of a trade union or an employers' association. This was justified by mixed and conflicting assumptions, such as that no definition was required because the definitions were clear from past industrial experience, or that definitions were too complicated to define and no singular definition could be given, or that it was better to leave the question for the courts to resolve. Second, the law required, for the first time, that trade unions achieve a representative status to be entitled to conclude a collective agreement.[32] Third, the law did not make majority support of the workers a requirement for earning representative status. To earn representative status, the law listed two separate sets of requirements. For a *special* collective agreement (covering only one establishment), the representative union was the union with the most workers covered by the collective agreement (including workers who gave ad hoc authorization to conclude a collective agreement) and at least a third of the total workforce in the establishment. For *general* collective agreements, covering an entire sector, or any other coverage that extended beyond the single employer, the law held that the union with most workers covered by the agreement was to be the representative union.[33] The rules are set forth in table 3.1.

Given the low level of employees' support required by the law, it would seem that the law failed with regard to the objective of providing stringent entry requirements. The reverse, however, is true. As demonstrated in chapter 2, at the time the law was passed the Histadrut enjoyed an 80 percent membership rate. Thus, the low requirements were translated into a twofold mechanism intended to entrench the Histadrut's position as almost the sole negotiator on behalf of workers. First, the Histadrut almost always enjoyed a

32. It is important to note that the law did not establish an equivalent requirement with regard to employers (Goldberg 1992; Ben-Israel 1986a). This was not deemed to be a problem at the time, as employers' associations were regarded as more of a contractual arrangement that was solely responsive to the Histadrut's operations. This asymmetry between labor and employers is in line with Offe and Wiesenthal (1985) view on "the two logics of collective action" and appears in other countries as well (Traxler 2000; Traxler 1993; Pestoff 1994).

33. Collective Agreements Law (1957), sec. 3–4.

Table 3.1. The rules for representative trade union status—a numerical example

Special collective agreement (limited to a single establishment)	General collective agreement (Industry-, occupation-, or statewide)
1,000 employees in the workplace, of whom:	10 employers are members of the employers' association
350 are members of the General Histadrut	10,000 workers are employed by the
100 are members of the National Histadrut	10 employers, of whom:
	100 are members of the General Histadrut
	50 are members of the National Histadrut
General Histadrut is the representative union	General Histadrut is the representative union
35% membership rate	1% membership rate
Can negotiate an agreement that covers all 1,000 workers	Can negotiate an agreement that covers all 10,000 workers
	Agreement can be extended by the Minister of Labor to other employers and their workers

higher level of membership than the other unions. Second, the low threshold required by the law, especially for earning representative status to negotiate a general collective agreement, ensured that the Histadrut would enjoy this status in every sector, almost regardless of its membership rate in the sector. Stringent entry standards, then, were not maintained by making representation status a hurdle that could not be passed. On the contrary, the law made earning representative status very easy, but it ensured that for the most part there would be only one union that could earn that status—namely, the General Histadrut. In the words of the Minister of Labor, Golda Meirson (Meir): "The law seeks to preserve the unity of the labor movement in Israel. Critics of the law who seek to preserve fragmentation are willing to give up the law altogether only because of the representation issue."[34] Moreover, the insignificant requirement for representative status for negotiating general collective agreements was explicitly intended to encourage broad negotiations and coverage as part of the overall corporatist scheme.[35]

Extending Broad Coverage of Collective Agreements   The law's second objective was to extend the coverage of collective agreements to a broad segment of the population. This was accomplished by three complementary measures. First, the law held that all the individual rights and obligations determined by the agreement would be automatically incorporated into the in-

34. See *The Knesset Protocols* D.K. vol. 19:187(1955)(Golda Meir, Minister of Labor). Mapai's position on "unity" was encouraged by the left-wing parties outside the coalition—D.K. vol. 19:154 (1955)(MK Riftin, MPM); ibid., 156 (MK Vilner, the Communist Party), and criticized by the right-wing parties—ibid., 168 (MK Magori-Cohen, Cherut). A similar objective was argued by the Minister of Labor in the debates over the Resolution of Labor Disputes Law; see D.K. vol.20:1787 (1956).

35. *The Knesset Protocols* D.K. vol. 19:147 (1955)(Minister of Labor Golda Meirson).

dividual employment contracts of all the workers who were covered by the agreement.[36] Second, the law held that the collective agreements applied to the parties to the agreement (i.e., the representative union and the employer or the employers' association), to the employers represented by the employers' association (i.e., in agreements not signed by individual employers), and to all the employees employed by the aforementioned employers.[37] The rules on coverage did not require membership in the representative union, or in any union for that matter, for the collective agreement to apply to individual employees. Thus, there is no legal connection between union membership and coverage of collective agreements. Third, the law introduced the mechanism of extension orders.[38] At the initiative of one or both parties to a general collective agreement, the Minister of Labor could extend the agreement, or parts of it, to a sector, a geographical area, and even to the whole state. Extension applies the agreement (or parts of the agreement) to employers who are not members of the employers' association that concluded the agreement and to their employees. The objective of extension orders is to prevent wage undercutting by nonorganized employers to whom the general collective agreements do not apply.[39]

To demonstrate the effects of extension orders, take the most typical corporatist example. Between 1972 and 1987 minimum wage was determined in collective agreements between the employers' associations, the state as an employer, and the Histadrut. According to the basic rules of coverage, this ensured a very broad coverage of employers and their employees. Yet to ensure the application of the minimum wage to the whole labor market, the Minister of Labor would issue a statewide extension order. As a result, every employer, including the employers of a single domestic worker, was obligated by the collectively determined minimum wage. During the corporatist phase, frequent

36. "Individual rights" designates rights (and the corresponding duties) that bind individual employees and their employer. These are distinguished from the party's rights or collective rights that prescribe the mutual rights and obligations of the parties signing the collective agreement. For example, a wage increase is an individual right because it prescribes a right to the worker and imposes a corresponding duty on his or her employer. By contrast, the union's right to receive an office and paid hours for union leaders within the workplace is a group right because it prescribes the right of the union and the corresponding duty of the employer. Individuals cannot claim this as their own right; it is the right of the collective.

37. Collective Agreements Law (1957), sec. 15–16.

38. Ibid., sec. 25–33.

39. *The Knesset Protocols* D.K. vol. 19:148 (1955) (Minister of Labor Golda Meirson). This was also a major point of controversy with regard to the proposed law, as it was argued that extending agreements imposed costs on small employers, which were negotiated with large employers, and was therefore anticompetitive. See, for example, ibid., 149 (MK Haim Ariav, the General Zionists Party); ibid., 166 (MK Avniel, Cherut); ibid., 168 (MK Cohen, the Progressive Party). A different type of argument was made by Cherut's MKs, who voiced the interests of the National Histadrut. Their argument was that the extension of collective agreements was designed to render the presence of unions other than the General Histadrut redundant because instead of negotiating at the enterprise level where the small unions are the representative unions, the extension orders would serve as trump cards. Cf. D.K. vol. 19:153 (1955)(MK Eliezer Shostak, Cherut).

use of extension orders was made, with extensions issued for various sectors, as well as statewide extensions (Kristal 2004).

Autonomy   The law's support for the corporatist system was not only in what it actively did but also in what it refrained from doing. The law displayed a passive and nonintrusive approach, with only a few legal rules that did not undermine the objective of securing autonomy. For example, one mandatory rule was that the collective agreement, like statutes, established a mandatory floor that could not be derogated in individual agreements.[40] A second required that collective agreements be concluded in writing and submitted for registration with the chief labor relations officer in the Ministry of Labor.[41] The officer was not authorized to use content-based discretion in his or her decision to register, and in fact the requirement was fulfilled merely by the submission of the agreement for registration. This requirement was intended to ensure that the agreements would be known and could be reviewed by the workers who were covered by them.

On other important issues, the law provided only default rules, of which three were of particular significance. First, with regard to the length of time collective agreements applied, the law determined, contrary to the principles of contracts law, that collective agreements continued to apply until terminated by one of the parties.[42] Thus, even if an agreement was signed for two years, it continued to govern the parties and the covered employees and employers until actively terminated and did not terminate automatically at the end of the contractual phase.[43]

A second default rule applied to the status of the agreement as providing a cap on employees' rights. While the view that collective agreements are mandatory and cannot be waived or derogated by individual contracts was broadly accepted, whether the collective agreement should be seen as exhausting all claims was a more controversial issue. On the one hand, the freedom of contract held that each employee could negotiate rights over and above what the collective agreement provided. The collective agreement was not deemed to bar the use of individual bargaining power. On the other hand, there was a concern that if the strong workers would negotiate individually, beyond what the agreement provided, the collective determination of wages and rights would be undermined. A compromise was reached asserting that agreements would serve only as a floor for rights but not as a ceiling unless the parties to the collective agreement determined otherwise.[44]

40. Collective Agreements Law (1957), sec. 22.
41. Ibid., sec. 10.
42. Ibid., secs. 13–14.
43. This accounts for one of the common practices in Israel, where negotiations on renewal of agreements often take place after agreements have reached the end of their contractual phase, and sometimes even years afterward (Danzinger and Neuman 2005).
44. Collective Agreements Law (1957), sec. 22. Also see the discussion in *The Knesset Protocols* D.K. vol. 19:147–48 (1955) (Golda Meirson, Minister of Labor).

Default rules were also used to achieve yet another compromise, with regard to the issue of monetary compensation for a breach of collective agreements. The Histadrut sought to withdraw the remedy of compensation from the sphere of collective bargaining.[45] Compensation for breach of agreements was not conducive to the resolution of disputes, it was argued, whereas injunctions requiring specific performance were better tailored to the needs of the negotiating partners. Even more than employers, the state was troubled with this position, as it had already experienced various wildcat strikes in breach of industrial-peace clauses in collective agreements. The Histadrut's objection to compensation for breach of damages was taken by some as a demonstration of its "irresponsible" position.[46] As in the controversy on the relationship between collective agreements and individual contracts, the proposed solution was to use a default rule prescribing that in collective relations the remedy of compensation for breach would not be allowed unless the negotiating parties to a general collective agreement held otherwise.[47]

The use of default rules in the Collective Agreements Law therefore gave rise to what was later designated as the "supremacy of collective agreements." According to this principle, on most matters relating to the status and content of collective bargaining, the negotiating partners have the power to decide the most suitable arrangement for themselves. Their decision is binding on the parties to individual contracts. The collective norm is therefore superior to individual norms. Moreover, the default rules are used in the same way as the derogation clauses and therefore also indicate that the legislature gave up its "natural" supremacy over collective agreements, making the collective agreements de facto superior to statutory provisions that affect the content of collective agreements. Thus, while the issue of recognition and coverage remained mandatory and ensured the domination of the Histadrut as the partner to employers in negotiating the broadly applied norms, matters of content were relegated to default rules and the supremacy of the collective norm. The application of mandatory rules to recognition and coverage and of default rules to content was therefore the basis of the "recognition and autonomy" formula that the Histadrut successfully endorsed in the first law on collective bargaining in Israel.

RECOGNITION AND AUTONOMY IN OTHER
COLLECTIVE LABOR LAWS

The same principles that characterized the legislation of the Collective Agreements Law can also be observed in the legislation of the two ancillary laws that were passed at the time—the Settlement of Labor Disputes Law

---

45. See *The Knesset Protocols* D.K. vol. 19:151 (1955) (MK Aharon Beker, Mapai, previously a Histadrut official).

46. Cf. ibid., 157–58 (MK Shoken, the Progressive Party); ibid., 167 (MK Cohen, the Progressive Party).

47. On the need for compromise, see the position of the Minister of Labor, Golda Meirson, ibid., 171.

(1957)[48] and the Employment Service Law (1959). Because the Collective Agreements Law provided the elements needed to secure recognition, the passage of the other laws reflected the Histadrut's effort to secure its autonomy in light of pressures to tightly regulate industrial relations generally and the privilege of the General Histadrut in particular.

Defending Autonomy: Labor Disputes   The Settlement of Labor Disputes Law was passed with much controversy, which indicated that despite the social partners' strong position, the corporatist system was constantly challenged. The right-wing parties argued that the pressing problem in industrial relations was extensive industrial unrest, making it necessary to impose a higher level of restraint on the Histadrut.[49] At the same time, the Knesset members on the left warned that passing the Collective Agreements Law would be the first stage of formalizing collective relations, leading eventually to binding arbitration arrangements in the Labor Disputes Law.[50] In this debate, the Histadrut's major objective was that any arrangement chosen must not undermine its right and effective power to strike. For the employers—and also for the National Histadrut, which took a liberal economic stand—the objective was to provide dispute resolution processes that would substitute for the use of strikes, leaving strikes only as a last resort in unspecified situations. The major instrument they sought to legislate was compulsory arbitration. By contrast, the leftist parties and most notably the Communist Party sought to avoid the law altogether and to reject any legislation that prescribed rights and obligations in the area of collective disputes resolution.

In this array of divergent opinions, the Histadrut's position prevailed. The law was enacted with three major parts. The first two provided the means of dispute resolution—mediation and arbitration, both of which avoided the problem of compulsory arbitration.[51] On the one hand, mediation could be instigated at the request of one of the parties or even at the initiative of the officer of labor relations. Once mediation was instigated, the parties had to comply with the process, but the central feature of mediation was that the officer or his representative could propose but not enforce solutions. By contrast, the outcomes of arbitration were binding on the parties, but the law held that both parties must agree to arbitration for the process to take place. At the time the law was passed, and ever since, compulsory arbitration, while often proposed, has never been accepted (Raday 1983a; Mironi 1990–1991; Finkelstein 2003).

48. For a discussion of the Settlement of Labor Disputes Law in the general context of labor dispute resolution processes in Israel see Mironi (1986), Raday (1983a), Ben-Israel and Mironi (1987, 1988).

49. See for example, *The Knesset Protocols* D.K. vol. 19:149 (1955) (MK Haim Ariav, the General Zionist Party); ibid., 150 (MK Moshe Kalmar, the National Religious Party); ibid., 157 (MK Shoken, the Progressive Party); ibid., 166 (MK Avniel, Cherut); ibid., 167 (MK Cohen, the Progressive Party).

50. See *The Knesset Protocols* D.K. vol. 19:155–56 (1955) (MK Vilner, the Communist Party).

51. Settlement of Labor Disputes Law (1957), sec. 5–37.

The third part of the law established the Council for Labor Relations, structured on a tripartite basis, granting the General Histadrut a monopoly on labor's representation, as well as a general consultation position. This third component actually legitimized the council that already existed at the time the law was passed, one that was also responsible for advising the Minister of Labor and Welfare on matters of legislation. This was a clear example of a tripartite institution legislating its own position in the corporatist scheme.

Defending Autonomy: Employment Bureaus　　The Resolution of Labor Disputes Law was an indication of the Histadrut's success in securing its autonomy and power even when potentially hostile legislation was being required by the political agents. A similar challenge to its autonomy appeared at the same time, when the problem of the employment bureaus was raised.

The employment bureaus existed even prior to the Histadrut, having been established by political parties in order to try and match Jewish workers in Palestine with Jewish employers and farmers.[52] The Jewish workers were at a disadvantage and needed the aid and persuasive power of the bureaus' staff because the employers preferred to employ Arab workers at lower wages. Once the Histadrut was established, for much the same reason, the bureaus were turned over to it. Because the employers objected to the bureaus and the supply of labor was much greater than the demand, the employment bureaus were viewed as acting only on behalf of the workers and not on behalf of both sides. As new unions were established, most notably the National Histadrut, each union opened its own bureaus. This led to strong rivalry between the bureaus for placements and consequently brought about the beginning of the "preferences" system, in which job seekers who were affiliated with the trade union were given preference when jobs were assigned.

The Employment Service Law sought to correct these problems by nationalizing the employment bureaus. At first this might have seemed to defeat the Histadrut's quest for autonomy and power, particularly given its insistence on preserving its role in the sphere of social provision. Yet the General Histadrut's consent to this move was based on its political affiliation with the governing party, Mapai. The party, headed at the time by David Ben-Gurion, aimed at nationalizing fundamental social services, such as education and employment placement services. Moreover, the law was intended to appease Mapai's coalition partners.[53] However, there was also a financial incentive to

52. The historical description of the employment bureaus is based on *The Knesset Protocols* D.K. vol. 24:1881–83 (1958).

53. The Coalition Agreement between Mapai and the Progressive Party, for the Seventh Government (1955); see *The Knesset Protocols* D.K. vol. 19:167 (1955) (MK Cohen, the Progressive Party); D.K. vol. 24:1881 (1958) (the introduction of the proposed bill on the Employment Service Law). The Progressive Party endorsed a more liberal view on markets, and the agreement on promoting the Employment Service Law was intended to appease its objection to other laws that were being prepared at the time the agreement was signed, most notably the Collective Agreements Law.

approve the law. In the 1950s, the bureaus administered by the General Histadrut were the major source of labor market mediation in the state. The state had begun funding the various bureaus, and de facto nationalization was on its way. It was clear that continuous funding would require some form of nationalization and that without state funding the costs incurred by the Histadrut would be prohibitive. Consequently, in 1956 the Histadrut's governing body decided to favor the distribution of work through a national employment service.

Despite the attempt to nationalize the employment bureaus, the Employment Services Law, like the other labor laws, maintained a corporatist tilt in favor of the Histadrut. The new preference system was to be determined by the bureaus' governing council, which was based on a parity system. As in the case of other laws, the workers' representatives were to be appointed by the Minister of Labor after consulting with the largest union (i.e., only with the General Histadrut), and the employers' representatives were to be appointed after consultation with all the relevant employers' associations. Much to the dismay of the National Histadrut, the General Histadrut's position as the sole representative of labor for the purpose of appointments, and as the second-largest employer, ensured that it could pack the governing council and hence have a disproportionate impact on the design of the preferences system. In addition, the law secured the Histadrut's interest in the evolving design of labor law and its impact on strikes. The law prescribed that the employment bureau would not interfere in industrial relations at the time of a strike. Thus the bureaus were prohibited from sending workers to substitute for striking workers, while at the same time employers whose workers were striking were exempted from compulsory affiliation with the service (and thus were able to hire substitutes at will).[54]

Thus, despite what may have seemed a grave infringement on the autonomy of the Histadrut, the damage to the General Histadrut was contained by the very partial withdrawal of the preferences system, which catered to the Histadrut's interests.

Promoting Recognition: Agency Fees In the midst of the process in which the legislature passed the laws of collective bargaining, the Wage Protection Law (1958) was passed. Although this law belongs to the general category of substantive labor standards, it also contributed to the collective regulation of labor by instituting a somewhat concealed recognition of agency fees for trade union activity by nonmembers.[55] According to this arrangement, an employee who was covered by a collective agreement and who was not a member of the representative trade union or any other union could be required to pay the representative union an agency fee. The law did not require employees to pay the agency fees but permitted the parties to the collective

---

54. Employment Service law (1959), sec. 44.
55. Wage Protection Law (1958), sec. 25.

agreement to deduct such pay directly from the employees' wages. In such situations the employer deducted the agency fee, like income tax payments, and transferred the money deducted to the trade union. The level of the agency fees was determined by the trade union itself, but in the Wage Protection By-laws it was capped to ensure that the agency fees would be lower than the membership fees. Thus, the law legitimized and provided the means for effective collection of fees from employees who chose not to be members of the representative union. The law also exempted members of nonrepresentative unions from paying agency fees to the representative union. Although they enjoyed the benefits of the collective agreements, it was considered a violation of their freedom of association if they were compelled to pay agency fees over and above their voluntary membership fees to the union of their choice. Yet despite the careful balances carved by the legislature, and in conformance with the corporatist principle of autonomy, the law left it to the social partners to determine the circumstances in which agency fees would be deducted.

At the time the agency fees arrangement was legislated, its role was relatively minor because most of the employees were members of the Histadrut. Other employees, such as teachers, were members of a competing union that was also a representative trade union in itself. Small groups of workers were members of other unions, and the "loss" the Histadrut suffered because of the law's exemption of these workers from paying agency fees was a small token to pay for the freedom of association. Despite the minor practical significance, this was an important component in building the corporatist legal infrastructure. It demonstrated a preference for the right to associate over the freedom from association. It further introduced an institution that was crucial in later years when membership in the Histadrut declined and its financing became a fundamental problem. These problems will be explained in greater detail in the chapter 5.

Promoting Recognition: Consultation Clauses and Tripartite Governing Bodies   Similar to the legislation of substantive norms described in the previous section, the procedural laws that were accepted in the late 1950s continue the tradition of consultation clauses and add to them. The three laws provide explicitly for consultation as a requirement before regulations are issued.[56] Like consultation clauses under the substantive law, the consultation clauses in the procedural laws ensure that consultation will be conducted only with the union representing the most workers in the state, namely, the Histadrut. Other unions are excluded.[57] Naturally, this was cause for protest by the right-wing members of the Knesset and was opposed most strongly by the representatives of the National Histadrut.[58]

56. Collective Agreements Law (1957), sec. 34; Industrial Disputes Law (1957) sec. 43 Employment Service Law (1959), sec. 90.

57. *The Knesset Protocols* D.K. vol. 21:1089 (1957) (MK Shostak, Cherut and the National Histadrut).

58. Collective Agreements Law (1957), sec. 27(2).

Moreover, the three procedural laws attempted to structure a tripartite governance scheme, maintaining the dominance of the Histadrut even beyond the tilted consultation clauses. The Settlement of Labor Disputes Law established a Council for Industrial Relations that is responsible for giving advice to the Minister of Labor on all matters related to industrial relations, including the need for extending collective agreements.[59] Labor and employers are represented equally on the council. A more important role is attributed to the Employment Service Board, which acts as the "supreme authority of the Employment Bureau."[60] In both the council and the board, the workers' representatives are appointed by the minister after consultation with the largest union in the state (i.e., the General Histadrut), and the employers' representatives are appointed after consultation with all employers' associations. Together with the governing boards of the Institute of Safety and Health (as determined by the Labor Inspection [Organization] Law) and the National Insurance Institute (as determined by the National Insurance Law), these laws complete the tripartite governance of all institutions dealing with the labor market and welfare issues, always guaranteeing the Histadrut's sole position and ability to pack the governing and consulting bodies with its own representatives.[61]

While these tripartite governing bodies were more or less active and effective during various periods, often depending on the ideological inclinations of the Ministry of Labor, most of them have become ineffective or extremely weak during the second (postcorporatist) phase of labor law. Thus, the arrangements written in the law books are not always implemented in fact. However, at the time surveyed in this chapter, the firm support for tripartite governing bodies, demonstrated by their recurring presence one way or another throughout all the labor laws that were passed, is highly indicative of the tripartite and corporatist foundations that influenced the legislature and that the legislature sought to secure.

Barriers to the Fulfillment of Corporatist Labor Law

As can be seen, except for the constitutionalization of labor's rights, the agenda prepared by the Histadrut on the eve of statehood was accomplished almost completely within a decade. The process of writing labor law was smooth, generally without controversy, and the failed attempt to legislate the Employment Contracts Law was the exception rather than the rule. While industrial relations were not always benevolent during the period 1948–1969 with a high level of industrial action, these disputes did not undermine the

59. Ibid., sec. 27(3).

60. Employment Service Law (1959), secs. 8–10.

61. Labor Inspection [Organization] Law (1954), secs. 26–28; National Insurance Law (consolidated version) (1995), secs. 15–16.

construction of the legal infrastructure for the corporatist regime. As one commentator suggested at the time: "[A]t the risk of simplification, labor legislation in Israel is not the outcome of struggle and compromise between labor and capital, but rather the expression of the will of the labor movement" (Zamir 1966, 304).

The discrepancy between the calm and unruffled legal front and the stormy industrial relations front indicates that law was somehow not fulfilling its expected function. While it provided a minimal statutory safety net to individuals, it had very little impact in terms of relieving tensions in the industrial relations system. In fact, despite the passage of statutes governing collective relations, these relations remained mostly extralegal. When one considers the decisions of the Supreme Court during these two decades, collective labor relations hardly appeared in its docket, nor did they reach the lower courts. In a handful of decisions, the Supreme Court primarily discussed the internalization of the collective agreement into the individual employment contract.[62] However, the relationship between the agents who signed the agreement received hardly any attention. Thus it seems that collective bargaining remained for the most part in the shadow of law, and labor disputes were resolved by means of negotiations and industrial action. As an anecdote, it is worth mentioning that collective bargaining received only bare mention in labor law courses in law faculties during that period. Students' casebooks mentioned collective labor law briefly, emphasizing its nature as "autonomous labor law." The emphasis indicates that labor law teachers, who were also the judges and leading labor lawyers of the time, viewed collective relations as an extralegal issue.[63]

The autonomous nature of collective bargaining might have been deemed a success of the corporatist paradigm of law. Yet autonomy in this sense was not truly satisfactory to the trilateral system. The employers and the state viewed the widespread use of industrial action by the Histadrut as undermining the effort to legally govern a more peaceful industrial relations system. At the same time, the Histadrut was concerned over the few decisions of the Supreme Court that narrowed its power in industrial action.[64]

The Histadrut's discontent with the law of strikes has been shown to have been of vast importance throughout the years surveyed thus far. The British Mandate government's narrowing of the unions' rights during strikes in 1927

---

62. Supreme Court HCJ 364/41 Yaákov Pelverbeum and Others v. Commissioner of Industrial Relations and Others, PDI 15(3):2547; Supreme Court CA 256/63 "Atlantic" Fishing Company Inc. v. Gad Rubin, PDI 18(2):294.

63. Class notes of Itzhak Bar-Shira (1954; School for Law and Economics, Tel-Aviv) and Tzvi Berenzon (various years, Hebrew University Faculty of Law), circulated by students. Not until 1970 did collective labor law appear as an important component in law studies, as observed in the class notes prepared by Itzhak Zamir (1970, Hebrew University Faculty of Law).

64. For example, Supreme Court CA 167/62 Leo Beck School Ltd v. Secondary School Teachers Union, PDI 16:2205; Supreme Court CA 20/56 Attorney General v. Naomi Dolzenski and Others, PDI 11:745.

and the Israeli legislature's attempt to regulate the employers' duty to pay wages to employees in 1968 are two examples in which legalization of industrial relations drove the Histadrut into opposition. The Supreme Court's sparse case law on strikes had a similar effect.

Consequently, the construction of the corporatist paradigm of labor law was not yet complete. There was, however, a way to move forward. After an unsuccessful attempt to establish a labor tribunal in 1958, in 1967 the Histadrut and the Industrialists Association signed a collective agreement in which they took upon themselves the obligation to lobby the legislature for the establishment of a labor courts system. Given the impasse on industrial action, the ministries of labor and justice were both in favor, hoping that the development of labor law by a designated courts system might bring about industrial peace. The catchy phrase coined by the then Minister of Labor, Yigal Alon, was "*shfita* instead of *shvita*" (adjudication instead of strikes). Soon the Labor Court Law (1969) was enacted, severing the jurisdiction over all labor disputes (both individual and collective), as well as social security matters, from the general courts system, granting the newly founded labor courts sole jurisdiction in these areas. This marked a new and distinct stage in the structuring of corporatist labor law. While the first phase was characterized by legislation, in the second phase hardly any legislation was initiated and the authoring of corporatist law moved to the courtroom. This transition and its effects will be described in the following chapter.

4 Adjudication in the Service of Corporatism, 1969–1987

In the first chapter I argued that the literature on corporatism in particular, and industrial relations in general, usually ignores the development of law, deeming the legal rule to be exogenous. Where there are exceptions, the study of legal developments is often focused on legislation. By contrast, adjudication is totally marginalized and receives hardly any attention. It may be hypothesized that this is a result of the assumption that judges are the civil servants of the legal system and that it is their role to implement the legal rule as developed by the legislature. In legal scholarship this view has hardly any support. Many fields of law have been developed predominantly by the courts, ranging from the common law in the area of contracts, property, and torts law, to constitutional law. However, the omission of judicial lawmaking is particularly surprising in the area of labor law, where labor courts and tribunals are involved.

Labor courts exist in many countries and can be distinguished according to their level of integration in the general legal system (Rogowski 1994). At one end of the continuum are administrative tribunals such as the National Labor Relations Board (NLRB) in the United States or the Conseils de Prud'hommes in France. Other states have established full-fledged judicial tribunals with powers matching those of the civil judicial system. As will be demonstrated, the Israeli labor court system, comprising five regional labor courts and the National Labor Court, falls into the latter category. However, the important role of the judiciary in establishing the legal infrastructure of corporatism cannot be captured without alluding to the role of the industrial relations system in establishing, staffing, and directing these courts. Although judges in the Israeli labor courts, as in most labor courts (France being the exception—Porcher 1994), are appointed by the state and therefore regarded as being insulated from the industrial relations system itself, the structure of the labor court system also ensures an affinity between the interests of industrial relations in general (rather than the interests of a particular party in a given dispute) and the mode of deliberations and reasoning within the courts.

This chapter will fall into two parts. In the first I will discuss the establishment of the labor courts, the objectives that were used to justify the separation of dispute resolution in the area of labor law from other legal spheres, and how the structure of the labor courts was intended to serve the needs and interests of the corporatist system. Second, I will discuss the contributions of the labor courts throughout the relevant period. I will argue that the labor court system has contributed much to the development of corporatist labor law in Israel. It has provided the necessary rules for recognition, centralization, concentration, limiting the use of industrial action and unilateral action, and the broad application of collective agreements. It has strengthened the autonomous sphere of the social partners while maintaining the necessary ingredients for recognition. It will further be demonstrated that these decisions can hardly be viewed as merely the mechanical implementation of legislation. The labor court system must therefore be viewed as a strategic partner in the corporatist system rather than its civil servant. Only by observing the labor courts' rulings until the late 1980s can we understand the level of perfection achieved in the construction of corporatist labor law.

The Foundation of the Labor Courts

The first proposal to establish a labor court was made in 1958, after an advisory committee had been appointed; the court was to be based on the same tripartite structure as was embodied in other laws (Berenson 1958). As was pointed out in the previous chapter, this was the period in which the legislature passed the infrastructure for collective agreements and corporatist negotiations (the Collective Agreements Law, the Settlement of Labor Disputes Law, and the Employment Service Law). The Labor Court Law would have fitted into this legislative project. The main objections at the time, however, came from the Ministry of Justice and the Supreme Court, which feared that the separation of labor disputes from the general judicial system would undermine the position of the general judicial system and serve as a precedent for future separations of disputes in other areas of the law. This indicates the presence of a pressure that has been overlooked in the corporatist literature. When the literature discusses the autonomy of the state and the relationship between the associations, especially between the trade unions and the state, the term "state" designates the legislature and the executive branches. The relationship is based first and foremost on political alliances. However, the judiciary is considered as important as the other branches, and its appointment process is not on a party basis.[1] The social partners therefore have a more limited influence on the judicial branch. The controversy over the 1958 proposal was therefore not between the state and the social partners but within the state itself. The legal system, the position of which was voiced by the peak-level agents within that system (the Minister of Justice and the Supreme Court), sought to insulate its own autonomy and concentration in the face of the corporatist system's challenge.

Further attempts to pass the Labor Courts Law did not materialize either (Zamir 1968).[2] Only when the interests of the corporatist triangle's vertexes merged, when each, for its own reasons, believed the labor courts were necessary at the time, did the triangle prevail over the judicial system. The draft proposal for the Labor Courts Law was submitted to the Knesset in 1967.[3] Despite the variety of rationales for the establishment of the labor courts, in essence all three sides expected the labor courts to resolve the problem of strikes. For the state qua employer (being represented by the executive branch), for the private employers, and for the right-wing parties in the Knesset, the expectation was that the labor courts would offer a venue for settling disputes without having the unions resort to strikes. The Histadrut and the center-left-wing parties in the Knesset expected that these courts would interpret the law of strikes more generously than the Supreme Court was doing in some of its early rulings, and that it would adopt a generally favorable disposition toward labor's side, unlike the formalistic legalism of the general courts. Absolute opposition to instituting a labor court was voiced only by the Communist Party, an insignificant minority in the Knesset. It is therefore wrong to think that the labor courts evolved out of consensus. In fact they evolved out of a dispute among the three corporatist agents over the "rules of the game" (rather than a particular industrial dispute). Rather than confront the law of strikes directly, the parties opted for establishing the labor courts, each side hoping the courts would legitimize the rules it favored. In a sense this was an autopoietic—"let's decide on how to decide"—solution (Rogowski 2000).

In the parliamentary debates, four arguments were put forward for the need to establish the labor court system.[4] First, there was a need to consolidate various administrative, quasi-legal processes that had been established by the legislation of the 1950s and that led to the dispersion of dispute resolution in the area of labor law and social security to numerous venues. Second, it was

1. This of course is not universally true, but in most countries judges are not appointed on the basis of their political position, although in some countries—the United States being the striking example—political and ideological positions are important. In Israel, political positions are not taken into consideration, at least not formally or visibly.

2. The most important proposal during the relevant period came in 1964 from Yehuda Sha'ari, a member of the right-wing Independent Liberals party. *The Knesset Protocols* D.K. vol. 41:327–29, 336–58 (1964).

3. Proposal: Labor Court Law (748 *Legislative Proposals* 15 [1967]).

4. See the Labor Minister's presentation of the proposal as recorded in *The Knesset Protocols* D.K. vol. 50:305–7 (1967).

argued that labor law and social security required special skills and expertise, not only in the legal field but also in economics and industrial relations. Moreover, judges must develop an understanding of industrial practices, the complicated structure of collective agreements, and their highly technical content. Third, it was argued that adjudication in the area of labor law must be devised to fit the special nature of labor disputes. Rather than provide a strict legal response to legal questions, the labor courts must be capable of adapting to the mode of communications appropriate to the industrial relations system.[5] They must also engage in alternative forms of dispute resolution, including the resolution of *interests disputes* (i.e., disputes on the establishment of future rights, such as an increase in wages, to which no legal response is usually appropriate).[6] The emphasis on the adjudication of interests disputes led to the fourth interest: to provide legal solutions that would reduce the need to resort to industrial action. In essence, a combination of the third and fourth arguments was the major reason for establishing the labor courts. As will be demonstrated, the original proposal was tailored to accommodate these two rationales, but as the legislative proceedings advanced, the Knesset erected a tribunal that was much bigger than had been imagined, in which the issues of industrial action were marginal in number. By the time the law was passed, it had undergone various changes, and the labor courts were denied some of the more significant (and controversial) legal tools to fulfill their mission in the area of industrial action. There was therefore a mismatch between the various objectives and the institutional design that was eventually constructed for the courts.

The proposal for the Labor Courts Law held, first and foremost, that the labor courts would usually sit with one "professional" judge and two lay judges, one from the employers' side and one from the labor side. The lay judges' affiliation would be relevant to their appointments process, but their loyalty was to the making of justice and not to their affiliated side. Appointments would be made by the Minister of Labor (unlike professional judicial appointments, which are made by a committee headed by the Minister of Justice), after consultation with the largest union (for labor representatives) and with the relevant employers' organizations (for the employers' representatives). The labor courts were therefore a reflection of the tripartite system, including the tilted preference for the General Histadrut that followed the tracks set by earlier

5. The comments made by several Knesset members on this issue are indicative of the tension between the legal and the industrial relations modes of communication and the need of the legal system to adapt itself. For example, one member held that "the lay-judges on the court will not be restricted, as the professional judges are, by the law of evidence and the legal precedents that delay and obstruct the process" (*The Knesset Protocols* D.K. vol. 50:374 [1976]). Another commented, "The judges must know how to compromise between the parties, to persuade them, and for that they need a whole different language. I don't argue that they must deviate from the law, but they must consider the relationship between law and justice" (D.K. vol. 50:394 [1967]).

6. For the problematic aspects of legal intervention in interests disputes, see Raday (1983a); Ben-Israel and Mironi (1988).

legislation. This was the basis of the solution to the disjuncture between the corporatist system and the judicial branch. The appointment of lay judges corresponded to the various objectives of establishing a separate labor court. These judges were to bring with them expertise from the field and the nonlegal wisdom to resolve disputes to the benefit of the parties, rather than merely applying the legal rule (Adler 1991). The labor courts were therefore designed to resolve disputes on the basis of communications that were typical of the industrial relations system rather than on the basis of the legal system's mode of communication. The bench was not designed to reach a legal consensus but rather to replicate corporatist negotiations. It was intended to present the labor courts not as just a final resort when all other negotiations had broken down but as a legitimate and preferred venue for resolving disputes in the course of negotiations.

To accommodate the role of the labor court system as a facilitator of industrial disputes, the law provided further measures. For example, it instituted a special procedure for collective disputes, which distinguished these processes from the resolution of individual disputes. The highly informal process in collective disputes brought together the various parties and allowed for court rulings on the basis of depositions filed by the parties, without any need for witnesses to testify. Furthermore, the law held that the parties were not formally bound by the law of evidence.

As the legislative proceedings developed, the Knesset extended the labor courts' jurisdiction over all labor and social security matters, broadly defined, while also granting it controversial jurisdiction over disputes among unions (which should be resolved by the industrial relations system, argued the left) and criminal proceedings (which should be decided by the regular courts system, argued the legal system). Consequently, right at the outset it already became clear that collective disputes, the raison d'être for establishing the labor court system, were numerically a marginal factor in the courts' docket, accounting at the time for less than 5 percent of the courts' overall caseload. This corresponded to the first objective listed earlier—the consolidation of dispersed jurisdictions—and to an extent also accommodated the building of expertise, but it had a diluting effect on the objective of providing alternative means of adjudication in labor disputes.

General criticism of the labor courts emanated from two distinct positions. The legal criticism of the Labor Courts Law held that there was nothing to prevent the resolution of labor disputes in the regular courts system.[7] While the regular judicial system might not be able to resolve interests disputes, these were few and did not in themselves justify the establishment of a whole judicial subsystem. To handle interests disputes there were alternative measures, some of which had been introduced in the Settlement of Labor Disputes Law a decade earlier and had in fact been underutilized. This also reflected on

---

7. For the legal criticism, see, for example, *The Knesset Protocols* D.K. vol. 50:374, 401–5 (1967). See also Zamir (1968).

the second argument. If previous efforts to encourage the parties to bring in neutral third parties to resolve their disputes had not resulted in a reduction of industrial action, there was no reason to assume that the labor courts would succeed. On top of that, the lawyers in the Parliament, as well as some key legal personalities (including some of the judges sitting in the Supreme Court), argued that the labor court system would pave the way for the separation of other courts, that it was liable to develop law in a fashion inconsistent with the developments in the regular civil courts system, and that the lay judges could not act as judges and their presence would delegitimize the labor courts.

The critique from the left, most notably from the leftist Zionist party (Mapam) and the Communist Party was that the law sought to limit the autonomy of collective bargaining and the right to strike.[8] They argued that establishing the labor courts to expedite hearings in the area of labor law was only a "justification" and that its true purpose was to initiate a creeping process leading to the termination of the right to strike and mandatory arbitration. Various features of the proposed law disturbed the leftist parties; concern over them was generally voiced also by some of the Labor Party's representatives. Most notably there was an objection to any kind of legal process that dealt with interests disputes and a fear that the law would entrust the labor courts with the power to issue injunctions against striking workers and to intervene in industrial action.

Despite the legal and the left-wing critiques, the law passed with strong support. As with previous laws, the final result was a centrist compromise led by the Labor Party.[9] The right succeeded in extending the jurisdiction of the labor courts to disputes among trade unions and between members of trade unions and the unions themselves. However, the right failed to introduce a clause prohibiting the use of industrial action when a dispute was pending in the courts. The left succeeded in weeding out the fact-finding procedure that was intended to be used in interests disputes. However, the left's request that the law would boldly state that the Court's power to issue injunctions would not be applied to strikes was not incorporated. Thus, both the left and the right's demands to introduce substantive provisions on the law of strikes into the "procedural" Labor Courts Law were rejected by the centrist position. It was precisely the courts' role to devise a way out of this controversy.

Shortly after the law was passed, the National Labor Court was founded, headed by Tzvi Bar-Niv, who had spent many years performing various legal roles related to the Histadrut and to labor relations. In an article, Bar-Niv provided a condensed yet apt statement on the position of the labor courts, stating, "The Labor Courts, although institutionally and constitutionally part of the Judiciary, are an integral component of the labor relations system, just as the judiciary as a whole is an integral component of the socio-economic and political system of any state" (Bar-Niv 1974, 558).

8. For Mapai's criticism, see *The Knesset Protocols* D.K. vol. 50:379, 384 (1967); the left-wing Mapam, D.K. vol. 50:378 (1967); the Communist Party, D.K. vol. 50:392 (1967).
9. The centrist compromise is presented in *The Knesset Protocols* D.K. vol. 54:2033 (1969).

The Contribution of the Labor Courts

To assess the performance and importance of the labor courts is no easy task. First, as noted above, the objectives of establishing the labor courts varied, and there was an institutional mismatch between the expectation that the courts would extend their jurisdiction into interests disputes and curb the use of strikes and the actual jurisdiction given to the system, which was solely over "legal disputes." Other objectives, such as the guarantee of expeditious and informal hearings, better adapted to the problems facing individual plaintiffs who are not represented by legal counsel, require an empirical comparison between the regular courts system and the labor courts. More relevant to the focus of this book is the question whether the establishment of the labor courts was associated with a reduction in the level of strikes. As will be demonstrated shortly, the answer is clearly no. More generally, it is possible to conduct various empirical analyses of the labor courts' performance, but these cannot depict its most significant contribution—the development of labor law. What had been a dormant body of law in the statutory phase became a living and dynamically changing area of law (Zamir 1978). For better or worse, the labor courts have become a central institution in the industrial relations system.

To demonstrate the courts' contribution to the development of the corporatist paradigm of law, I will focus on two areas—the law of trade union recognition and the law of industrial action. Although, as mentioned, collective labor law composed only a small share of the overall cases brought to the courts, this is where the courts were expected to contribute the most. This was in fact the major justification for the labor court system's establishment.

The analysis of the labor courts' cases in the first two decades after the system was established indicates its contribution in developing a rich jurisprudence in the area of labor law. To the legal system it provided the expertise, and to the industrial relations system it provided the policy compromises that could not have been made in legislation. As will be demonstrated, the Court's rulings were highly sensitive to the corporatist nature of the industrial relations system and tried to function within the confines of corporatism. Thus, while legally it was a highly active court, in terms of policy it was relatively conservative (as measured by adherence to the social status quo).

The Role of the Labor Courts in Perfecting the Law on Trade Union Recognition

As explained above, the establishment of the labor courts was a method of mediating conflicting interests in a corporatist system. The fundamental conflict that justified the labor court system was in regard to the legal infrastructure. The extensive legislation of the first twenty years was characterized by the Histadrut's powerful domination of the legislative agenda. It has been demonstrated that in some situations the Histadrut initiated the process, whereas at other times it was actively engaged in the legislative process, and the Labor Party (Mapai) voiced the Histadrut's position in the Knesset. The laws that were passed occasionally provided compromises on controversial issues, such as the nationalization of the employment bureaus. Matters on which a consensus or a compromise could not be devised, such as a law of industrial action, were removed from the legislative docket. Such was the case with the status of trade unions. From the outset, the Histadrut objected to the British Mandate government's efforts to implement the Trade Unions Ordinance from 1947, and it later objected to regulatory attempts in Israel.[10] The Histadrut viewed any attempt to intervene in its internal matters (broadly defined) as an infringement of its autonomy.

Consequently and inevitably, the labor courts were entrusted with the task of developing the law of recognition. I use the term "law of recognition" to designate the range of issues involved in recognizing the agents to collective bargaining. Which organizations are deemed to be trade unions? Which trade unions are representative? When can rival unions obtain recognition? When does internal rivalry within the union affect the rules of recognition?

Unlike the legislature, which could avoid confrontation by abstaining from legislation, the labor courts were presented with real legal disputes that had to be resolved one way or another. The expectation was that the labor courts would devise solutions using their legal authority to overcome the Histadrut's objection to lawmaking in this area. Indeed, the courts' early rulings on trade union recognition are carefully designed, sometimes cunning, and often conceal value-laden outcomes beneath positivistic legal rhetoric.

Most notably, the development of the law on trade union recognition was responsive to two basic features of corporatism—concentration and centralization.[11] The case law on trade unions spanned various questions relating to the definition of "trade union," its status, the status of its organs, its powers, and its relationship with the members. Most of the judicial decisions in this area were based on general legal principles and not on the direct interpretation of statutes because statutory law intentionally avoided them. Only a handful of decisions rested on statutory interpretation, but even these identified serious

10. The initial attempt to pass a new Law of Associations to regulate not-for-profit associations, to replace the Ottoman legislation was in 1964. The proposed bill excluded trade unions on the basis of an argument that international covenants on the freedom of association required such exemption (*The Knesset Protocols* D.K. vol. 42:1794 [1967]). In 1967, still within the debate over the law, the parliamentary members of the center and left emphasized again that the Histadrut must remain outside the scope of the law because it had broad political and social objectives that rendered it different from other associations (MK Idelsson from Mapai—ibid., 1642, and MK Joseph Kushnier (Mapam)—ibid., 1788). This reasoning was echoed by the Minister of Justice when a later proposal was finally accepted (1980) (D.K. vol. 87[2]:738 [1989]).

11. It is interesting to note that shortly after the Labor Court was established, its president identified these features as the major problem for the Histadrut. He was well aware of the tension within the Histadrut, as power was exercised by secondary units such as workers' committees and even ad hoc bodies that did not have any formal standing. He identified this as the result of tension between formal (centralized) power and real (decentralized) power (Bar-Niv 1974, 559).

problems with the statutory language, most notably problems of circular definitions. Thus, the case law should be viewed as a creation de novo by the labor courts. While the legal logic of these cases may sometimes seem odd, their logic from an industrial relations standpoint is clear. The case law in this area is the paradigmatic example of constructing the necessary enabling conditions for corporatism. There are hardly any cases that fall outside the corporatist paradigm. The first case in which the Histadrut lost on matters relating to recognition, centralization, and autonomy did not occur until 1992, thus extending the time frame that I attribute to the corporatist phase of labor law.

Generally, the case law sought to ensure the hegemonic position of the Histadrut in the industrial relations system and to avoid fragmentation of interests representation. What this required was ease of recognition for the Histadrut as the representative union, while the recognition of other unions needed to be made more difficult. A related agenda was to ensure concentration by precluding rival unions from earning the status of a representative union. To resolve the problems associated with centralization, it was the court's task to preclude the Histadrut's organs from taking part in collective bargaining and industrial action. Moreover, this required the immunization of the Histadrut's centralized position from challenges by individuals and small groups among the rank and file. Together these cases upheld the slogan "one Histadrut—a strong Histadrut." (Ben-Israel 1986a; Mundlak 1996; Raday 1983b; Shaked 2003). Following are what in my view are the most important contributions of the National Labor Court in this area of law between the years 1969 and 1987.

1. *Finding the Histadrut to be a primary organization.* The Histadrut was held to be a primary organization rather than a federation of trade unions.[12] This was based on the historical evolution of the Histadrut, which preceded its trade unions and had actually created them over the years according to its own bylaws. Consequently, the trade unions and other representational structures within the Histadrut (such as the enterprise-level workers' committees and the regional workers' councils were granted power only to the extent permitted by the Histadrut's bylaws.[13] This was of particular importance in denying the workplace-based workers' committees the power to negotiate collective agreements or to declare a strike, despite (and actually because of) their proximity to the workers themselves (Raday 1983b, 1971; Shaked 2003). An additional implication of the "primary organization" approach was that the Labor Court refused to adjudicate lawsuits brought by one of the Histadrut's organs against the Histadrut itself. The Labor Court held these to be a kind of

---

12. See, National Labor Court 35/5-1 Leon Markovitz—General Histadrut, PDA 6:197; National Labor Court 43/5-3 Bank Egod—Bank Egod's Workers' Committee, PDA 16:99.

13. National Labor Court 35/3-8 Tzvi Markovitz—Association of Workers in Kupat Cholim, PDA 6:125.

family affair that had to be resolved within the Histadrut itself, whether politically or through its internal dispute resolution system.[14] Given the Histadrut's power at the time, the effect of "privatizing" these disputes was to
guarantee the centralized authorities within the Histadrut an autonomous
sphere without judicial intervention.

2. *Protecting the Histadrut's membership.* One of the implications of the
Histadrut's being a primary organization, rather than a federation, was that its
members were allowed to be members of one trade union representing their
affiliation to a branch (an industrial union) and one trade union representing
their affiliation to an occupation. The flip side of this coin was that the Histadrut denied membership in its trade unions to those who were not members
of the Histadrut itself.[15] For example, when the Engineers Union sought partial autonomy from the General Histadrut and wanted to allow non-Histadrut
members to join, the Labor Court upheld the Histadrut's objection to this
practice.[16] This was at a time when the General Histadrut was fiercely trying
to prevent the professional unions' quest for autonomy and their attempt to
break away from the Histadrut's organizational structure.

3. *Defining "trade union."* Although the legislature had used the term
"trade union" in various statutes, it had never defined the term, assuming this
matter should be left to the courts. In a small number of cases the Labor
Court produced a list of criteria that were very easy to comply with.[17] In
terms of recognition, there was no need for any official recognition by the
state, nor was it necessary to formally register as an association. Thus, what
mattered was the substance of activity, not the formalities. A trade union was
required to have published bylaws (the content of which was not part of the
definition), to be voluntary in terms of both entry and exit of members, to be
independent of an employer's domination (although a company union was
not prohibited per se), and to have the intention of providing ongoing and
stable representation (rather than ad hoc "spontaneous" associations). Interestingly, the Court never asked whether the Histadrut itself complied with
these requirements, such as the voluntary entry requirement, at the time
when the Histadrut was a monopolistic health-care provider. At the same
time, in a handful of cases on this topic, no organization that wanted to obtain recognition as a trade union from the Court ever succeeded in fulfilling
all the conditions. The minimal requirements were therefore a hurdle never
placed before the Histadrut but an impassable obstacle for all others. The
only trade unions outside the Histadrut were therefore those it acknowledged

---

14. National Labor Court 44/5-3 Lawyers Association—General Histadrut, PDA 16:62;
National Labor Court 52/4-9 General Histadrut—State of Israel, PDA 25:171.

15. While early case law permitted membership in the Civil Servants Union to nonmembers
of the Histadrut, this was actually because the Civil Servants Union was established with the aid
of the Histadrut but was not part of its organizational structure.

16. National Labor Court 44/5-2 Zerach Shaket—General Histadrut, PDA 17:140.

17. National Labor Court 33/4-7 Tel Aviv University—Academic Staff Association at Tel-
Aviv University, PDA 5:85.

or accepted of its own free will, albeit always reluctantly, concerning which no courtroom confrontation was necessary.

4. *Defining the status of the Histadrut's internal organs.* Like the organs of a corporation, the organs of the Histadrut derive their vitality from its one and only pulsating heart—its bylaws. Thus, in defining their status the court took a dual approach: it assessed their status according to the above-mentioned test of what a trade union is, and it sought the answer to the same question in the Histadrut's bylaws (Ben-Israel 1986a; Raday 1983b). The result of this twofold inquiry was that the trade unions established by the General Histadrut (also designated "histadruts"—such as the Engineers Histadrut and the Histadrut of the Nurses and Orderlies) were trade unions in themselves.[18] They fulfilled the case law's definition, and not surprisingly they were also approved by the General Histadrut as trade unions in its bylaws. By contrast, the workers' committees did not fulfill either test. There is no case in which the legal test provided a solution other than the one determined by upholding the Histadrut's bylaws. It may therefore be concluded that the legal definition of a trade union fitted the General Histadrut's own definition like a glove.

5. *Prohibiting dual membership.* In the context of determining the representative union in situations of interunion rivalry, the Labor Court held that (a) a person may not be a member of two competing unions and (b) when such dual membership occurs, the later membership is to be voided.[19] This prohibition was introduced by analogy to political parties, where dual membership was prohibited by statute. Two complementary rationales were offered by the Labor Court for this prohibition. First, it was held that because the Histadrut's bylaws prohibited dual membership in a competing union (outside the Histadrut), the courts would not take part in upholding membership that was rooted in the breach of a contractual obligation of its members to the Histadrut. This argument was somewhat at odds with the general law of contracts, where a contract signed in breach of another contract is not void but merely subject to the remedies for a breach of contract. Thus, the Court also explained that dual membership (and dual membership dues) appeared to be nepotistic and opportunistic behavior. While this might have been true in the past, when the labor bureaus were administered by the unions on behalf of their membership,[20] it is somewhat unclear what the Labor Court thought people with dual membership stood to gain once the labor bureaus were nationalized. Despite the controversial reasoning for the prohibition, it remained in place until the postcorporatist litigation of the late 1990s.

6. *Establishing the law of new unions and breakaway unions.* Acknowledging freedom of association as a fundamental human right, the Labor Court

18. National Labor Court 31/3-4 Nurses and Orderlies' Histadrut—State of Israel, PDA 4:85.

19. Cf. National Labor Court 30/5-1 Postmen's Union—State of Israel, PDA 1:7; National Labor Court 37/4-7 General Histadrut—State Attorneys' Union (unpublished, 1977); National Labor Court 42/5-2 General Histadrut—Senior Workers at Paz, PDA 14:367.

20. See chapter 3.

did not deny the formation of new unions, nor did it object to breakaway unions—namely, unions trying to sever themselves from the Histadrut. This, however, was merely the theoretical starting point. In reality, the Labor Court's case law made sure that the Histadrut would provide concentrated representation.[21] This was achieved through several measures. First, as noted above, despite the minimal requirements for an association to be a trade union, the Court never acknowledged that all these features applied to new organizations. Second, the Court held that if workers wanted to break away from the Histadrut, they could freely do so as long as they first resigned their membership in the organization. Only then could they organize other workers without using the Histadrut's infrastructure. Because the Histadrut was an almost monopolistic health-care provider at the time, the significance of this rule was that organizers who wanted to break away from the Histadrut had to persuade the rank and file to resign their membership in their health-care provider; only then, once they were no longer covered by any health insurance, could they organize their workers in a new trade union. No union organizer could ever succeed in breaking away from the Histadrut under these conditions.

7. *Identifying the representative trade union.* The definition of "representative trade union" was the only component of the trade union recognition law that appeared in statute. The definitions were presented in chapter 3.[22] In a nutshell, the Collective Agreements Law required a very low threshold of membership level. The implication of this low threshold was that in most situations (especially regarding general agreements, which are more important for corporatist bargaining) there would always be a representative trade union. Moreover, given the high concentration of membership in the Histadrut (at least in the past, when the law was enacted), the low level of membership that was required ensured that generally it would always be the Histadrut that served as the representative union, rather than competing unions.

8. *Determining the bargaining unit.* The statutory requirements for a representative union were found to be difficult to implement in situations where a group of workers tried to sever themselves from the Histadrut (a "breakaway union"). The problem was rooted in the cyclical definition of the statute.

As the example in table 4.1. shows, assuming multiple bargaining units are allowed (option B), if a breakaway union achieves an adequate level of repre-

---

21. The Labor Court paid tribute to the importance of the freedom of association in most important decisions, but not once did the Court explicitly address the tension between the freedom of association and the Histadrut's hegemonic position. See, for example, National Labor Court 35/5-1 Leon Markovitz—General Histadrut, PDA 7:197 (sec. 5); National Labor Court 38/5-1 Mizrachi Bank Workers Union—General Histadrut, PDA 21:283 (sec. 7a); National Labor Court 44/5-2 Zerach Shaket—General Histadrut, PDA 17:140 (secs. 9–10); National Labor Court 42/5-2 General Histadrut—Senior Workers at Paz, PDA 14:367.

22. The Collective Agreements Law (1957), secs. 3, 4, 15, 16. Also see table 3.1.

Table 4.1. Representative status for a special collective agreement: Determining the bargaining unit

To see the extent of the problem, assume an undertaking with a thousand employees (this analysis would apply to either a general or a special collective agreement). Of these, eight hundred are administrative staff and members of the Histadrut (H). Two hundred are knowledge experts who want to break away from the Histadrut and negotiate their own wages. They all join the breakaway union (B).

Section 3 of the Collective Agreements Law states that the representative union is the union in which most workers to whom the collective agreement applies are members, and membership must consist of at least a third of the workforce *to whom the agreement applies.* Section 15 holds that the parties to the collective agreement (employer and the representative trade union) decide to whom the agreement applies. Which union is representative?

Option A: One bargaining unit	Option B: Two bargaining units
One representative union	Two representative unions
H has most members (800 of 1,000)	H has the most members among the administrative staff, and B has the most members among the knowledge workers
H will conclude a collective agreement that covers 1,000 workers	H will conclude one agreement for 800 workers, and B will conclude one for the other 200
Due to the coverage of the agreement over the whole workforce, it was correct to assess representative status out of 1,000 workers	Due to the split coverage of the agreements (administrative/experts), it was correct to assess representative status out of 800/200 workers
This is a corporatist equilibrium (representation is assessed for all workers together)	This is a noncorporatist equilibrium because it allows each group of workers to split from the whole

sentation within a small faction, it will become the representative union for that particular group. This poses a threat to corporatist bargaining, which seeks comprehensive coverage of its agreements. The workers who would have the greatest incentive to sever themselves from the large bargaining unit are those with the greatest economic leverage. These are the workers for whom solidarity in bargaining means having to compromise their market power. The Labor Court sought to deny elite rank-and-file workers the power to detach themselves from the broader bargaining unit by holding that (with minor exceptions), the bargaining unit is always the broadest unit possible.[23] This precluded any possibility that small groups would carve out a space for their own bargaining units.

9. *Rejecting a duty of fair representation.* The previous components of the case law on trade unions indicate that the Labor Court ensured that the Histadrut would organize a large, and therefore also a very heterogeneous, group of workers. The possibility that small groups would voice their dissatisfaction with the Histadrut's bargaining policy and break away into small unions was

23. National Labor Court 42/5-2 General Histadrut—Senior Workers at Paz, PDA 14:367.

almost nil. Without the power of exit, the only thing workers had was the power of voice. The Labor Court frequently noted that dissatisfaction with the Histadrut's policy was an "internal affair" of the Histadrut and must be resolved within its political institutions. Yet it was difficult for small groups to dissent because of the Histadrut's highly centralized nature, the leadership's distance from the rank and file, and the political affinity of the leadership of small units within the Histadrut with the general leadership. This is not to suggest that no such political uprising was possible. There were instances of revolt within the Histadrut mostly by political means. A legal attempt to use law to protest against the union was made by suggesting that the Labor Court apply the American "duty of fair representation." This doctrine holds that the union must fairly represent all its members. Failure to represent them fairly may lead to the nullification of any unfair agreement that was concluded with an employer or an employers' association. However, the Labor Court was quick to dismiss this legal proposition, except for situations that seemed to overlap with claims that were also based on antidiscrimination law (e.g., gender). In this it fortified the union's autonomy from judicial review of its internal policies.[24] In doing so, the Labor Court left it to the Histadrut to balance these different roles with limited judicial interference (Mironi 1981).

10. *Preserving autonomy for the Histadrut and its internal affairs and for the negotiating social partners.* Consistent with the Labor Court's rejection of the duty of fair representation, it was also reluctant to intervene in the Histadrut's autonomy or in the autonomous negotiations between the trade unions and the employers (Raday 1983b). On the one hand the Court repeatedly held that the Histadrut was not immune from judicial review. The Court held that the membership of individuals in the trade union was a contractual relationship that could be reviewed by the law of contracts. It further held that the Histadrut was not a private agent but rather a semipublic one to which both private and public law applied. Therefore, doctrines of administrative law that permitted judicial review of administrative action could also be applied to the Histadrut. On the other hand, the Court never used these doctrines, and it resolved challenges to the Histadrut's practices by emphasizing that the Histadrut's balancing of competing interests was its own internal affair. Similarly, until the early 1990s the Labor Court suggested that it had the power to review the content of collective agreements, but it has done it on only two occasions when an agreement was bluntly discriminatory against women.[25] The Labor Court's active conservatism with regard to the entry of new unions and the centralization of bargaining structures was therefore very different from its passive conservatism with regard to interference in the bargaining process and the balancing of conflicting interests by the social partners. This was the

24. National Labor Court 36/4-7 Guy Cherut—El Al, PDA 8:197.
25. National Labor Court 33/3-25 Edna Chazin—El Al, PDA 4:365; National Labor Court 37/3-71 Elite—Sarah Lederman, PDA 9:255. The Supreme Court's Naomi Nevo case (1987), which also demonstrates this type of intervention, will be presented in the following chapter as one of the indicators of the transition from the corporatist paradigm of law to the plural one.

major characteristic of the corporatist paradigm of law: strong regulation of entry to the bargaining arena, although once the identity of the partners had been secured, the law gave them a very high level of freedom and autonomy.

As this step-by-step description demonstrates, the various components of the judge-made labor law intertwined with and forestall attempts to break the concentrated and centralized nature of representation, while at the same time the Labor Court refrained from intervention in content. Because most of these components were constructed by the Labor Court, I have described them as "active conservatism." They demonstrate activism in the sense of an extraordinary judicial originality in constructing statutes and broad principles to fit the corporatist agenda. They are conservative because the Labor Court sought to preserve and entrench the system of interests representation that existed at the time. This is not surprising because this is the same system that established the Labor Court itself.

The Role of the Labor Court in Industrial Action

As on the issue of trade union recognition, the statutory law on industrial action was very partial. The various legal measures that were tried to reduce the high level of industrial action included the voluntary conciliation and arbitration rules in the Resolution of Labor Disputes Law (1959); emergency regulations that were issued from 1960 onward; the 1969 amendment to the Settlement of Labor Disputes Law, requiring the notification of intent to strike and a cooling-off period of fifteen days; and, the most far-reaching, the 1972 amendment to the Settlement of Labor Disputes Law, holding that some strikes do not receive legal immunity.[26] These measures failed, each for its own reason (Raday 1971; Zamir 1974), indicating the limits of law as a means to address the problem of industrial action. The voluntary conciliation arrangements did not succeed because the parties did not want to use them. The emergency regulations were often successful; however, when mass refusal to comply with them occurred (although infrequently), the state could not penalize everyone, and the process merely strengthened the Histadrut. The prior notification requirement and the cooling-off period were generally helpful but of little use in the large number of wildcat strikes in which the striking workers ignored restraints on strike activity (e.g., the need to obtain the approval of the Histadrut to strike) to begin with. The harsh measures provided by the 1972 amendment to the Settlement of Labor Disputes Law were not utilized because they were likely to intensify the rank and file's objections to regulation and intervention in industrial action. Consequently, the employers themselves did not use the new law, and it remained for the most part ignored. None of these measures was reflected in the data on the use of strikes in Israel, and both wildcat and authorized strikes continued to erupt with little con-

26. Settlement of Labor Disputes Law (1957), secs. 3–5, 37A-E.

straint (Chermesh 1993; Shirom 1970; Zamir 1974). More important than the weak legal restraints was the practice of negotiating with the employers the payment of wages for strike days as part of the strike's settlement (Zamir 1974, 557). Consequently, strikes, whether legitimate or not, incurred very little risk to the strikers.

On the face of it there was no explicit mention of strikes in the Labor Court's Law. In fact, it has been demonstrated that the corporatist compromise rejected demands by both the right and left to incorporate into the law references to strikes (e.g., the prohibition to strike at the time a dispute is pending or a restriction on the Court's remedial power with regard to strikes). However, the law granted the labor courts the power to issue remedies, just like the district courts in the regular court system. This was the valve through which the Labor Court in its formative years introduced the injunction against strikes. From the outset, this power of the Court quickly brought employers to litigate in the labor courts in an unprecedented manner. Interestingly, despite the fact that the regular courts already had the power to use this remedy, employers rarely resorted to judicial relief before the labor courts were established.[27] This is indicative that the labor court system was not perceived simply as an employees' tribunal but rather as an industrial tribunal that was more accommodating to employers and employees alike.

Shortly after the National Labor Court was established, it started to issue injunctions, although cautiously. On this thorny issue, the Court delivered a clear message. There was no hesitation in the cases of the first years with regard to the actual authority and jurisdiction to issue injunctions. The emphasis instead was on a careful implementation of its authority. In the first cases, the Labor Court was insistent that injunctions in collective relations were rare and that the Court should ensure against "government by injunctions."[28] This is perhaps one of the most powerful corporatist statements of the Court. The Court further emphasized that injunctions are not a means to conclude a case but an incentive for the parties to resume negotiations. Thus, the first steps the Court took, somewhat in contrast to the typical inclination of the judicial system, sought to restrain its intervention by legal means in industrial disputes. At the same time, the Court did not seek to remain an outsider to the dispute. It held that injunctions, when administered, are often only temporary, requiring the parties to return and report to the Court on the pace of negotiations and their outcomes.[29]

Following the first cases that established the legitimacy of and the limits for using an injunction, the Court turned to outline in more detail the rules on the

27. A rare example of the court's use of injunctions before the Labor Court was established can be found in Supreme Court CA 167/62 *Leo Beck School Ltd v. Secondary School Teachers Union* PDI 16:2205. This decision was one of the incentives for the Histadrut to support the establishment of the Labor Court.

28. National Labor Court 30/5-2 Engineers Histadrut—State Service Governorship PDA 2:71; National Labor Court 32/4-6 Maintenance Workers Committee in El-Al—El Al, PDA 3:393.

29. National Labor Court, 32/4-6, Maintenance Workers Committee in El-Al—El Al, PDA 3:393.

permissible use of industrial action.[30] The Court noted that it is legitimate to govern industrial action by law, just as it is common to govern military action by international law. It described its task as that of implementing and devising the rules of the game. A short time thereafter, the Court started developing these rules one by one. It is noteworthy that in the initial steps of writing the rules of the game, the court dealt with cases that involved wildcat strikes that were initiated by the workers' committees. Developing the limits of industrial action in these cases aided in legitimizing the regulatory process because wildcat strikes that are unauthorized by the central organs of the Histadrut were deemed to be a serious threat to the corporatist project. One of the important early cases that demonstrated the Labor Court's strategy on this matter was that of a strike initiated by the workers' committee in the Israeli Shipyards.[31] In that case, the workers' committee decided to initiate industrial action despite the Histadrut's objection. The Labor Court issued an injunction against the striking workers, holding that while the law permitted an entity of workers that was not a union to give advance notice before a strike, such a notice was legitimate only when there was no representative trade union. Consequently, the strike was declared a wildcat strike—and hence illegitimate.

The Israeli Shipyards case, as well as other cases from the formative years of adjudication in the Labor Court, complements the case law the Labor Court developed with regard to representative trade unions, described earlier in this chapter. It sought to undermine the power of small factions. To that extent, it upheld the Histadrut's bylaws, which in the present context prohibited workers' committees from declaring a strike, and it upheld the law, which stated similar objections to the militancy of small groups. The result of both strategies was a coherent effort to move power away from the local to the centralized venues. Injunctions by the Labor Court, which seemed to be at the outset a considerable threat to the autonomous and nonregulated sphere of industrial relations and labor representation, proved to be yet another useful tool in the effort to promote the centralized power of the Histadrut. This did not necessarily lead to loud applause for the case law by the Histadrut, but neither did it produce a terrible outcry. The Court succeeded in reforming the law by drawing on the common-law method of incremental lawmaking, advancing the law in less controversial cases, and responding to the fears of the Histadrut while addressing the needs of the employers.

In the first decade the Labor Court developed a law of strikes from scratch. While there were no clear limitations on industrial action until the Court was established, the Labor Court succeeded in designing a coherent, complicated, and constantly growing body of law.[32] However, describing the development

30. National Labor Court 31/4-4 Workers Committee in the Cables and Electric Wires Company—Cables and Electric Wires Company, PDA 4:12.

31. National Labor Court 33/4-3 Moshe Shitrit—Israeli Shipyards Inc., PDA 4:337. Also see Raday (1971).

32. For a short summary of the legal principles governing the injunction, see Mundlak and Harpaz (2002).

of the law of strikes without discussing its implementation is incomplete. Unlike the law of trade union recognition, where cases were few and far between, the matter of industrial action also received casual attention in the regional labor courts. Most cases were not precedent-setting, not only because routine litigation rests into a rhythm that is not constantly peaked by precedents but also because the developing law of strikes was by its nature antilegal. As noted, the first cases held that the use of law in industrial action should be limited to avoid the rule of injunctions. This seems to be a perfect statement on the ambivalent relationship between law and corporatism. Law is a necessary enabling condition, but excessive legalism can be disabling.

During the years the Court developed the law of strikes it also developed the judicial practice of handling strikes. Drawing on rules of procedure for collective disputes that were very flexible, the labor courts developed patterns of chaperoning industrial disputes. The use of interim injunctions that was upheld in the first years led to a constant interaction where an injunction was merely a gate to successive meetings for judicial review. However, this was not the typical judicial review. The court would ask to receive an update on the negotiations between the parties and their likely outcome. Occasionally the court would make suggestions and even caucus with each of the parties. In the first of several studies concerning the level of the courts' responsiveness to employers' petitions, Galin and Shirom (1978) found it to be only 21 percent in the early 1970s.[33] They explained the small share of cases in which the courts issued an injunction by pointing to the practice of judges to mediate cases rather than simply adjudicate them. In later years this tendency has somewhat changed, in tandem with the changing nature of the industrial relations system and the Court's function in that system.

The functions of the Labor Court in developing labor law by means of scholarly precedents and its function as an industrial mediator in the more mundane day-by-day litigation interrelate. During the first ten years the Court, in its lawmaking function, designed a complex system of rules of the game. The Court held that when a strike does not comply with one or more of the rules, the Court *will be inclined* to issue an injunction against the workers at the employer's request. Yet when a strike complies with the rules of the game, the Court will *usually refrain* from issuing an injunction unless a "balance of interests" test (mostly balancing the interests of harm to the employer and the public on one side and to the freedom to strike on the other) indicates otherwise. Consequently, while a simplistic account suggests that the Court was very "legalistic" in its precedents, an alternative account suggests that it designed a law that contained many exceptions and left much discretion to the judge. The Court did not seek to bind itself in a web of rules

---

33. Other studies include Weiss (1989) studying the 1980s, and Mundlak and Harpaz (2002) studying the 1990s. The Labor Court's responsiveness during its first years will be compared with the decades that followed in chapter 5.

but rather to free itself from formalistic rules and allow itself as much leeway as possible. For any legal outcome desired, there was an appropriate set of rules that could justify it. This strategic view of law aided the Court in what it perceived to be its main role—an industrial mediator. However, the Court's achievement was partial. On the one hand, it brought expertise, developed the law, and mediated conflicting claims. At the same time it did not contribute to a decline in the share or rate of industrial action. Law just didn't seem to matter enough.

In the labor courts' failure to affect the relatively high rate of industrial action in Israel lies an important lesson about the relationship between law and industrial relations. Particularly in the corporatist period, law is argued to be the product of the social partners' needs and interests. A simple reading of law seems to suggest that the Labor Court revolutionized the body of law dealing with the rights and obligations of the parties at the time of a strike. Yet when the law is read in the proper industrial relations context, it is clear that the rules merely enhanced the parties' strategic repertoire and enabled them to bring about a well-respected institution to engage in the process of dispute resolution. Law could not do much beyond what the parties were prepared or willing to do in themselves.

Summarizing the Construction of Corporatist Law

From the beginning of the British Mandate in Palestine until the 1980s, the industrial relations system gradually adopted corporatist characteristics. Observing the three basic institutional features of corporatism, as described in part 1, the system was based on (1) autonomy and recognition, (2) concentration and centralization, and (3) encompassing bargaining. The discussion in part 2 has indicated what role the legal enabling conditions played in making corporatism possible. It is important to note from the outset that law did not create the corporatist system. Law was for the most part constructed by the social partners, as part of the corporatist negotiations, and was tailored to the needs of the corporatist system. The instrumental use of law by the industrial relations system also impacted its content. This has been demonstrated by numerous examples throughout these chapters. To summarize the content of the law, it is possible to draw on its three functions, which were presented in the introduction.

Labor Law's Metalevel

Labor law's metalevel determines where the particular norms will be drafted. During the corporatist years, the metalevel was geared toward emphasizing the centrality of collective bargaining and negotiations within civil society while downplaying the role of private contracts law (market ordering) and regulation (public ordering). This was achieved through the following measures.

- *The legislative process*. Consultation before and after legislation, which ensured that statutory norms would not infringe on the autonomous sphere of the social partners.
- *The "supremacy of the collective norm."* The centrality of collective bargaining ahead of individual contracts was ensured by the recognition of the collective agreements' binding force and their mandatory effect. While collective bargaining was held to be bound by legislation, the prominence of collective agreements was ensured through various measures. First, statutes abstained from intervening with wages and dismissals. Moreover, the impact of executive orders that extended collective agreements was as important as were the statutory standards. Second, several statutes made it possible to derogate the statutory standards by means of collective bargaining.
- *Facilitating and promoting the making of norms by collective bargaining*. The state took active measures to promote the centrality and exclusive position of the social partners. It preserved the role of the Histadrut in important areas of social welfare—namely, health care and pensions—as well as in ancillary areas such as the annual vacation funds. This encouraged membership in the trade union, ensuring concentration and a high level of union density.
- *Facilitating and promoting the autonomy of the social partners*. The state abstained from intervening in the autonomy of the social partners, therefore avoiding, for example, compulsory arbitration or interference in the content of collective agreements.

In sum, the most important task of labor law in the corporatist phase was to encourage the making of norms by means of autonomous self-regulation by the corporatist associations. The centrality of its first function accounts for labor law's limited role with regard to its other two functions.

Labor Law's Regulation of the Labor-Capital Relationship

What seems to be the most important function of labor law was in fact downplayed in the corporatist phase of labor law. In the sphere of individual rights and obligations, most norms governing the employment relationship were merely reflections of norms that were developed in collective bargaining. Legislation merely ensured the application of these norms to the working population as a whole. Fields of law that were not negotiated by the social partners—for example, antidiscrimination law—remained embryonic during the corporatist years of labor law. The only area in which the law intervened in the relationship between labor and capital's collective agents, clearly assigning rights and obligations to the two sides, was that of industrial disputes. However, even the continuing disagreement over the rules of the game in this area resulted in a corporatist solution—to establish the labor courts that stem from and adjudicate within the corporatist triangle.

Labor Law's Regulation of the Labor-Labor Relationship

Like the norms governing the relationship between labor and employers, the component of labor law seeking to govern the insiders-outsiders problem that pervaded the labor side was limited. The strong evidence for labor market segmentation along ethnic and national lines, which was strongly endorsed by the Histadrut, is documented in sociological and economic studies. However, segmentation was not considered a "legal" issue. Other than the assertion of a general principle of nondiscrimination in the Employment Service Law, the problem of segmentation does not appear in either statutes or case law. This invisibility stems not from neutrality, of course, but from the autonomy and recognition that were precisely intended to shield the industrial relations system from judicial scrutiny.

IN the following chapters I will demonstrate how the corporatist construct of labor law has changed since the late 1980s. Postcorporatist labor law is distinct from the corporatist model in two significant ways. First, the legal arrangements have changed. The objective of labor law's metafunction is no longer to elevate the collectively negotiated norms above all others. It acknowledges the disintegration of the autonomous system and has replaced it with more recognition of both contractual and regulatory instruments. These in turn have resurrected the importance of the two other functions of labor law. Second, the new law no longer originates with the industrial relations system but rather seeks to construct a new industrial relations system by means of prescriptive rules that define the rights and obligations of the various agents. Thus, at present both the content and the relationship between the legal system and the industrial relations system have been reversed.

Part III

FADING CORPORATISM

Nothing dramatic happened in 1987. No economic or political revolution took place in Israel. The changing nature of industrial relations and labor in Israel is not part of anything like the Soviet perestroika but has been an incremental, albeit rapid, process of disintegration of the old order. As noted in chapter 2, this process can be traced to the political elections in 1977, in which the political order was shocked by the overthrow of the Labor Party and first rise to power of the right-wing Likud Party. Because the political change occurred in periodical elections, however, it did not shake the political system altogether. Most institutions enjoyed continuity after the 1977 political drama, and the institutions of the industrial relations system survived the change as well. Yet over time the political changes were accompanied by other economic and social changes that, it has been argued, had the effect of destabilizing the industrial relations system. What happened to law in the process of change?

It seems that changes in labor law began after the industrial relations system had gradually started to fade. Changes were subtle, and their significance is only made clear by looking at their cumulative impact over time. All the same, the argument developed in this part of the book is that slight changes reflect a deep structural change in which the objectives of labor law were altered. From a body of law that was initiated, developed, and influenced by the agents of the industrial relations system, it has become a body of law that governs the industrial relations system. The hierarchy of lawmaking has been reversed.

The gradual nature of transformation makes it difficult to start this part of the book with a clear depiction of change. Two events that took place around the same time have been chosen to illustrate the buds of change in labor law: the legislation of the Minimum Wage Law (1987) and the case of Naomi Nevo.

Legislation: The Minimum Wage Law

Since 1972 the Histadrut and the Federation of Israeli Economic Organizations (the federation of employers' associations) had been negotiating collective agreements on minimum wage. These were nationwide agreements that were routinely extended by the Minister of Labor and Welfare to almost all the employers (and employees) in the country. Thus, the normative effect of these agreements was identical to that of a statute (Getenyu 1990). Such agreements were an apt demonstration of the corporatist method.

Only three years after the minimum wage agreements began, several proposals to enact a minimum wage law were brought to the Knesset by a member from the left-wing (Ratz) party and a right-wing (Likud) member.[1] Unlike previous proposals in the area of labor law and social security, which were usually drafted by the Ministry of Labor after consultation with the social partners, as demonstrated in the previous chapter, these proposals were brought by individual Knesset members. The Labor Party's Knesset members put forth arguments that were typical of the corporatist phase, holding that the legislature in a democratic country should not intervene in setting wages and that collective bargaining was the more appropriate venue for determining the minimum wage.[2] In this debate, the Labor Party's position still prevailed and the centrality of collective bargaining remained secure.

However, in 1977, after the Labor Party lost the elections for the first time to the right-wing Likud, further proposals to legislate minimum wage were submitted, only this time by several Knesset members from the Labor Party. Particular noteworthy was the proposal submitted in 1981 by Yeruham Meshel, a Knesset member of the Labor Party and the general secretary of the Histadrut at the time.[3] The various proposals were rejected.[4] Yet the almost unprecedented proposals by the Labor Party were followed by yet another strategic innovation—the Likud-headed government submitted a draft proposal for legislating minimum wage.[5] In 1984–1988 a national unity government was established, based on both the Labor Party and the Likud. During these years complex political maneuvers, accompanied by numerous private

---

1. Proposed Bill on Minimum Wage Law (1975) by MK Yoram Aridor (Likkud) and other proposals are documented in *The Knesset Protocols* D.K. vol. 76:1563–64 (1975). Numerous subsequent proposals were surveyed in later debates in D.K. vol. 104:1974 (1986).

2. *The Knesset Protocols* D.K. vol. 76:1545 (1975).

3. *The Knesset Protocols* D.K. vol. 93:1749 (1981).

4. *The Knesset Protocols* D.K. vol. 81:602–3, 617–18 (1978).

5. Proposal: Minimum Wage Law (1978 *Legislative Proposals* 1367). The legislative process on this law was exceptionally slow, and the proposal remained idle for several years.

proposals from all wings of the Knesset, led to the final proposal that was passed by the Knesset in 1987.[6]

The lengthy process of legislating the minimum wage law (over a decade) was marked by two symptoms of the gradual disintegration of the corporatist system.

The Breakdown of Consensus

Until the 1977 elections, in which the Labor Party fell from power, the Histadrut and the employers' associations presented a joint position against the legislation of a minimum wage. This was part of the tradition whereby the social partners consented to legislation as long as it did not infringe on what they deemed to be the crucial components of collective bargaining—wages and dismissals. This joint position, however, changed as the Histadrut realized the extent to which its power in collective bargaining had diminished. The first national minimum wage agreement determined the minimum wage at a level of 44 percent of the average wage at that time. Later agreements led to the erosion of the minimum wage, ranging from 25 percent (1980) to 39 percent (1975). While the minimum wage fluctuated from one agreement to another, the hyperinflation of the 1980s indicated to the Histadrut that it could no longer shoulder the task of ensuring the minimum wage by means of collective bargaining. By 1977 the Histadrut's general assembly had decided to promote a minimum wage law that would be based on automatic indexation of the wage to the average wage at a level of 60 percent. By contrast, during these years the employers' associations, represented by the Coordinating Bureau, continued to argue that the automatic indexation of the minimum wage would have severe economic implications for the private sector. While in the past both sides to the bargaining table had favored the bargaining option, during the 1980s the Histadrut's inability to raise the minimum wage was translated into a preference for legislation, while the employers' ability to halt the rise in the minimum wage was translated into a continuous preference for bargaining.

The social partners' position on legislation at the initial stages of the legislative process in 1975 aptly demonstrated the overriding assumption that characterized

---

6. *The Knesset Protocols* D.K. vol. 102:2739 (1985)(Minister of Labor outlines the proposed activities for the ministry); D.K. vol. 102:3424 (1985) (Private proposal); D.K. vol. 104:2078 (1986) (another private proposal is submitted to the Knesset); D.K. vol. 105:1986 (1986) (Knesset agrees to take the private proposals off the agenda but on the condition that the government will bring its own proposal instead). Under D.K. vol. 105: 3899–3902 (1986), the government did not bring its own proposal, and consequently four additional private proposals were brought to the Knesset: Proposal: Minimum Wage Law (1986 *Legislative Proposals* 1749) (government's proposal submitted); Proposal: Minimum Wage Law (1986 *Legislative Proposals* 1823) (Knesset's Labor and Welfare Committee integrates government's proposals with private proposals after intensive consultation with social partners, ministries, the State's Central Bank, the National Insurance Institute, and others). D.K. vol. 107:2168 (1987) [first vote of the law—approved]; D.K. vol. 107:2560 (1987) [Second and third vote of the law—approved].

their position in the past—legislation was to be promoted only by agreement. The changing position of the social partners over time marked a different role for legislation—as an instrument for advancing the partisan position of one side to the bargaining table. The locus of effective power had shifted from bargaining power to political power by means of lobbying and litigation.

The Fragmentation of the "State"

In the corporatist phase, the state was represented by the Labor Party (Mapai), which enjoyed a majority in the Knesset and also dominated the ministries of labor and finance for most of the time. Therefore, there was usually a unanimous position on social and economic matters, which cut across the legislature, the executive, and even the politically independent judiciary. Legislative proposals were drafted by the Ministry of Labor, generally accepted by the Ministry of Finance, and enjoyed the approval of the majority of the Knesset members. The voices of the opposition in the Knesset, on both the left and the right, were marginalized, and all laws eventually took the form of a corporatist compromise.

After the 1977 elections, the hegemonic position of the Labor Party evaporated. This did not lead spontaneously to a revolt against the Histadrut or against corporatist negotiations in general. However, the changing coalitions after 1977 did lead to higher levels of conflict between the legislature (the Knesset) and the executive branch. Moreover, because of the difficulty in forming a coalition, a disjuncture emerged between the Ministry of Labor and Welfare and the Ministry of Finance. While the corporatist literature emphasized the need for centralization among labor and a high degree of centralized coordination among the employers, the 1977 change of affairs highlighted the need for coordination among the state agents as well. The absence of coordination led to a more disharmonious legislative process in the Knesset, with the frequent use of private proposals by individual Knesset members instead of the carefully drafted proposals that were prepared by the Ministry of Labor in the past. Moreover, the political process brought about a disharmonious relationship between the legislature, which took the Histadrut's side and favored the legislation of the minimum wage, and the executive branch, which took sides with the employers and objected to it. The trilateral nature of corporatist legislation was replaced by a relatively pluralist system.

Thus, with regard to both questions presented at the beginning of this book, the corporatist features of labor law have been replaced with new ones. First, law has ceased to be an output of the industrial relations system and has turned into a method of prescribing to the industrial relations agents the norms with which they must comply. Second, law's metafunction has been transformed, from upholding norms making by consensus in civil society as an instrument for advancing corporatist negotiations to a preference for regulation that is not necessarily conducive to ongoing negotiations.

Adjudication: The Naomi Nevo Case

While acceptance of the Minimum Wage Law in 1987 marked the beginning of a transformation in the legislative arena, the previous chapter highlighted the fact that corporatist law has been equally influenced by judge-made law. It is therefore necessary to observe what happened in the courtroom at the same time. Because the Labor Court is relatively insulated from the changing political forces in the legislature, it might have been possible for the Court to continue to facilitate the needs of the corporatist system. However, to choose one pivotal change in the judicial branch, we may turn to the seminal case of Naomi Nevo.[7] The case, which ended in 1990, started approximately at the same time the Minimum Wage Law was enacted. While the proximity in time is certainly not coincidental, the relationship between these changes in the legislature and those in the courts is indirect. Neither branch of government has any direct influence over the other. It seems that changes in the legislature coincided with those in the courts because the corporatist system had already begun to show signs of instability and the breakdown of binding norms, acceptable rules of the game, and shared ideology.

Naomi Nevo was a researcher in the Jewish Agency. According to the collective arrangement that prevailed in the Jewish Agency at the time, she had to retire at the age of sixty, unlike her male peers, whose retirement age was set at sixty-five. The collective arrangement was negotiated by the Histadrut and the Jewish Agency, but the unequal retirement age in this arrangement was no different from that which appeared in most collective agreements. Naomi Nevo argued that her forced retirement at the age of sixty was discriminatory, although at the time there was no explicit law that required equal treatment in retirement of men and women. The National Labor Court continued its corporatist tradition, refusing to intervene in the content of the collective agreement. But Naomi Nevo petitioned against the Labor Court to the Supreme Court, sitting as a High Court of Justice. While Supreme Court intervention in the Labor Court's rulings had been rare in the past, the former often deferring to the expertise of the latter in the field of labor law, the Supreme Court accepted the petition in this case, holding that the differential retirement age was discriminatory and therefore void. In the interim, the legislature had also passed the Equal Retirement Age Law, after lobbying by feminist NGOs.

Although there had been two previous cases in which the Labor Court intervened in the content of collective agreements for the purpose of voiding discriminatory practices, it was the Naomi Nevo case, when observed in retrospect, that

---

7. The case commenced in the Tel-Aviv District Labor Court and was then appealed to the National Labor Court: 46/3-73 Naomi Nevo—Jewish Agency, PDA 18:497. In a petition against the Labor Court's decision to the Supreme Court, the decision was reversed: HCJ 104/87 Naomi Nevo v. National Labor Court and others, PDI 44(4):749.

marked the end of the corporatist model of labor law.[8] First, while previous interventions in collective bargaining for the purpose of voiding discriminatory agreements remained isolated episodes, the Naomi Nevo case marked the beginning of a flourishing legislation and adjudication of antidiscrimination norms. Moreover, the outcome of the case indicated that individual rights had emerged as trump cards over collective concerns. Second, the Naomi Nevo case indicated that the labor court system was no longer insulated from intervention by the general judicial system, even in its own area of expertise. The degree of autonomy accorded to the Labor Court was always a thorny point of controversy within the judicial system (Barak 1989; Goldberg 1989). This case marked the beginning of the Labor Court's co-optation into the general judicial system and a departure from its origins as a tribunal in the service of the industrial relations system. Thus, while the legislation of the Minimum Wage Law was indicative of the fragmentation of the state, the Naomi Nevo case denoted further complexities evolving from the interaction between the labor and the general courts system. Third, the case also demonstrates the beginning of NGOs' intervention in the field of labor. The exclusive influence of the social partners—employers' associations and trade unions—was diluted by the entry of new associations. Unlike the social partners, these associations were not formally recognized, and they can be characterized as pluralist interest groups rather than all-encompassing associations.

In sum, like the legislation of the minimum wage, the Naomi Nevo case served as an indication of the ongoing fragmentation of the corporatist triangle and the beginning of an amoebic pluralist polygon.

Overview: The Transformation of Labor Law's Objectives

Taking into consideration both the Minimum Wage Law and the Naomi Nevo case, it seems that the corporatist nature of labor law had lost some its prominent characteristics. However, the change was even more fundamental than these two examples show. During the 1990s very little was left of the corporatist labor law. These changes will be discussed in detail in this part of the book. Unlike the description of the corporatist phase of labor law, part 3 will not be developed on a chronological axis because changes were rapid and the period of time studied here cannot be subdivided. Instead, the discussion will be based on labor law's three functions, as explained in the introduction to the book.

In chapter 5 I describe the changes in labor law's metafunction. From a body of law designed to ensure the supremacy of the corporatist collective

8. In 1973–1974, the Labor Court intervened twice in collective agreements for the reason of gender-based discrimination: National Labor Court 33/3-25 Workers' Committee of Air-Stewards in El-Al—Edna Chazin, PDA 4:365; National Labor Court 37/3-71 Elit Chocolate Industries of Israel Ltd.—Sarah Lederman, PDA 9:255.

norm over other legal norms, labor law has moved on to downplay the role of collective bargaining in favor of individually bargained norms (i.e., norms grounded in contract) and statutory norms (i.e., regulation).

In chapter 6 I describe the changes in labor law's function as a power-breaking mechanism in the relationship between employers and labor. This process is designated as "juridification"—that is, a process in which law constructs numerous new rights and obligations in the workplace. These legal rights, as well as the legal rhetoric that has taken over the governance of the workplace, substitute for the many layers of collectively negotiated norms in the corporatist heyday.

Finally, in chapter 7 I discuss labor law's distributive function in the internal dimensions of corporatism—the distribution of rights, privileges, and opportunities among workers. Although Israel's corporatism was always tainted with dualism on the labor side, even the law's function with regard to this dualism, as well as the nature of this dualism itself, changed. Labor law, which was aimed at erecting dualist tendencies that served Israel's warped version of corporatism, has been tilted in the postcorporatist phase toward eradicating untamed market forces and recapturing some of the sense of centralization that was achieved in the past by the corporatist pact.

Together the three chapters reflect on the deep structural change that the Israeli legal and socioeconomic systems have experienced over the past twenty years.

support of the Ramon-governed Histadrut, he left his position in the Histadrut and returned to the national political arena.

The passage of the National Health Care Law in 1994 was a dramatic example of postcorporatist law. On the one hand, the odd process whereby the law was passed contained corporatist ingredients. It was clear that the law could not pass without the approval of the Histadrut. On the other hand, in a break with past situations in which the Histadrut's objection had led to an impasse, this time the political agents adopted an original and effective way to gain the Histadrut's support—conquest. Oddly enough, it was in the corporatist phase that scholars have observed the influence of the Labor Party over the Histadrut's political bodies. Yet it was in the postcorporatist case of healthcare reform that the party exploited its domination in the most militant and adversarial way. It therefore seems that the underlying characteristic of this reform was its adversarial nature. The political party no longer acted as a mediator of interests. Legislation was no longer based on consensus building that was later reflected in the law itself. Instead, the law was the final outcome of competition between the state and the Histadrut.

The consequences of health-care reform have been demonstrated in the second chapter, which describes the rate of decline in the Histadrut's membership. While the decline in membership had already started by the 1980s (Cohen et al. 2003), the dip in membership after 1995 was significantly greater. Moreover, because of the dramatic effect of the health-care reform, the more interesting challenges to the Histadrut's hegemonic position in labor law came shortly thereafter, when past glory was no longer matched by present status.

CHANGING THE RULES OF RECOGNITION: LABOR LAW REFORM

As described in detail in the previous chapter, labor law crafted a latent yet dense network of protections around the Histadrut. Given the homage paid to freedom of association, the law did not prohibit associations outside the Histadrut. Instead, it merely provided rules of recognition, centered on the legal requirements for forming a trade union, and—more important—a *representative* trade union. As demonstrated in the previous chapter, these rules made unionization outside the Histadrut or unauthorized rank-and-file activity within the Histadrut difficult to carry out. How did the authors of the legal rule respond to the changes in the Histadrut's position? Generally, there were two types of legal positions. The first of these held that if the law on trade union recognition were to be maintained, the legal system could preserve some of the corporatist past. The second position held that the rules of recognition that were tailored to the corporatist system were no longer feasible or desirable and that the law of recognition had to be changed to accommodate new forms of representation. Both views assumed that the law of trade union recognition had to be relaxed, but the former sought to do so in order to maintain some vestige of corporatism, while the latter sought to overwrite corporatism altogether.

Because the law of recognition was authored by the Labor Court, the two positions were highlighted within the Court in several cases that challenged the old law. The legislature did not actively participate in designing the corporatist law of recognition, nor did it have any significant role in rewriting the law.[5] The idle approach taken by the legislature was a result of its choosing not to intervene in collective labor disputes at a time when it was clear that there was no consensus among the social partners on the rules of the game. Moreover, for those who favored the liberalization of the labor market and the withdrawal of collective bargaining altogether, doing nothing was a good solution. The protective measures devised by the law twenty years earlier were no longer effective. By contrast, the Labor Court could not avoid resolving disputes brought to it by the parties themselves. Most decisions did not change the previous case law dramatically, but they indicated that the Histadrut's hegemonic role in collective bargaining was no longer taken for granted and did not serve as the guiding principle for the court.

Some of the Labor Court's cases merely relaxed the previous case law. One such example is the judge-made law that prohibited dual membership in trade unions and voided the later membership. The previous chapter explained that the court's prohibition of dual membership in a trade union and the automatic voiding of the later membership were intended to ensure that unions could not break away from the Histadrut. However, in the 1990s the Labor Court held that dual membership was prohibited *only* if it was also conflicting, thus relaxing the effects of the corporatist rule.[6] A similar effect was achieved in a dispute between the Teachers Union, at the time an organ of the Histadrut, and the High School Teachers Union, an independent trade union. Unlike prior rulings, the Labor Court opted for a pragmatic solution, holding that the employer must conduct a survey and ask the teachers with dual membership to determine which membership they wished to maintain.[7] This change, while subtle, indicated a move away from the strict pro-Histadrut rules that characterized the corporatist law of recognition to the establishment of membership on the basis of individuals' choice.

In some areas of the law, the postcorporatist Labor Court was required to rule on questions that had not been determined in the past. This was not because these problems had been nonexistent in the past but because they were not brought to court. One of these was the issue of union security clauses in collective agreements. In 1992, a case was brought to the Labor Court, challenging

5. A few proposals to amend the Collective Bargaining Law and the Wage Protection Law, with regard to agency fees, as well as other proposals that touch on the issue of recognition, were raised after the health-care reform in order to strengthen the Histadrut (Ben-Israel 2001; Neuman 1996). However, these proposals did not materialize and did not even pass the initial stage of the legislative process.

6. National Labor Court 53/5-1 Israeli Medical Association—General Histadrut, PDA 25:516.

7. National Labor Court 55/4-24 High School Teachers Union—State of Israel, PDA 31:439.

for the first time, the legality of union security clauses, which appeared in a collective agreement in Zim, an Israeli shipping commpany.[8] The Labor Court held that union- and closed-shop arrangements were illegal because they violated the freedom of association and its alleged corollary—the freedom not to associate.[9] The reasoning of the Labor Court in this case, as in previous cases, can be challenged. However, again as in previous cases in this area, it is important to assess the decision in light of the industrial relations context, rather than strictly in terms of statutory interpretation. As in the new case law on dual membership, the Labor Court emphasized the free choice of workers, as opposed to the collective goals and objectives emphasized in the decisions of the past. This case marked a transition from upholding the needs of the corporatist system for concentration to affirming individuals' rights to liberty, free choice, and the freedom of association.

LEADING CASES: AMIT AND RESEARCH
WORKERS UNION

In two leading cases, the controversy over the need for a renewal of the law of trade union recognition was most evident. The first was a case in which a newly formed association, Amit, asked to be recognized as a trade union, although not necessarily as a representative trade union. In a split 3–2 decision, the Labor Court ruled that Amit was a trade union.[10] The decision was brought to the Supreme Court and challenged on the grounds that the Labor Court had substantially erred in its decision.[11] The Supreme Court, sitting in a special panel of seven judges, decided unanimously to uphold the Labor Court's minority position—holding that Amit was not a trade union.[12] The Supreme Court did not, however, determine that Amit could never be a trade union, and it provided several guidelines on what changes were needed for the association to be recognized as a trade union. However, seven months after the Supreme Court's decision the Amit union decided to terminate its activity.

In a second case that was determined a few months after the Amit case, the Labor Court recognized the newly established trade union of the Research Workers in the Public Security and Defense Institutes as a trade union and, moreover, as a representative trade union authorized to conduct collective

8. National Labor Court 52/4-12 General Histadrut and Sea Officers' Union—Zim, PDA 26:3.

9. The court emphasized, however, that its decision did not undermine agency shop arrangements, which are explicitly recognized by the Wage Protection Law (1958). On the issue of agency shop arrangements, see the following section on the Amit case.

10. National Labor Court 55/4-30 Amit, "Maccabi" Trade Union—Municipal Governments Authority and Others, PDA 29:61.

11. Decisions of the National Labor Court cannot be appealed to the Supreme Court, and judicial review by the Supreme Court is limited to matters in which a substantial legal error has occurred. This arrangement is considered one of the features that render the labor courts a separate system of law.

12. Supreme Court HCJ 7029/95 General Histadrut and Others v. Amit, "Maccabi" Trade Union, PDI 51(2):63.

bargaining.[13] The two cases posed different challenges to the corporatist system. The Amit union was intended to be a broad trade union representing workers throughout the country, undermining the concentration of representation by the Histadrut. By contrast, the Research Workers Union was intended to represent only a small number (i.e., several thousands) of workers in four government-controlled establishments.

To understand the legal controversy regarding the Amit union, it is necessary to trace the reasons for its establishment. In 1994, when the legislative process to enact the National Health Care Law began, Maccabi—one of the health-care providers competing with the Histadrut-owned health care system—considered ways of increasing its leverage in the competition expected once the law passed. As explained earlier, the health-care reform disassociated health care from the trade unions. At the time the reform took place, two health-care providers were dominated by the General Histadrut and the National Histadrut, and two were independent of the trade unions—Maccabi and the United Health Care Fund. The reform held that health-care providers must be independent, and that each resident in the country must be insured in one of the providers of his or her choice. However, in one of the drafts to the National Health Care Law, it was proposed to insert a clause allowing financial interaction between sick funds and trade unions. This was intended to appease the General Histadrut, which was the most weakened by the proposed law. Amit was therefore a device that originated from one of the clauses in the legislative drafts (and that was later slashed from the proposed bill).

The Amit trade union was founded by Maccabi, a worldwide Jewish and Zionist organization that provides various services to the Israeli population and to the Jewish population in the Diaspora. One of the services provided within Israel is health care. The dispute between Amit and the General Histadrut was an interunion clash the particulars of which are slightly complex, but it is nevertheless important to set them out in relative detail. As explained in the chapter 3, the Wage Protection Law (1958) legitimized the agency-shop security arrangement. According to this arrangement, workers covered by collective agreements but who were not members of the trade union signing the agreement had to pay agency fees to the representative union. While membership fees to the Histadrut were 0.9 percent of the worker's wage (with a cap), the agency fees were 0.7 percent (with a cap). This arrangement was intended to prevent free-riding behavior. However, the law also held that a worker who was a member of another union (i.e., not of the representative union that signed the collective agreement) was exempted from paying agency fees and only had to pay the membership fees to his or her union of choice. This exception was intended to uphold the freedom of association because if workers had to pay both voluntary membership fees and legally mandated agency fees, they would most likely forgo the right to join the union of their choice. Because

13. National Labor Court 55/4-28 Researchers in the Ministry of Defense Union—General Histadrut, PDA 31:54.

coverage of an agreement could not be waived, as it was determined by law, the only option for the workers would be to forgo affiliation with their own union.

In the past, when the Histadrut had organized most of the workers in Israel, many of whom joined because they wanted to be members of the Histadrut's health-care provider, the Histadrut had not been troubled to any considerable extent by this exception. Its resources were not dependent on the contributions of the small share of workers who were members of other unions. However, as health-care reform loomed, it was clear that many workers would no longer have the same incentive to remain with the Histadrut. The Amit union, with its objective of being a statewide union, organizing workers in both the private and public sectors and in various industrial fields and occupations, could have undermined the collection of agency fees from workers who were covered by the Histadrut's collective agreements, which still covered a majority of the working population. The Histadrut therefore brought an interunion dispute to the Labor Court, arguing that Amit was not a trade union and therefore that its members could not enjoy the exemption from paying agency fees.

The majority opinion in the Labor Court decided that, as a matter of fact, Amit was committed to the representation of workers as individuals, with a lesser interest in collective bargaining. Yet the court held that this was immaterial. On the basis of the characteristics the Labor Court had developed in the past, the majority held that Amit should be recognized as a trade union.[14] The dissenting opinion provided a more critical analysis of Amit. It noted that Amit had been founded by Maccabi and that its executive board was staffed by high-ranking officials of Maccabi. There were no democratic elections to the board. The recruitment of new members was performed in the Maccabi Health Care clinics. Most importantly, however, the dissenting opinion noted that membership fees in Amit were lower than the agency fees paid to the General Histadrut and that in return the worker also received supplementary health coverage in Maccabi's clinics. Thus, to reap the full benefits provided by membership in Amit, the worker had to join Maccabi Health Care. The benefit was therefore twofold: the workers joining Maccabi would be exempted from paying membership or agency fees to the Histadrut, and they would receive additional health coverage. The dissenting position depicted Amit as a tax haven for workers who did not want to pay agency fees, which thus gave them an incentive to join the Maccabi health-care fund. If it had tried to attract new members so as to become a representative union and negotiate collective agreements instead of the Histadrut, that would have been legitimate. As the majority opinion pointed out, however, Amit was not interested in collective representation but only in providing personal services to its members (such as legal advice and representation in individual employment

14. See chapter 4.

disputes). The dissenting opinion concluded that Amit was not a trade union since its objectives were foreign to the interests of labor.

The Supreme Court unanimously reversed the decision of the National Labor Court, upholding the dissenting opinion instead. It held that Amit in its present form could not be a trade union. It was established to advance the interests of Maccabi in improving its position in the competition over members in the health-care market. Thus, while it was independent of any one particular employer, it was not independent of market forces foreign to the interests of labor. Moreover, the Supreme Court agreed with the dissenting opinion that an association that does not want to pursue collective bargaining cannot be a trade union. Trade unions, by definition, are situated in the sphere of collective representation and not in that of individual support to workers. In essence, the controversy was not only about this particular case but also about the meaning of terms such as "collective" and "associations," echoing the difference between corporatist and pluralist associations.

The Supreme Court's ruling appears to demonstrate that the corporatist foundations of collective labor law remained in place. All the same, the Labor Court did not seek to draw a strong border and defeat the entry of new unions, as it did with cases in the corporatist phase. It portrayed Amit as part of a new pluralist reality, in which trade unions compete for members on the basis of different strategies. The majority's rhetoric was therefore not focused on the need for concentration, centralization, or solidarity. It was based on competition, innovation, and spontaneous organization and on the minimal role that the state should play in determining what a trade union is and how it should function.

The Supreme Court's position, following that of the dissent, also emphasized that competition over members' votes is legitimate and may even be desirable. However, Amit was denied recognition because of the opportunistic objectives behind its establishment and, in particular, the use of Amit as a method of attracting new members to Maccabi's health-care services. While in the corporatist phase the Labor Court intentionally provided guidelines beyond the factual circumstances of the case to ensure that no such unions would evolve in the future, the Amit decision was structured in the opposite manner. The Supreme Court subtly provided Amit with concrete guidelines on how to correct its bylaws and operations. The Court also acknowledged that the determination that Amit was not a trade union could be changed once Amit changed its operations.

If there was any doubt whether the outcomes of the Amit case continued or broke away from the corporatist adjudication on trade union recognition, the Researchers Union case certainly indicated that the court was pointing in a new direction. In this case the Labor Court unanimously recognized the Researchers Union as both a trade union and a representative trade union. This dispute was brought to court by a group of research workers in four state-owned establishments engaged in security-related manufacturing and research.

In the past, all the workers in these establishments had been represented by the Histadrut, although the negotiations for the research workers were always conducted separately from those of the other workers (e.g., production and clerical workers). The research workers, who were considered the core workers of these establishments, deemed the Histadrut's representation of their interests to be unsatisfactory and therefore desired to represent themselves. Their efforts to change the Histadrut's policy from within had been unsuccessful, and they decided to organize themselves in an independent union outside the Histadrut.

As in the Amit case, the Histadrut challenged their status in the Labor Court. However, unlike the Amit union, the Researchers Union posed a dual problem. The workers needed recognition not only as a trade union but also as a *representative* union, because, unlike Amit's, the only objective for their organization was to negotiate collective agreements with their employer—the state. The first of the two problems was quickly resolved by the Labor Court. The Court emphasized that, unlike Amit, this was a grassroots organization, established for the ongoing advancement of its members' rights at work. The second problem was more complicated because the research workers did not constitute a majority of the workers. Therefore, even if all the research workers had joined the new union, they could not have achieved the necessary majority required to be recognized as a representative union. In the past the Labor Court had held that the state-as-an-employer was considered one bargaining unit for the purpose of identifying the representative union. It further determined that the bargaining unit was not negotiable and was always determined as the largest bargaining unit possible. The only way to avoid this detrimental consequence for the Researchers Union was to challenge the Court's previous ruling on bargaining units. The research workers' request was especially difficult in this context because they asked to be recognized as a separate bargaining unit characterized by two cumulative characteristics: (1) research workers (2) in the defense industry. Nevertheless, the Labor Court approved their request, and given their majority membership in this carefully tailored bargaining unit, they were recognized to be a representative union entitled to negotiate and conclude collective agreements. Unlike the Amit case, the Researchers Union case was decided by the Labor Court unanimously, with only concurring opinions that did not affect the final outcome.

In this decision, the Labor Court displayed a preference for the interest of a small group that had succeeded in organizing and separating its members from the concentrated Histadrut structure. The Court's reasoning tilted the balance in favor of individual preferences over both the collective interests of a broader group of workers and the corporatist interest in preserving solidarity. Despite the Histadrut's concern that the researchers' separation from the broad bargaining unit would lead to further efforts by small groups to organize independently outside the Histadrut, to this day only a few other cases have raised this issue.[15] The law of recognition, however, was significantly transformed by this case, especially when put in context with the Amit litigation.

THE NEW CASE LAW ON RECOGNITION AND THE
MARGINAL ROLE OF FREEDOM OF ASSOCIATION

Throughout the new case law on trade union recognition, the growing emphasis on individual choice, partially grounded in the freedom of association, was not intended to strengthen the sphere of collective bargaining, nor was it intended to impede it. However, it was clear—especially in the Zim case, which prohibited the use of union security arrangements in collective bargaining—that the decision would weaken the already fragile Histadrut.[16] But what may seem like a paradox is in fact a demonstration of an inherent tension in the freedom of association itself (Leader 1992).

Freedom of association is not a monolithic right but rather a bundle of rights that includes the individual's right to associate in a trade union, the collective right of self-determination, the right to disassociate, and the right of effective unionization. These rights are sometimes in conflict with one another. For example, the Labor Court had to decide a few cases that challenged decisions of the collective that excluded individual interests and preferences.[17] The cases discussed in this chapter indicate yet another tension. The more the court acknowledges individual choice as part of the individual's right to associate (or disassociate) with the union of his or her choice, the more the effective solidarity pact that characterizes corporatism is undermined. Thus, the freedom of association can serve as a trump card for both sides in situations of

15. In another case an independent union argued to be the representative union of the state-employed veterinarians. The Histadrut objected, but in 2004 the parties succeeded in reaching an original compromise of joint representation. Similar solutions were also achieved by the General Histadrut and the religious Mizrachi union (2004), and a different form of cooperation was attained between the General and the National Histadruts with regard to workers employed by temporary work agencies (see chapter 7 for a detailed analysis).

A much more significant blow to the General Histadrut was the 1999 breakaway of the Teachers Union, one of the strongest unions that operated within the Histadrut. However, this breakaway was not affected by legal changes and could have taken place in the past as well.

A potential shattering separation was emerging in 2006 when the Service Workers Union sought to separate from the Histadrut and become independent. This is the largest trade union within the Histadrut. The separation reached the courts on the day it was announced, as the Service Workers Union sought an injunction recognizing that the workers-members remained with the Service Workers' Union despite its separation, or at least that a poll must be conducted among the members. Extralegal pressure brought the case to an end and the Service Workers Union back to the Histadrut's courtyard. Despite an unfavorable preliminary injunction in court, most of the legal questions that were raised remained unanswered.

16. See supra note 8.

17. For example, the court had to determine whether the bylaws of the Mizrachi Histadrut, a trade union organizing religious workers, were valid, given that they required its members to observe Orthodox Judaism. National Labor Court, 48/5-1 The Mizrachi Bank Workers Union—General Histadrut, PDA 21:283.

conflict between unions and individuals or small groups. To be effective, the collective must have some power to keep the solidarity pact intact, while in order to promote individual choice the law must grant individuals the possibility of associating and disassociating at will.

Generally, corporatism rests on rules of recognition that promote freedom of association, in the sense of effective bargaining on behalf of a large solidarity base that is not dependent solely on individual choice. As demonstrated in several examples throughout the discussion thus far, members did not join the Histadrut solely because they identified with its objectives and supported its policies. The state did much to ensure the extensive membership of workers and nonworkers alike in the Histadrut, thus ensuring some legitimacy for the formal power delegated to the Histadrut. Leaving health care, pensions, and, in the early stages, the employment bureaus in the hands of the Histadrut while at the same time extending the coverage of collective agreements to most of the workforce characterizes a system that seeks to draw on association to advance social objectives rather than individual preferences. By contrast, pluralist systems of industrial relations in which the state's role in promoting recognition is very limited, as is the case in the United States, adhere to a different construction of the right to association. The right of association in pluralist regimes is consistent with the general individual approach to human rights, which emphasizes the promotion of individual choice and an uninhibited sphere of action in which government must not interfere.

It is interesting to observe that in the case law on recognition, in both the corporatist and postcorporatist phase, the Labor Court consistently refrained from basing its decisions on the freedom of association. The bracketing of the freedom of association that appears throughout the judicial construction of the rules of recognition is peculiar. It seems that the courts are making extraordinary efforts to avoid the inherent tension within the freedom of association and to preserve that freedom for cases in which there are explicit prohibitions on it.[18] Exposing the tension between different conceptions of "freedom" would have revealed the full complexity of the corporatist project, as well as that of the postcorporatist project. Neither is neutral in dealing with individual preferences, collective action, or solidarity. Both corporatist and postcorporatist decisions favor the interests of some over those of others. The removal of freedom of association from judicial decisions is therefore an instrument for concealing complex and value-laden distributive outcomes.

Only at a later stage was the freedom of association revived, but always in a context not directly involved with the rules of recognition. Freedom of association has been used to develop the protection against abusive dismissals of workers who try to organize their fellow workers, and to devise the rules on

---

18. The only case in which the Court has admitted that freedom of association was at stake was one in which a police organization challenged the restriction on association in the police force. Supreme Court HCJ 789/78 David Ofek v. Minister of Interior Affairs, PDI 33(3):480.

labor-management consultation and negotiation rights, the rights of disclosure, and the rights of the parties in the transfer of operations from one employer to another. These rules will be explored in greater detail in the following chapter. It is clear, however, that they fashion rights and obligations that govern the relationship between the bargaining partners. Yet they still do not formally intervene in the controversial area of recognition and in the mediation of interests among different groups of workers.

From Social Partners to Interest Groups: The Rise of the Social NGOs

Complementing the change of law in the area of trade union recognition is that particular segments of the workforce are gradually coming to be represented by pluralist interest groups. The emergence of social movements and associations outside the corporatist structures is explained as an outcome of the fading of old identities and the emergence of new ones that fill in for those lost (Kriesi 1999; Freeman, Hersch, and Mishel 2005). As old political structures become unstable, there is a growing diversity of interests that seek an organized method of representation. Whereas the Histadrut and the employers' associations were in the past considered the social partners in policymaking, today they are still considered bargaining agents, but their macrosocial role has declined. Into this gap many new associations in civil society have entered, and they have begun to play an active role in affecting policy. Like the representation of particular groups of workers by the new associations, the general representation of interests in society has been transformed. Rather than being based on the sole distinction between labor and capital, it is currently a more dynamic and segmented form of representation that corresponds to the growing disposition to multiculturalism in Israeli society (Mautner, Sagie, and Shamir 1998; Shafir and Peled 2002).

Nongovernmental organizations (NGOs) are not a new phenomenon in Israel, but their number and the extent of activism they display have increased dramatically since the end of the 1980s (Gidron, Bar, and Katz 2003). While NGOs perform various functions in civil society, the reference here is mostly to those that represent the interests of groups that also have a direct interest in the structure of the labor market and the welfare state. These include human rights organizations, associations that voice the concerns of regional interests, political associations that are not represented as political parties in the Knesset, and even employers' and employees' interest groups that fall short of being a formal employers' association or a trade union. It is noteworthy that most NGOs that also have an impact on social law, and labor law in particular, do not view their own mission in terms of labor market regulation. Except for some of the small employers' and employees' organizations and the handful of NGOs that define their mission solely in terms of transformation within the labor market (e.g., organizations that represent migrant workers, the unemployed, or Arab workers), NGOs take a position on labor issues only to the extent that it coincides with their general mission. For example, for groups representing women, labor market conditions are viewed through the prism of women's rights and not from a labor rights perspective.[19] This epitomizes one of the major differences between corporatist representation of interests, which is modeled around the centrality of the labor-capital conflict, and the pluralist mode of representation in which there is no a priori hierarchy of social distinctions or conflicts. The pluralist social agenda is shaped by the pluralist interest groups in a dynamic manner (whereby groups are formed in response to the social agenda and then take part in further influencing it and also deterring it from its present track). By contrast, in a corporatist regime the labor-employers-state division is a constituting characteristic, and therefore it cannot be changed by the corporatist players without undermining the corporatist structure itself.

While corporatist associations are characterized by the dual principles of recognition and autonomy, the NGOs described here for the most part do not enjoy explicit recognition by the state, but they do maintain their autonomy. Arguably, their autonomy is even stronger than that of the corporatist associations because of the lack of recognition. Many NGOs do not even have any desire for state recognition in the sense that corporatist associations do. They seek limited recognition only, in the sense of being consulted in legislative proceedings or acquiring some standing in the courts. However, they reject any state declaration of a "most representative" status. Consequently, they are not centralized, nor do they seek concentration that is achieved by means of state intervention, as is typical of the corporatist associations. This results in fragmented representation and a dynamic relationship among the associations, characterized by alternating spells of rivalry and coordination and a voluntary, yet incomplete, division of labor. In most situations the "relational" characteristics of corporatism are also irrelevant to these groups. They do not formally negotiate with the state, certainly not with employers. They cannot formally construct rights for their members, and at most they can influence the legislature or the courts in the process of authoring the new law of the workplace.

The NGOs evolve by voluntary means (also designated in the literature as "spontaneous"). Many of the new NGOs are not grassroots associations. They are formed by social activists and funded by contributions and international funds. Most NGOs have a small membership, and therefore they are not based on members' contributions. This creates a gap between the NGO and its constituency, which in a sense replicates the gap developed by the Histadrut over the years between it and its own members. However, given the absence of state recognition, which accounted for the Histadrut's lesser reliance on the active support of its dues-paying members, the NGOs are directed according to the interests of the professional leadership and the need to demonstrate activity in the social field for which they receive the external funding. For example, an

---

19. Whether these two perspectives collide is a question that is addressed extensively by the literature, but I draw my analysis here from Fraser and Honneth (2003).

NGO that represents the interests of migrant workers may have a handful of members who do not pay dues, may be funded by international funds, and may be led by a group of social activists. The migrant workers it represents are not members, and therefore the NGO is not a trade union. The workers are "clients" who receive individual aid. Their interests are also represented by means of the NGO's attempts at lobbying and litigation, but the migrant workers themselves do not control the agenda of the NGO or its mode of operation. This is not because migrant workers are denied membership, but because the new NGOs simply do not rely on members for the management of the association. The above example is not limited to migrant workers but can also be observed with various distinctions in large NGOs (such as the Association for Civil Rights in Israel—ACRI) or NGOs with many active members (such as the Eastern Rainbow, which represents the Sepharadic Jews, or the Women's Lobbying Group, which represents the interests of women). All these NGOs represent the interests of their groups, which are defined by the organization's managerial team and the board of directors.

The absence of recognition and grassroots support and the professional orientation of the leadership account for the NGOs' intensive reliance on legal strategies, with the intention of influencing the authors of law—both the legislature and the courts. This is not the sole strategy of the NGOs. They also develop educational resources and are engaged in the empowerment of their clients and in raising public awareness, but legal strategy is central to many of them. Some seek to influence only the legislature, others focus on litigation, but many pursue at least one of these avenues of action. Of course, each of them can be reduced to various substrategies. Influencing legislation is conducted by the diffusion of alternative information that challenges the information provided by the state and by lobbying, drafting proposals for statutes, and drawing public attention through the media. Litigation strategies include both fundamental challenges brought to the Supreme Court and day-to-day representation in the lower courts. However, all these strategies seek to change the law, whether formally or through its administration in action.

It is difficult to quantify the impact of NGOs on the new labor law, but there are various indications as to their growing importance. In the legislative arena, NGOs and not the social partners were responsible for advancing the law against discrimination at work. Since 1988, numerous statutes and statutory amendments have developed the law of antidiscrimination. While groups representing women initiated the process, influencing the legislation of the Equal Retirement Age for Women and Men (1987) and the Employment (Equal Opportunities) Law (1998), other groups have followed. The gays and lesbians' NGO affected the first amendment to the Employment (Equal Opportunities) Law, prohibiting discrimination on the basis of sexual orientation (Yonai 1998). Various civil rights organizations effected further changes in 1995, prohibiting discrimination on the basis of a broad list of categories, including age, nationality, and ethnicity. An NGO representing the interests of people with disabilities succeeded in the partial passage of the Equal Rights of People With Disabilities

A similar process, although on a lesser scale, can be observed in the courts. While NGOs are often those who initiate litigation on behalf of their clients, the courts also, at their own initiative, have begun turning to NGOs as the representatives of interest groups. For example, in a case where the issue of migrant workers' rights in the judicial system was raised, the National Labor Court asked the Israeli Association of Civil rights (ACRI) and the Workers Hotline (an NGO representing the rights of migrant workers) to submit their position on the legal question at stake.[26] Consequently, an official committee that was commissioned to reconsider the Labor Courts Law proposed to amend the law that grants standing to the largest trade union and to employers' associations in court, and to extend standing rights to organizations that engage in the implementation of statutory rights relevant to the legal dispute.[27]

At first glance, the influence of NGOs on law may seem reminiscent of the corporatist phase, in the sense that law is affected by civil society instead of governing it. The NGOs affect the making of law in both the Knesset and the courtroom and are later recognized as the representatives of interests for further development of the law. This may seem similar to the process whereby the Histadrut dominated the legislative proceedings and then ensured its position in subsequent legislative processes by ensuring the incorporation of consultancy clauses. However, this superficial similarity glosses over the vast difference between the corporatist and postcorporatist phases of lawmaking.

One characteristic of the corporatist process of establishing regulatory norms was the precedence of corporatist negotiations over the legislative process. Where corporatist agreement was not reached, statutes were not successful either. By contrast, the pluralist regulatory phase is characterized by interest groups' proposals that are endorsed by groups of legislators that are formed ad hoc around the issue at stake (e.g., legislators who support the advancement of women's rights in the labor market, cutting across the typical political left and right). The statutory reforms may therefore be characterized as a majoritarian achievement in the legislative process rather than a reflection of consensus. In the courtroom, similarly, the judicial decisions that advance the rights of various identity groups or of identifiable communities of workers (such as migrant workers) are not intended to uphold the labor market's status quo, as was typical of the corporatist phase, but are instead aimed at changing the behavior of the labor market's participants.

The replacement of corporatist negotiations with the pluralist legal strategies of NGOs marks a shift in the relationship between the law and autonomous norms making. The autonomous making of norms has been replaced by the determination of conflicting interests by the authors of state law (legislators and judges). The new participants in the evolving pluralist system no longer seek to

26. National Labor Court 1541/01 Xue Bin—A. Dori Inc. (2002, unpublished interim decision).

27. The Committee to Assess and Propose Amendments to the Law of Procedure in The Labor Courts, headed by Itshak Elyassof (former judge of the National Labor Court) (report filed in November 2002).

negotiate labor market norms among themselves. They are not centralized, not concentrated, and they derive their power from professionalism rather than from grassroots support or state recognition. Their ethical framework is often removed from that of class representation and leans heavily toward individual human rights and claims of equality among groups of workers; only to a much lesser extent are they concerned with the rights of labor vis-à-vis employers.

THE two changes in interests representation—the decentralization and decline of labor's representation in favor of identity groups and small groups of workers—indicate that corporatist autonomous lawmaking by means of collective bargaining has lost its prominent central position in the legal system. The evolving structure of interests representation therefore denotes the breakdown of the corporatist model with regard to lawmaking. Consequently, the state's law no longer reflects the corporatist structure but is assumed to be a means for ranking competing claims and promoting one claim over another. However, another outcome of the changing nature of interests representation can be observed with regard to the centrality of the norm established by collective bargaining. Whereas these autonomous norms were regarded as the central norms in the corporatist system, they have been partially devalued in the new labor law. This will be described in the following subsection.

The Declining Centrality of the Collective Norm

The centrality of the collectively bargained norms to the corporatist system was upheld by labor law through various measures. On the one hand, collective agreements were deemed by the Collective Agreements Law (1957) to be superior to individually negotiated norms and therefore binding on the parties to the employment contract. On the other hand, although statutory norms were considered superior to collective agreements, some of the laws, as has been explained in the previous chapters, included derogation clauses that allowed the parties to collective bargaining to change the statutory norms. Another measure that was introduced for the purpose of placing the collectively negotiated norm at the center was the extension order, which turned the collectively negotiated norm into secondary legislation. These three features attest that the collective norm was considered of a higher normative caliber than all individual contracts, as well as an important method of writing and revising regulatory norms. Complementing the normative centrality of the collectively negotiated norm was the reluctance of the courts to intervene in its content. The strict regulation of entry into the collective bargaining sphere enabled the courts to forgo the need to constantly monitor and supervise the parties to collective bargaining.

   These features of the corporatist labor law have been overturned in the postcorporatist phase. In this section I have listed several legal changes, which resulted in the weakening of the collectively bargained norm. None of them can be presented as a major rewriting of labor law. However, cumulatively they clearly represent a coherent statement of the law, according to which the centrality and immunity of the collectively negotiated norm, which characterized the corporatist paradigm of law, no longer obtain.

The Decline of Upward Regulation—Extension Orders

The use of extension orders in the corporatist phase was to deny employers the benefit of disassociation from an employers' organization. At the same time, they allowed the bargaining partners a greater level of control regarding both the content of the orders and the scope of extension. The bargaining partners were solely responsible for the content of the agreement that served as the basis of the extension order. Employers therefore preferred this method of broad regulation, which evolved from negotiations, over regulation that evolved from political coalition building by the legislature.

Despite the advantages of the extension orders to the parties, the decline of corporatism has brought about the gradual marginalization of extension orders. The diminishing use of extension orders has been documented empirically in a comparison spanning the years 1957–1998 (Kristal 2004). In most economic branches, extension orders have not been used in the postcorporatist phase. Whereas the share of industrywide collective agreements that were extended ranged from 20 to 60 percent annually in the period 1957–1980, since 1980 it has gradually declined, reaching 0 percent for several years during the 1990s. This is a result partially of the disappearance of sector-level collective agreements in many branches and partially of the reluctance to extend the few agreements that were signed. The effort to provide comprehensive regulation of wages and working conditions over an industry or sector by means of extension orders has been almost abandoned.

A different type of extension order is one that extends statewide collective agreements and applies them to *all* the employers in the state. These tend to be less detailed than the extension orders that cover only particular economic branches. Yet, as described in the previous chapter, they did play an important role in the corporatist arrangements of the past, determining the minimum wage, cost-of-living adjustment, convalescence payments, and even the transition to a five-day workweek. However, among the several statewide extension orders, two of the more important ones have been terminated and replaced by statutory standards: the minimum wage law described in the opening section of this chapter and the requirement to provide prior notice before dismissals.[28]

---

28. The extension orders issued over collective agreements that set minimum wage were replaced by the Minimum Wage Law (1987), and those that extended the duty to provide prior notice before dismissals were replaced by the Prior Notice Before Dismissal and Resignation Law (2001).

The use of extension orders has not been abandoned altogether, and one general extension order providing employees with daysoff in times of mourning was approved late in the postcorporatist phase.[29]

All the same, it is important to note that the statute governing the process of issuing extension orders has not changed over the years. However, the legal system more generally has started to question the necessity and morality of extension orders. The opponents of the orders argue that it is immoral to impose collectively negotiated norms on employers (and their employees) who show no interest in such coverage. Furthermore, the law authorizes employers' associations (but not trade unions) to collect agency fees from employers in an economic branch covered by an extension order. The collection of agency fees, in a situation where most employers are heavily obligated by the extension orders and receive very few rights and privileges, is deemed particularly coercive. By contrast, it is possible to portray extension orders in a less antagonistic fashion. The alternative description suggests that while the state has legitimate power to regulate the labor market, the use of extension orders allows the state to forgo its power and delegate the power of norms making to the social partners, who must develop it by means of negotiation. Thus, while extension orders are indeed more coercive than voluntary arrangements, they can be considered less coercive than the legislature's regulatory power. It is all a matter of the choice of benchmark for comparison.

These two competing perspectives on extension orders first surfaced in the Labor Court in 1996, in the postcorporatist phase.[30] In this case, an employer who was not a member of an employers' association contested various extension orders that had been made to collective agreements in 1974, 1978, and 1988. Because an extension order continues to be in effect until it is affirmatively canceled or such time as the collective agreement that was extended is terminated, these orders continued to apply together with the applicable collective agreements. The employer challenged the extension orders on the basis of the constitutional right to property and the freedom of occupation, both constitutional rights enshrined in the Israeli Bill of Rights that was written in 1992.[31]

The Tel Aviv District Labor Court, and the National Labor Court on appeal, held that the extension order violated the right to property and the freedom of occupation. In itself this ruling was well within the constitutional jurisprudence developed by the Israeli Supreme Court. In fact, all the legal measures that regulate the labor market are considered to infringe on employers'

29. Official State Publications (Yalkut Ha-Pirsumim) 4895 Y.H. (2000), 4002.

30. The case was first brought to the Tel-Aviv District Labor Court 54/3-1381 Chamber of Commerce Tel-Aviv Yafo and Others—Minister of Labor and Others (1996, unpublished) and then appealed to the National Labor Court 56/3–303 Chamber of Commerce Tel-Aviv Yafo and Others—YAD Electronics Inc., PDA 30:249.

31. Basic Law: Freedom of Occupation (1994), and Basic Law: Human Dignity and Liberty (1992), sec. 3. For a more detailed description of constitutional developments in Israel, see chapter 6.

property rights. However, the Bill of Rights does not prohibit the infringement of constitutional rights as long as any such infringement is "by a Law fitting the values of the State of Israel, designed for a proper purpose, and to an extent no greater than required or by such a law enacted with explicit authorization therein."[32] The important question, then, is not whether an infringement of a property right has occurred but whether such an infringement is lawful. While constitutional review applies to the entire gamut of legal instruments—legislation, secondary legislation, collective agreements, and even private contracts—extension orders are more vulnerable to judicial review than other instruments. With regard to the constitutional review of legislation, the courts are very cautious when it comes to striking down legislation because of the respect accorded to the democratic separation of powers. With regard to the constitutional review of contracts and collective agreements, the courts are cautious when it comes to interference, upholding the freedom of contract as a constitutional right in itself. Extension orders, however, are not an act of the legislature (being extended by the Minister of Labor and Welfare), and they do not benefit from a presumption of consent and the freedom of contract. Their objective is exactly the opposite—to govern when there is no consent and to regulate when the legislature does not intervene.

Both the district court and the National Labor Court held that extension orders generally pass the constitutional hurdle of property rights. The Labor Court's view seems to indicate that extension orders are legally immune to constitutional review, and it would therefore appear that the fruits of the corporatist legal model are still existent and well accepted in the postcorporatist law. However, the National Labor Court avoided awarding carte blanche approval to all extension orders. Because the extension orders at stake were issued many years before the enactment of the Bill of Rights, the Court held that it would be wrong to interfere in a stable economic system on which many people are dependent. It did state, however, that in the future new extension orders must be scrutinized for their constitutional validity. Since the case was decided in 1997, no such constitutional challenge has been brought to court, mainly because the actual use of extension orders has declined dramatically and is now almost nonexistent. Extension orders have become a legal institution with far-reaching implications but little practice in actual fact.

The Decline of Downward Regulation—Derogation Clauses

While extension orders made it possible to "upgrade" norms that had been negotiated in general collective agreements and turn them into secondary legislation, the corporatist law also accommodated the reverse process. Contrary to the supremacy of legislation over all contractual instruments, derogation

---

32. Basic Law: Human Dignity and Liberty (1992), sec. 8; Basic Law: Freedom of Occupation (1994), sec. 4.

clauses allowed derogation from the statutory standards by means of collective bargaining. In chapter 3 I provided various examples of derogation clauses in the corporatist legislation. Although only a handful of laws introduced the possibility of derogation by collective agreements, these clauses were of practical importance. It has also been demonstrated that the use of derogations interacted with the use of extension orders, whereby an instance of derogation from the statutory standard could later be extended by means of an extension order to a broad segment of the labor market.

Unlike the early legislative project of labor law, the numerous laws legislated since 1987 do not allow derogation. This is symptomatic of the legislature's view that collective bargaining is no longer the dominant source of labor market norms. In the absence of derogation clauses, statutory standards have attained an absolute supremacy. While there are two notable exceptions to the absence of derogation clauses, these in fact only point up the general breakdown of corporatist law.

One exception can be found in the Employment of Employees by Manpower Contractors Law (1996). Generally, the law prescribes that employees hired through temporary work agencies are entitled to wages and working conditions equal to those of employees who are employed directly. The use of a derogation clause in this law was intended to strengthen the trade unions and encourage collective agreements in conformance with the corporatist use of derogation.[33] However, as the detailed discussion of this arrangement in chapter 7 reveals, it departs in several important respects from the corporatist use of derogation clauses. In a nutshell, the use of derogation in this law is indeed a corporatist measure, but it was implemented in noncorporatist circumstances and therefore had perverse effects that fragmented the trade unions and decentralized collective agreements and their coverage. It is an important example of the transitional stage of labor law in Israel at present.

The second exception to the abstention from introducing derogation clauses can be found in the Prevention of Sexual Harassment Law (1998). This law is typical of the postcorporatist phase. It evolved from the lobbying and activism of NGOs and legislators engaged in the protection and empowerment of women. Like many other laws enacted during the 1990s, it is not concerned with wages or economic working conditions but with antidiscrimination norms and concerns of human dignity (Kamir 1998). It is tempting, however, to identify within it the reflexive features that were typical of corporatist law. The Prevention of Sexual Harassment Law does more than define the norms of conduct; it also requires an extensive intraorganizational change. It requires employers to prepare a set of bylaws concerned with the diffusion of information, to conduct inquiries on allegations of sexual harassment, and to instigate disciplinary measures when allegations are substantiated. It therefore tunnels deep into the governance of organizational culture.

---

33. Employment of Employees by Manpower Contractors Law (1996), sec. 13.

norm. This derivative is absolute, and it is intended to prevent any pressure on individual employees to consent to wages and working conditions that are less desirable than those determined by the collective agreement. Individual agreements that derogate from the collective norm are assumed to be against the interests of the individual employee, but they also run the risk of generally undercutting the collective norm and thus threatening the solidarity setting of norms altogether (Yadlin 1999).

The second derivative holds that individual negotiations can improve on the terms of the collective agreement unless the parties to the agreement determine that the collective norms constitute a cap on individual benefits. In chapter 3 it was argued that the second derivative led to a corporatist compromise in the legislative process of the Collective Agreements Law. On the one hand, it is assumed that individuals are free to improve their own conditions and that the statutory standards and collective agreements merely present a minimum that generally cannot be derogated. On the other hand, allowing individuals to negotiate their own terms, over and above those determined in the collective agreement, can undermine the solidarity representation of interests that is carefully weighted and balanced within the collective agreement.

While the supremacy of the collective norm remained uncontested throughout the corporatist phase of labor law, its two components have undergone a partial erosion in the postcorporatist phase (Margaliot 2001). In one direction, the Labor Court recognized that there are instances, despite the general prohibition on derogation of the collective norm by individual bargaining, in which a worker claiming rights waived in individual bargaining will be held to be in bad faith.[46] In the other direction, the Labor Court also gradually recognized instances in which employees who have bargained individually for rights that improve on the collective agreement may be disassociated from the collective agreement altogether. That is, they will not be entitled to claim rights to which they are formally entitled by the collective agreement if the individual bundle of rights generally improved their employment benefits (e.g., in wages) but also derogated from them in several respects (e.g., in job security).[47] Hence, the Labor Court weakened the solidarity pact held together by the collective agreement in favor of advancing individualized justice. Together, these two changes lend more weight to individual bargaining than did the corporatist phase of labor law.

Growing Intervention in the Content of Collective Agreements

A final symptom of the declining status of the collective norm is the growing judicial tendency to intervene in the content of collective agreements. As

46. While there are several cases that suggest the possibility, the most direct is National Labor Court 97/3-237 Ezrah Shmueli—Israeli Broadcasting Authority, PDA 36:557.
47. National Labor Court 57/4-4 General Histadrut—Moriah Hotels (1996, unpublished).

demonstrated in the previous chapter, during the corporatist phase the Labor Court rarely intervened in collective agreements. The Naomi Nevo case described at the introduction to part 3 illustrates the court's willingness to intervene in discriminatory agreements even in more ambiguous situations. The Supreme Court preferred the equality principle over the autonomy of the industrial relations system and the primacy of the collectively bargained norm.

In the aftermath of the Naomi Nevo case, the Supreme Court's view infiltrated the Labor Court, and the latter has gradually come to display a more interventionist stance. Over the years, several agreements have been struck because they were found to be discriminatory. In fact, the seminal cases on employment discrimination deal with discrimination that is rooted in the collectively negotiated norm rather than in unilateral action on the part of employers. After the Naomi Nevo case, the Labor Court intervened in the content of collective agreements that it found to endorse unequal promotion processes for men and women or deny spousal benefits for same-sex couples, as well as collective agreements that mandate early retirement. These instances of intervention resonate with the growingly multicultural agenda and the pluralist structure of interests representation discussed in the previous sections.

However, the Labor Court's intervention in the content of collective agreements extends beyond the problems of employment discrimination. One area in which the law has fluctuated somewhat during the postcorporatist phase concerns the duty of fair representation. The American doctrine requiring the trade union to "fairly" represent all the bargaining-unit members had been rejected by the court in the corporatist phase (Mironi 1981).[48] In keeping with the corporatist model of labor law, the Court was unwilling to substitute its judgment for that of the social partners. However, in the Zim case mentioned earlier in this chapter, in which the Labor Court prohibited the use of closed- and union-shop union security clauses, one of the justifications offered was that these clauses violate the duty of fair representation.[49] Although the matter of union security clauses that affect nonmembers has little to do with the right of fair representation, which is aimed at protecting bargaining-unit members, the court's recognition of the duty suggested that in other cases it might be willing to intervene in the union's judgment in bargaining and internal affairs. In and of itself, the Zim decision in general, and the reference to the duty of fair representation in particular, marked a deviation from the formerly held corporatist premises.

The Court's position, however, was not unequivocal. In later decisions the Labor Court held that the duty of fair representation would be considered only in cases of discrimination on familiar grounds (such as gender, sexual preference, nationality, and the like).[50] The firm distinction between discrimination issues and other types of categorization (e.g., occupational differences)

---

48. See chapter 4.
49. National Labor Court 52/4, see supra note 8 and accompanying text.
50. Cf. National Labor Court 1143/01 Dov Winkler—General Histadrut, PDA 39:153.

is generally typical of noncorporatist regimes, most notably the United States (Freed, Polsby, and Spitzer 1983). However, occasionally the Labor Court was even willing to put this distinction aside and intervene in circumstances that did not correspond to the notion of employment discrimination on familiar grounds. In yet another case dealing with the Zim Company, the court was confronted with a claim by a seaman who argued that he had been denied promotion because the collective agreement gave priority in promotions to land workers. The court accepted the argument and struck down the priority system.[51]

To understand the significance of this decision, it is important to note that within Zim, workers are covered by different agreements signed with different organs of the General Histadrut. These are not different bargaining units because the Histadrut is the sole representative trade union of all the workers in Zim. The different agreements are therefore merely a result of the Histadrut's internal structure of interests representation. While mariners have their own trade union within the Histadrut, the land workers are represented by the regional workers' committees. Admittedly there is little coordination between the different agents. Nevertheless, the priorities system for the land workers was negotiated by the Histadrut, which also represents the seamen. As in all such agreements, the trade union balances, explicitly or implicitly, the interests of all workers and gives preference to one set of interests over another. This may be a "good" or "bad" preference. The assumption underlying collective labor law is that no one is better informed than the bargaining agents regarding what should be deemed good or bad. Giving priority to land workers may be unfair, but it might also be fair because seamen enjoy a higher status and greater benefits in Zim. There is no one single ethical guideline for determining fairness in such cases. This was not a case in which one union excluded the members of another, as all workers were represented by various organs of the same union. This was not a case in which fairness was used to endorse a preference for men over women. What it involved was a mere preference for one group, defined on the basis of its occupation, over another. The Court's willingness to intervene in this case was therefore unprecedented and went beyond the bounds of discrimination that the Court allegedly observes.

From Consensus-Building Law to
Power-Breaking Law

This chapter is the first of three describing the extent of change in labor law that has taken place in tandem with the decline of the corporatist regime in Israel. In a nutshell, I have argued that two of the central premises of the corporatist paradigm of labor law have significantly changed. First, the centralized, class-based structure of interests representation that prevailed in the past has

51. National Labor Court 400024/98 General Histadrut—Sea Officers' Union, PDA 36:97.

been transformed into a pluralist and multicultural form of representation. Second, the centrality of the collectively governed norm has been undermined, with a growing preference for market regulation and public norms imposed by the legislature and the courts. The two processes are separate but are inter-related. The centrality accorded to the collectively bargained norm was em-bedded in the centralized and all-encompassing structure of corporatist interests representation. At the same time, the stability of the corporatist institutions was made possible, in part, by the legal recognition of the collectively bar-gained norm's centrality. These pillars of the corporatist paradigm of law were interdependent and inseparable. It is therefore not surprising that they changed in tandem.

The causal relationship between these two components of transformation cannot be elucidated, since they are concurrent phenomena. There is no clear chronological order, and the transformation described in this chapter has taken place in a rather short period of time, considering the pace of legal re-forms. It is therefore better viewed as a single coherent process, which can be described as an *hourglass effect*. The collectively bargained norm is situated in the middle of the norms governing the labor market, in neither the public nor the private sphere. It is governed by the corporatist institutions at the level of civil society. With the disintegration of the corporatist institutions, the collec-tive norm has been replaced by both private (market) and public measures of regulation—namely, statutes and the judicial development of mandatory norms. The middle sphere of regulation is being squeezed from both directions—hence the hourglass image. Similarly, the corporatist institutions that are formally rec-ognized and strongly supported by the state, yet removed from the state, are being weakened. Substituting for them are the pluralist institutions on the one hand (e.g., the NGOs) and state agents on the other.

The more important question, which was posed at the outset, concerns the relationship between the changes in the industrial relations system and the le-gal system. Can a clear causal relationship be established in this context? Oth-erwise stated, has the decline of the corporatist industrial relations system led to the breakdown of corporatist labor law, or have the changes in the legal structures induced the decline in corporatist forms of representation? The sim-ple answer is that primacy must be imputed to the change in the industrial re-lations system as the catalyst. This can be substantiated first and foremost by the chronological sequence; as noted in chapter 1, the decline of the corpo-ratist system began in the early 1980s and perhaps even a few years earlier, while most of the legal episodes described in this chapter came to pass at least a decade later. This, however, is not merely a technical assessment of the chronology. From a substantive point of view, the hourglass effect was in re-sponse to the instability that appeared in the corporatist system. The new agents in civil society and the lawmaking agents (the legislature and the courts), who have become increasingly important, clearly took upon them-selves the role of substituting for the weakening corporatist regime and its out-puts (the collectively negotiated norm).

The causal description provided here does not, however, suggest that the legal system merely reflected the outputs of the industrial relations system, as is sometimes assumed in the literature of industrial relations. While this may have been a good approximation of the relationship between the two systems in the heyday of the corporatist regime, it certainly cannot be a good description at a time of transition away from corporatism. When the industrial relations system was based solely on tripartite negotiations among a limited number of well-defined agents, the state's monopolistic power to legislate was heavily influenced by the norms produced by the parties themselves. However, the destabilization of the corporatist pact has led to a more complex system of lawmaking influenced by agents and interests outside the traditional industrial relations system. Consequently, it would be wrong to assume that the legal changes could have been easily predicted or traced back to the industrial relations system. In a sense, labor law has been extricated from the monopolistic control of the industrial relations system and is currently influenced by other social subsystems. It would also be wrong to assume that the particular legal response to the weakening of the industrial relations system was inevitable. The agents accorded with the formal power to regulate the labor market could have taken other paths. They could have preserved the corporatist structures of the law or even reinforced them. A refusal to pass the Minimum Wage Law, to intervene in collective agreements, to accept the growing role of the NGOs operating outside the formal structure of the industrial relations system, or to uphold the centrality of the collectively bargained norm and penalize employers for failing to negotiate—any and all of these measures might have resulted in different legal rules and perhaps even in a different fate for the industrial relations system. Of course it is difficult to hypothesize the outcomes of counterfactual situations, but it is just as difficult to assume that the changes described here were inevitable.

While in this chapter I presented the infrastructure of the new legal system—namely, where, how and by whom regulatory norms are currently designed—in the following two chapters I will take a look at the substantive norms themselves. In the next chapter I will discuss the juridification of the employer-employee relationship, and in the subsequent chapter I will observe the effects of the changing norms on the dualist nature of the Israeli labor market. The changes in labor law's metafunction will also account for the changing content of the norms that govern the labor market themselves.

6 The Juridification of the Employment Relationship

Defining Juridification

The central characteristic of corporatist labor law was that it sought to develop regulation based on norms that do not directly rely on the state's monopolistic power to regulate. Insofar as "law" is perceived narrowly—as the body of norms produced by the state's agents—then corporatist law sought to minimize it. As demonstrated in the previous chapters, the state provided a minimal set of rules that prescribed the structure of collective bargaining and elevated the collectively bargained norm to a position as the primary source of norms governing the labor market. The substantive norms imposed on the labor market by the state originated from collective bargaining as well and were later applied to the entire labor market by means of extension orders, legislation, or judicial interpretation according to the "industrial norm."

In the previous chapter I described the effects on labor law of the corporatist system's disintegration with regard to law's metafunction. It was demonstrated that since the agents influencing the law have changed, the law no longer reflects corporatist—concentrated, centralized, and autonomous—negotiations. Moreover, the centrality of the collectively bargained norm has declined, leading to a greater role for individual agreements on the one hand and for mandatory employment standards on the other. This in turn has led to extensive intervention by the agents authoring the law—namely, the judiciary and the legislature—in the labor market. The legal system has turned from providing inducements to self-regulation in the corporatist phase to direct regulation of the labor market. This process is designated "juridification."

There is no clear consensus regarding the definition of juridification or what distinguishes it from more general terms such as "regulation." (Gladstone

1997). For example, Clark (1985) describes it as the process whereby the state directs social and economic life. Simitis (1987) emphasizes that juridification is a byproduct of industrialization, whereby there is a gradual replacement of a society based on contractual agreements by one based on regulatory law. Following Simitis and Teubner, Mitchell (1998) emphasizes that the term "juridification" connotes not only the proliferation of legal norms but also the dysfunctional problems associated with it.

As used in this book, juridification is the process of establishing mandatory legal norms that substitute for extralegal regulation of social or economic relationships. In this process, legal norms replace extralegal norms and legal sanctions replace social or economic sanctions, such as shame, loss of authority, decline in stock value, and diminishing reputation. Two types of questions on juridification may be distinguished.

The first type asks why individuals or groups decide to lobby the legislature or file a petition in court, seeking a legal remedy in situations where legal intervention was uncommon in the past. Moreover, why are some issues advanced by legislation and others by litigation, while others remain outside the legal discourse altogether? The answers to these questions are for the most part sociological rather than jurisprudential. They require a grasp of how law is used in social reform processes. They were partially discussed in the previous chapter. It was argued that the rise of NGOs outside the traditional corporatist structure of interests representation, coupled with the absence of state recognition on the one hand and of a broad grassroots base on the other, has led to an increasing reliance on legal strategies to advance their claims.

The second type of questions asks which norms should be associated with juridification. If the court or legislature prefers to leave the establishment of norms to the contracting parties or to the parties taking part in collective bargaining, then juridification doesn't fully materialize. A fully juridified process ends in imposing a public norm, rather than leaving the task to nonpublic parties (individuals, trade unions, and employers' associations, or other agents in other contexts—such as a stock exchange, professional guild, and the like). Complete juridification requires the intervention of either the legislature or the courts, in a manner that limits or withdraws the representation of interests and the making of norms from the extralegal spheres (markets, politics, or intimacy).

In this chapter I will emphasize the legal norms that are being developed in the postcorporatist process of juridification. The discussion is not intended to question the particular balancing acts that have been performed and the norms that were constructed by the courts and legislature. Rather, my purpose is to demonstrate how the new norms diverge from the norms that characterized the corporatist regime. In this I argue that juridification is not merely a matter of legal imperialism (Ben-Israel 1990) but also a process of compensation for the decline of extralegal norms.

The process of juridification is taking place in both the individual and the collective legal contexts. In the first section of this chapter I observe the juridification of the collective relationship, which is characterized by growing intervention in the *process* of collective bargaining. In addition to general observation of the changing role of collective labor law, two particular features of the new juridification will be highlighted: bargaining in the public sector and the changing nature of the law on industrial action. In the second section of this chapter I will discuss the process of juridification in the area of individual employment law. The proliferation of individual negotiations over employment conditions is itself a result of corporatism's decline. To fill the vacuum, the authoring agents of law have decided to devise what will be described as an Employees' Bill of Rights.

Juridification of Collective Bargaining

From Gatekeeping and Autonomy to the Regulation of Collective Bargaining

In the previous chapters I argued that the metafunction of corporatist labor law was to elevate the collectively bargained norm to a position as the prominent mode of labor market regulation. What this required was that both individual bargaining and direct governmental regulation be trumped. To achieve these two objectives, the state intervened by establishing rules of the game that governed the process of collective negotiations but abstained from providing detailed substantive norms. While this image of collective labor law could apply to very different systems of collective bargaining, the rules of the game that were adopted in Israel were particularly suited to the corporatist nature of the system. The adaptation of collective labor law to the corporatist nature of the industrial relations system had a threefold aspect:

1. Very strict keeping of the gate to ensure centralized representation of interests, coupled with provisions that were designed to ensure a broad membership within the corporatist regime
2. Abstention from state intervention in the process of collective bargaining and in the content of the norms concluded by the few negotiating agents approved in the first stage
3. A guarantee of broad coverage of the collectively negotiated norms by means of rules that extended coverage to all employees directly, or by means of extension orders

The weakening of the corporatist industrial relations system made it necessary to rethink the objectives of labor law. Two components of the postcorporatist labor law were discussed in the previous chapter. First, the law weakened the gatekeeper's function, allowing the entry of new agents to the collective bargaining arena. At the other end of the collective-bargaining chain, the centrality of the collectively negotiated norm was gradually eroded. In this section I would like to illustrate the change in the midlevel tier—the relationship between the legal rule and the autonomy accorded to the collective bargaining partners. This change is part of the process of juridification. While at first glance it may seem to be at odds with the general tendency to relax the legal rule, as was the case with regard to gatekeeping, it is in fact a complementary process. Because bargaining is more dispersed, and because the Histadrut has been weakened and can no longer perform its role as the representative of labor on the basis of its organizational power, trade unions have come to rely more extensively on the aid of the state.

Juridification has taken place on several fronts, from the law of organization to the law governing negotiations, and extending to the termination of the collective relationship. In the process of juridifying collective labor law, the major and almost sole actor has been the Labor Court. The legislature has been relatively idle, taking an active position on only one issue (the law of organization), and even in that case it has for the most part codified prior decisions of the National Labor Court. Because the Labor Court has been the one to develop the new labor law, it had to draw on general legal principles rather than detailed legal rules provided by the legislature. The two principles on which it has relied most are the freedom of association and the employees' property rights in their workplace. In the following subsections I will first outline the new labor law that developed during the postcorporatist phase and then analyze the court's reliance on the human rights of association and property and how they were put to use in the process of juridification.

THE NEW COLLECTIVE LABOR LAW

The new collective labor law includes case law that was developed to address problems within the industrial relations system resulting from the disintegration of the corporatist regime. In corporatist negotiations, the rules of the game were composed of norms informally developed and accepted by the bargaining partners. They were never written, and they had no formal legal status. Consequently, the new law that developed in the postcorporatist phase did not overwrite or amend the old law but merely filled in legal gaps in order to regulate behavior that had been previously rare in the industrial relations system. While most of the new legal rules were not innovative from a comparative perspective, the fact that they were not developed in the Labor Court until the 1990s is what requires attention. Most of the "new" problems that were brought to the court during the 1990s and onward had been previously—in the corporatist era—resolved outside the courtroom, or they had never arisen because the informal rules of the game forestalled any such behavior.

The first case of this type was brought to the Labor Court in 1996.[1] In this case, an employer dismissed four employees who tried to organize their peers at work, to enlist the Histadrut as their representative union, and to commence negotiations with the employer on a collective bargaining agreement.

1. National Labor Court 56/3-209 Mifalei Tachanot Gat/Tapuz—Israel Yaniv, PDA 33:289.

Other cases that followed featured a similar employers' response with only slight variations.[2] These types of cases are prominent in the body of law regarding collective bargaining in noncorporatist regimes, most notably in the United States (Weiler 1990). However, in Israel there had been no previous examples of dismissals for the reason of organization attempts.[3] The corporatist regime was comprehensive, which meant that most workers were organized and most employers were bound by collective agreements either directly or through extension orders. There was little incentive for employers to adopt a confrontational approach with workers on the issue of organization in a trade union. Moreover, because the more important collective agreements were signed at the branch and state levels, the issue of workers' organization was of little importance.

The declining scope of the corporatist system has brought about a greater incentive for employers to fight organization drives by their employees. First, many employers are no longer covered by collective agreements, and therefore there is fiercer competition over wages and working conditions, a situation that did not exist in the past. Second, the extent and scope of collective agreements negotiated at the branch level has declined as well. Moreover, there are several economic branches in which there are no branch-level collective agreements at all—for example, transportation. It is not surprising, then, that the first cases concerning employers' efforts to put a stop to an employees' organizing drive were in the transportation sector.

The Labor Court responded by establishing new rules that prohibit employers' retaliatory actions against workers who are trying to organize. The Court held not only that the dismissals of the organizers are illegal, but that—contrary to the general rule on dismissals in Israel—reinstatement is the appropriate remedy in these cases. Furthermore, the Labor Court extended this type of protection to situations in which an employer disproportionately dismisses organized workers at a time of redundancies.[4] The Court also declared the Histadrut to have reached representative trade union status in a situation where the employer put pressure on the employees to forgo their membership in the trade union, thus causing the union to fall below the minimum membership needed to be a representative union (a third of the workers).[5] This

2. National Labor Court 1013/02 General Histadrut—"Matnas" Kiryat Malaahi, PDA 39:295; Be'er Sheva Regional Labor Court 1037/02 General Histadrut—Sharforn Inc. (2003, unpublished); Haifa Regional Labor Court 301670/96 Veinberg—Company for Education and Culture Institutions Nesher (2003, unpublished); Tel-Aviv Regional Labor Court 1070/01, General Histadrut—National Sport, PDA 37:32(regional cases); National Labor Court 1008/00 Horn and Leibovitz Inc—General Histadrut, PDA 35:145.

3. There are indications, however, that workers were discriminated against on the basis of the trade union with which they were affiliated, and, most notably, if they were members of trade unions operating outside the General Histadrut. This problem was addressed mostly by the nationalization of the labor bureaus in 1959, as described in chapter 3.

4. For reinstatement after dismissals during an organizing drive see 56/3–209, supra note 1, and 1037/02 supra note 2. For reinstatement after redundancy layoffs, see National Labor Court 1998/4-10 Delek, Israeli Petrol Company—General Histadrut, PDA 33:367.

5. National Labor Court 1037/02.

rule—which was provided in 2000—marked the first time that collective labor law dealt explicitly with the procedure for organizing and establishing representative status for the union. Again, while such procedures are set out in detail in noncorporatist regimes, such as in North America, they had been regarded as foreign to the logic of corporatism.

The case law on organization and the protection of employees from dismissal because of trade union activity was codified by the legislature in a surprisingly noncontroversial amendment to the Collective Bargaining Law in 2001.[6] The ease with which this amendment was passed can be accounted for by two complementary explanations. First, the amendment for the most part repeated what was already known to be "the law." Second, the law was limited mostly to the negative measure of prohibiting discrimination against organized workers. It did not impose a positive requirement to support an organizing drive. The only addition to the statute in the amendment, which was generally unnoticed in the parliamentary debate but which was also partially based on prior rulings, held that employers must provide access to the workplace to union organizers.[7] This was intended to avoid some rulings in American labor law that made organizing difficult.[8]

The second frontier of the new collective labor law deals with the rights and duties of the bargaining partners in negotiations. In this matter, the Labor Court developed the duties of consultation, negotiation, and disclosure in the process of bargaining.[9] Following the law in most countries, the Labor Court refrained from asserting a right to codetermination. While the Court determined a relatively broad scope for negotiations rights, it emphasized that the law cannot require the parties to agree. However, because of the weak nature of the procedural rights in this context, the Court did not hesitate to apply the more minimal right to consultation to a broad range of issues, including—most notably—the employer's decision to relocate, sell its business, and outsource work to contractors, as well as other matters involving the rights and obligations of the negotiating parties.[10]

6. Collective Agreements Law (1957), amend. 6 (January 10, 2001).

7. Haifa District Labor Court 1996/4-10; 1997/41–8 Haifa Chemicals—David Raviv (1997, unpublished).

8. Most notably, the statutory amendments sought to prevent the adoption of property-based restrictions that were consolidated in the United States in Lechmere Inc. V. NLRB, 502 U.S. 527 (1992).

9. National Labor Court 52/4-2 Bromides Compounds Inc.—General Histadrut, PDA 23:456 (duty of consultation); National Labor Court 40000058/98 General Histadrut and National Committee of Administration Workers in State-Owned Hospitals—State of Israel, PDA 35:103 (duty to negotiate); National Labor Court 52/4-30 High-School Teachers Union—State of Israel, PDA 24:479 (duty of disclosure); National Labor Court 1998/4-10 Delek, Israeli Petrol Company—General Histadrut, PDA 33:367 (duty of disclosure); Tel-Aviv District Labor Court 100098/00 Workers' Committee at the American Gas Company—The American Gas Company (2000, unpublished) (right to disclosure).

10. National Labor Court 98/3-7 Menashe Mo'adim—Ministry of Security, PDA 33:441; National Labor Court 97/99 General Histadrut—Kur Industries Inc., PDA 34:510; National Labor Court 359/99 Leah Levin—Broadcasting Authority, PDA 33:441.

As in the development of the law on the organization of workers, there is nothing extraordinary about the case law developed by the Labor Court from a comparative perspective. Nor did it encounter strong objections, at least not at the preliminary stage of development. Nevertheless, in the past these questions did not arise in the Labor Court because negotiations were taken for granted on an even broader set of issues than those mandated by the present law.[11]

A third frontier for the development of the new collective labor law includes issues involving the continuity of collective rights. One such issue concerns the rights of workers at times of reorganization and privatization. In these matters, the Labor Court emphasized the principle of continuity in the collective relationship, together with the individual rights of employees to continued employment in the new establishment and the right to compensation at the time of transfer.[12] Beyond the continuity of the individual employment relationship, the Court also emphasized the continuity of the collective relationship. Interestingly, the Court sustained the corporatist approach and held that the parties to the collective agreement should reach an agreement on the compensation workers deserve at the time of transfer. At the same time, the Court held that the workers are entitled to compensation during a transfer, regardless of whether the parties to the collective relationship agree on this matter. Hence, it is implied that the postcorporatist solution to an impasse in negotiations may be that the court must determine the compensation the workers deserve.[13]

A related issue had to do with employers' efforts to terminate the collective relationship. In chapter 3, I presented the statutory corporatist solution to this issue. At the time the Collective Agreements Law was passed, the legislature was satisfied with ensuring the continuity of the collective agreement beyond the contractual time frame agreed upon. However, relying on the principle of autonomy in negotiations, the legislature did not prohibit or even denounce the termination of a collective agreement. There were only a few such cases of termination, and these were generally marginal. Such action did not form part of the social partners' strategies. However, in 1996 and almost a decade later, in 2005, the Labor Courts presented two options for resolving such matters.[14] In both cases, the majority's approach preserves the corporatist position of nonintervention, despite a strong emphasis that such withdrawal from collective bargaining is undesirable. A dissenting approach in both cases presented a

11. National Labor Court 37/4-17 Engineers Histadrut—State of Israel, PDA 9:373.

12. National Labor Court 54/4-1 General Histadrut—Israeli Aviation Industry, PDA 29:601; Supreme Court HCJ 8111/96 922/97 General Histadrut and the Israeli Aviation Industry v. National Labor Court and Others, PDI 58(6):481.

13. National Labor Court 98/3–7, supra note 10.

14. In 1996–97: Haifa District Labor Court 57/4-11 General Histadrut—Haifa Chemicals (1996–97, unpublished); National Labor Court 57/4-44 Haifa Chemicals Inc.—General Histadrut, PDA 30:216.

In 2005: National Labor Court 52/05 Histadrut Ha-Maóf—Kiryat Gat (2005, unpublished).

juridified norm that renders such withdrawal to be in bad faith and against public policy.

The different opinions are, therefore, not about the desirability of collective bargaining but about the limits of the law's power to intervene in such circumstances, contrary to the premises of autonomy underlying collective bargaining in general and the corporatist version of it in particular. While the dissenting position viewed the law as an omnipotent instrument that could revive the collective relations, the majority took a humbler view of the law's power. The majority opinion carried on the corporatist tradition of granting autonomy to the negotiating partners. However, unlike in the corporatist phase, this position was now detrimental to the Histadrut.

In sum, the new collective labor law is characterized by a juridification of the negotiations process. This process is marked, first of all, by the trade unions' need for judicial intervention in their relationship with employers. The internal norms of the industrial relations system are ill equipped to deal with various employers' strategies, such as the dismissal of workers because of an organizing drive, the refusal to negotiate and disclose information to the trade union, or a decision to terminate the collective relationship altogether. These strategies were for the most part outside the repertoire of strategies deemed valid by the social partners themselves in the heyday of the corporatist regime. The use of these strategies after the decline of corporatism can be attributed to both the declining legitimacy accorded by employers to collective bargaining and the fact that collective bargaining agreements are no longer comprehensive in terms of coverage. The actual need to approach the Court to resolve disputes is therefore a result of the instability within the industrial relations system.

In most cases, the Court has deviated from its traditional response in the corporatist phase, which was to remain outside the collective relationship and let the parties arrive at their own solutions. The Labor Court has adopted a new position according to which it must provide substantive legal solutions and remedies for conflicts within the industrial relations system. In this process the Court must determine the rights and duties of the parties to the collective relationship and hence arrive at the complete juridification of the collective relationship. These solutions include the mandatory prohibitions of retaliation for trade-union-related activity and procedural rules that are intended to encourage the parties to reach an agreement. However, while the Court was aware that abstention from complete juridification of the collective relationship could be detrimental to the trade union, it also refused to fully secure the position of the Histadrut (and other trade unions) by granting de facto veto power.

THE DEVELOPERS' TOOL KIT

This analysis of the juridification process would not be complete without a study of the method used by the Labor Court in developing the new collective labor law. The basic problem the Labor Court faced in the process was the mismatch between the Collective Agreements Law adopted in 1957 and the problems brought to the Court from the mid-1990s onward. The law was corporatist in nature, while the problems were of a different brand. Seeking a renewal of the statutory framework for collective bargaining was generally not a feasible option.

The Labor Court was troubled by the crisis in the industrial relations system and could not refrain from adjusting the law of collective bargaining to the new reality. It should be remembered that although collective disputes form only a small fraction of the Labor Court's workload, their resolution had been the justification for the establishment of the Labor Court as a tribunal separate from the general court system.[15] The lay judges representing labor and employers, as well as the judges themselves—many of whom came from legal practice that was well embedded in collective labor law—viewed the need for the continuity of the collective relationship more favorably than the legislature did. Moreover, the nonneutral effect of reliance on the "old" labor law was more visible when concrete cases came to the Labor Court, especially when such cases concerned high-visibility collective disputes. Consequently, unlike the legislature, the Labor Court had to address the new problems that were laid at its doorstep by the parties to collective bargaining. However, how this should be accomplished was not altogether clear. It was clear that the Court could not rely on the legislature for a new direction. It had to construct the new direction itself. To that end, it relied on constitutional values and human rights as its basic tool in designing a new approach. Two rights were particularly significant—the freedom of association and the right of property.

The freedom of association had been an underutilized right in the case law of the past. This was demonstrated in the previous chapters with regard to the development of the gatekeeper's function of collective labor law. I have argued earlier that the Labor Court denied the relevance of the freedom of association in almost all cases that dealt with interunion rivalry, as well as in the cases concerned with what a trade union is and the determination of the representative trade union.[16] This was argued to be a result of the corporatist task of concealing the trade-offs intrinsic to the freedom of association itself. The court evinced no desire to resolve situations in which breakaway unions tried to sever themselves from the corporatist negotiations, by holding that the rights of some must be sacrificed for the rights of others. Implicit in the construction of the freedom of association by the Labor Court was the view that this right is a highly individualistic one that places obligations only on the state. Each individual has a right to join a union and disassociate from a union, and no direct restrictions can be imposed by the state unless they are necessary to preserve the public order or other legitimate interests.

From this view two important components were missing. First, the freedom of association is not only a negative right but also a positive right that is

15. See chapter 4.
16. See chapters 4 and 5.

closely related to the right to work, the right to dignity, and the right to adequate subsistence. It therefore requires the state to take positive measures beyond merely allowing individuals to join the union of their choice. The state must also guarantee that the association can *effectively* carry out its task of promoting its aims—collective bargaining and labor market regulation by means of collective agreements. Although this may be deemed to be the basic premise of corporatism, the corporatist regime was sufficiently strong as not to require the benefits of constitutional protection. The advantage of concealing the coercive nature of association in Israel, whereby most employees were driven to membership in the Histadrut and coverage by its collective agreements, was greater than any advantage that might have accrued if the positive dimension of the freedom of association had been highlighted. The second component missing from the old case law on the freedom of association was the explicit recognition that this freedom places obligations not only on the state but also on other agents, such as the employers (horizontal application).

While the new case law regarding the gatekeeper's task of collective labor law sustained the narrow reading of the freedom of association, a different construction of the right appeared with regard to the new collective labor law. The Labor Court derived most of the new rules from a positive reading of the freedom of association, with a horizontal application of the right vis-à-vis employers. This was the basis of the newly devised protections from abusive dismissals and the right to negotiations and disclosure.[17]

In addition to the freedom of association, the Labor Court constructed a parallel right that appears to be more of an oddity—the right of property. While this right generally plays an important role on the employers' side in the application of constitutional law to the employment relationship, the Labor Court designated a property right of *employees* in their workplace. The premise according to which employees have a property right in their workplace is almost unprecedented in Israeli labor law.[18] The potential rationales for acknowledging a property right for employees in their workplace are diverse and are based on a relational theory of property rights (Michelman 1981;

17. It should be noted that in the early stages of these rules' development, the Labor Court opted to continue neglecting the freedom of association and preferred to construct the rights of a trade union on the basis of the general duty to act in good faith in contractual (and quasi-contractual) relationships. See, for example, National labor Court 52/4-2, supra note 9.

18. Only one decision of the Labor Court in 1973 mentioned the property rights of employees in their workplace. National Labor Court 33/3-9 Tsori Pharmaceuticals and Chemicals Company Inc.—Dr. Tsvi Riks, PDA 4:477. The significance of a property right, however, was merely to sidestep the common law of contracts according to which reinstatement is not possible even when employees are dismissed in breach of the employment contract. The Labor Court therefore noted that the workers' interest in their workplace is more than merely contractual, and thus reinstatement is a feasible remedy. When this decision was brought to the Supreme Court (HCJ 254/73 Tsori Pharmaceuticals and Chemicals Company Inc. v. National Labor Court and others, PDI 28(1):372), it was held that even if workers do have a property right, reinstatement is not possible. Because the property right argument was not successful in achieving the Labor Court's objective of allowing reinstatement, the discourse of property rights has been abandoned in subsequent case law.

Radin 1996; Simon 1991; Singer 1988). However, the Court did not provide any theoretical underpinning for this innovative assignment of property rights. The right of property simply appeared in one case in 1999, being presented almost as a truism. In subsequent cases the Labor Court merely cited its previous decisions as a precedent and did not add any theoretical layers to its decision.[19] It seems that the property right developed not from theoretical concepts but rather as a pragmatic response to Israel's idiosyncratic human rights legislation.

In the 1992 Basic Law: Human Dignity and Liberty, the legislature listed only a few constitutional rights, which were simply those that succeeded in passing the political hurdles of legislation at that time. However, this Basic Law was intended to serve as the first of several Basic Laws, and therefore the list of rights was not exhaustive. After the Basic Law was passed, the Supreme Court held it to be of constitutional caliber, thereby superseding "regular" legislation.[20] The political consequence of this position, together with several other decisions in which the Supreme Court displayed too much activism to suit some political factions, was opposition to the continuation of the human rights legislation. Various parties, especially the ultraorthodox Jewish parties, claimed that the Supreme Court had used the Basic Laws as a means of usurping too much power. Since then, constitutional human rights legislation has ceased. Consequently, the list of human rights that appears in the two Basic Laws that were passed is incomplete and generally incoherent (Gavison 1999; Hirschl 1998; Hofnung 1996). For example, it omits some of the more important rights, such as freedom of speech. More pertinent to the issue of labor rights, the partial outcomes were strongly tilted in favor of employers, mostly because of the recognition of the right to property and the absence from the list of social and economic rights for workers.

The Labor Court's recognition of the workers' property right in their workplace is therefore not so much the outcome of a relational theory of property but a method of enlarging the repertoire of constitutional rights the Labor Court can rely on. Drawing on a balancing test of rights, the Labor Court wanted to avoid the need to counterpoise the employers' property right against the workers' interests, regarded as of lesser value. Absent a strong theoretical justification, the right of property was used to develop a set of rights for both trade unions and individual workers. In none of the cases in which it was used was it necessary, nor did it serve as the sole justification for the

19. A partial list of cases includes National Labor Court 98/3-7 Menashe Mo'adim—State of Israel, PDA 31:441; National Labor Court 375/99 Israeli Company for the Development of Kfar Manda (1977)—A'abed el Chamid Gaber, PDA 35;245; National Labor Court 40000058/98 General Histadrut and National Committee of Administration Workers in State-Owned Hospitals—State of Israel, PDA 35:103; National Labor Court 1008/00 Horn and Leibovitz Inc.—the General Histadrut, PDA 35:145; National Labor Court 400024/98 General Hisadrut and Sea-Officers Union—Zim, PDA 36:92; National Labor Court 1189/00 Ilana Levinger—State of Israel, PDA (2000, not published).

20. Supreme Court CA 6821/93 Bank Ha-Mizrachi Ha-Me'uchad v. Migdal, PDI 49(4):222.

Court's decision. Generally, it has served mostly as a heuristic device to justify a sense of fairness.

The Labor Court's need to develop a constitutional framework to decide the new cases suggests that it was seeking legitimacy. The Court sought to do more than merely resolve concrete disputes. Resolution of a dispute on the basis of existing statutes would have halted the development of labor law, as it would have required adherence to the principle of autonomy that appears throughout the corporatist phase of labor law. With the growing weakness of the industrial relations system in general, and of the Histadrut in particular, adhering to the principle of autonomy would have led to tilted outcomes, merely exacerbating the decline of the industrial relations system itself. Consequently, the Labor Court needed to do away with the principle of autonomy altogether and devise legal means of dealing with the new problems that appeared once the corporatist system had lost its internal cohesion and norms. Constitutional values and rights served as useful means of legally addressing the new problems without having to explicitly admit the inadequacy of the old labor law.

The use of constitutional values and rights also demonstrates the changing direction of lawmaking. In 1947 the Histadrut signaled its desire for a constitution that would include recognition of social and economic rights. In chapter 3, we saw that this was one of the few objectives set for the new nation by the Histadrut that was never accomplished. The constitution was to reflect an agreement within civil society, and the failure to adopt one was due to the absence of agreement, mostly with regard to the relationship between religion and state. Consequently, social legislation in general, and labor law in particular, developed outside the realm of constitutional law and on the basis of the corporatist pact. In the 1990s the influence came from the opposite direction. The Basic Law that formulated the new Bill of Rights, the Supreme Court's decisions expanding the list of rights beyond those listed explicitly in the Basic Laws, and the decision to accord the Basic Laws with a higher normative power—these have become the sources for writing the new labor law.

In the process of reversing the nature of fundamental legal values—moving from the outputs of the industrial relations system back to its building blocks—the institutional position of the Labor Court has changed as well. In contrast to its initial establishment as a forum intended to serve the particular needs of the agents in the industrial relations system, the Labor Court has become the regulator of that system. This difference is not a wholesale reversal of roles because the court was intended to be an agreed-upon forum that could advance the resolution of fundamental disputes over the rules of the game, most notably in the area of industrial disputes.[21] However, the change in the Labor Court's function is more than just a matter of degree, as will be discussed in the following section.

---

21. See chapter 4.

Regulating Industrial Action

In the previous subsection, the new collective labor law was presented as the result of new employers' strategies to which the industrial relations system had no response and the legal system no immediate answer. A similar problem arose in the postcorporatist phase with regard to the workers' use of industrial action. This area, however, merits particular attention for several reasons. First and foremost, one of the major reasons for establishing the Labor Court system outside the general judicial system was in response to the failure of the legal system to construct agreed-upon rules governing the use of strike activity. Second, at times of strikes, especially when the strike is used as part of an economic dispute (i.e., an interests dispute over the determination of future rights rather than a legal dispute over existing rights), the traditional role of the judiciary is tested. This is where the Labor Court, it is assumed, displays its unique adjudicative position. Hence, the study of the law on industrial action is also a study of the Labor Court's role after the transformation of industrial relations.

CONSTRUCTING THE LAW OF STRIKES

In chapter 4, I outlined the Labor Court's role in developing the law of strikes with regard to the corporatist phase of labor law—that is, until 1987— and showed that the Court constructed the law of strikes from scratch. In a nutshell, in the period before the Labor Court was established, the law of strikes was underdeveloped. This was mostly due to the failure to achieve a consensus, or even a lesser agreement, between the social partners over the desirable limits on the workers' use of industrial action. Once the Labor Court was established, it began setting limits on industrial action. The Histadrut's fear that the Labor Court would use the remedy of injunction to intervene in industrial action was immediately confirmed. By the mid-1980s, the law was stable, well developed, highly discretionary, and constantly tested and implemented in day-to-day litigation. The discretionary nature of the law on injunctions against striking workers afforded the Labor Court much leeway in tailoring the mode of judicial intervention to the industrial conflict underlying the legal dispute.

However, from the early 1990s onward, new types of questions began to reach the Labor Court. Unlike the issues dealt with in the past, regarding the rules of the game that applied during industrial action (e.g., the requirement to provide prior notice by an authorized organ of the Histadrut or the requirement to observe industrial peace clauses in collective agreements), the questions that were raised in the 1990s touched more fundamentally on the legitimacy of industrial action in a democratic regime. These questions asked what the game was and whether it was legitimate to begin with, not what its rules were. These issues were most evident in situations where strikes blurred the boundaries of familiar legal distinctions like those between the economic and the political spheres. The fact that the precedents concerning these issues appeared only in the mid-1990s was not due to the emergence of a new phenomenon in the industrial relations system (as was the case with the dismissal of workers for organizing). On the contrary, strikes against government policy were actually an integral part of the corporatist regime. However, they were resolved by extralegal norms. Judicial precedents appeared only when the industrial relations system ceased to accept certain practices, and particularly the corporatist practice of integrating the economic and the political into one system. It was at this point that legal rights began to substitute for nonlegal rights and sanctions.

Rather than surveying the new law of strikes, I will demonstrate the transition away from corporatism by focusing on the Bezeq case (Ben-Israel 1986b; Raday 1995; Shaked 1999; Mundlak 2002).[22] The workers in Bezeq, Israel's leading telecommunications company, initiated a strike to protest the government's effort to open Bezeq's statutory monopoly over international calls to competition. Bezeq petitioned the Labor Court to issue an injunction against the workers, arguing that the strike was political and that the workers were not allowed to protest such a decision during their working time. The Court had to decide whether the Bezeq workers' strike was more like a conventional strike, because it addressed issues of employment conditions or industrial relations, or more like a political demonstration aimed at the state and not at the employer.

The majority opinion of the National Labor Court distinguished this case from a political demonstration because the workers' claim was that the government's decision would seriously damage their work security and culminate in massive layoffs. The majority opinion further held that a strike in the public sector that is aimed at the sovereign's actions, which may have an effect on the workers' employment conditions and which is intended to secure these conditions, should not be viewed as a political strike. Bezeq and the Attorney General petitioned the Supreme Court to overrule the National Labor Court's decision. The Supreme Court distinguished between the economic (conventional) strike and the political strike, and designated a new category—the quasi-political strike. The Court held the quasi-political strike to be a valid strike as long as it is limited to a short period of time. Subsequent decisions have established the "short time" as several (1–8) hours.[23]

In constructing the law on this issue, the underlying premise highlighted by the Court was the concern that political and quasi-political strikes threaten

22. National Labor Court 53/4-4 General Histadrut—Bezeq, PDA 25:367; Supreme Court HCJ 1074/93 Attorney General v. National Labor Court and Others, PDI 49(2):485.

23. This time frame was established in a series of cases during a wave of political strikes against the government's efforts to conduct an economic reform (1996–97), see National Labor Court 57/41-50 Association of Banks in Israel—General Histadrut and others (1977, unpublished) (strike approved for half a day); National Labor Court 57/41-33 Airports, Seaports and Trains Authority—General Histadrut (1977, unpublished) (strike approved for four hours); National Labor Court 57/41-36 Industrialists Association—General Histadrut (1977, unpublished) (two hours); National Labor Court 56/41-41 General Histadrut—Airports, Seaports and Trains Authority (1996, unpublished) (one hour).

democracy. In a nutshell, it was argued that the sovereign, which is democratically elected, makes decisions on the basis of the "common good." When workers strike in protest against the sovereign's decisions, they seek to impose an illegitimate pressure that distorts the democratic process. The workers' ability to exert economic constraints on employers and, more important, on consumers and the users of services gives them an unfair advantage over the rest of the citizenry, which has access to the ballot box only every few years.

The democratic argument put forward in the Bezeq case is very persuasive, but it suffers from a serious fallacy. It contrasts a surreal description of democracy with a concrete description of what striking workers do. The ideal portrayal of democracy ignored the role of lobbyists hired by Bezeq, and by competing companies, domestic and international, that wanted access to the new competitive niche. These lobbyists were backed by enterprises with ample resources and a vision of profits to be made, which enabled them to dictate the political rules of the game. Consequently, the judicial logic underlying the Bezeq case is rooted in the view that the collective organization of labor is inherently political and in tension with democracy, whereas the collective organization of capital, by contrast, is a natural component of capitalist society that resonates with the democratic ideal.

The concern of the Supreme Court about preserving democracy highlights the move away from corporatism in several respects. First, it is based on a distinction between a public sphere governed by democratic decision making and a private sphere in which the strike is one of the instruments that are legitimate solely for bargaining over wages. According to this view, strikes must not spill over from the private into the public sphere. This distinction could not have been neatly implemented in the heyday of corporatist negotiations, when the state was implicated not only as an employer but also as an active bargaining agent with the social partners. However, despite the decline of corporatism, the role of the state as an active agent in the labor market did not disappear. On the contrary, the state remained involved, only differently. Instead of being a partner to negotiations, it took on the stronger role of regulator. Drawing boundaries on the basis of a distinction between public and private therefore failed to recognize the de facto role of the state as a coemployer, in the sense that it took an active part in determining the work conditions, employment security, and wages of a growing segment of the workforce, particularly in the public sector (broadly defined).

Second, the Labor Court's majority opinion in the Bezeq case characterized the legitimacy of the strike on the basis of the affinity between the workers' concerns and their employment security. The Supreme Court's position was based on the public/private dichotomy and a choice between two bilateral relationships—workers/employer and workers/state. In the first relationship the workers appear qua employees (private), whereas in the second relationship they appear qua citizens (public). This liberal distinction is difficult to implement in a corporatist regime where the role of the social partnership is extended beyond the mere determination of wages. In a comparative perspective, the

Institute, and sometimes also public companies like the Ports Authority. Moreover, the Court held that not only do such agreements constitute a cluster of special and general agreements, but any change in the agreement with regard to one employer requires the consent of all employers and unions that are party to the agreement. The legal framework for the plural agreement was, therefore, the Labor Court's innovative and creative solution to ensure that all the public-sector employers and unions would be packaged together in an arrangement resistant to factional change.

The typically corporatist solutions of the past were therefore based on collective agreements and did not rely on the regulatory regime. Some of the corporatist solutions resulted in extremely complicated and difficult-to-manage arrangements, such as the indexation agreements (State of Israel 1989b). Others created a web of agreements that courts have found difficult to untangle (Adler 1987). Yet it seems it was the decline of corporatism, rather than any attempt to untangle the web, that was the trigger for a different solution to the challenge of maintaining wage restraint in the public sector. One of the more interesting postcorporatist legal arrangements that functionally seeks to substitute for past corporatist solutions is section 29 of the Budget Foundations Law (1985).[33]

According to the law, any wage or benefits arrangement, individual or collective, that was concluded in the public sector and that deviates from the standard wages and benefits usually accorded to state workers must be approved by the Minster of Finance (or his agent, the Head of the Wage and Labor Accord Department in the ministry). For the purpose of this law, "public sector" is defined broadly to include all institutions that are at least partially funded by the state (including, for example, universities and health-care providers). Failure to obtain approval for a "deviant" agreement results in voiding the agreement. While in the first few years this arrangement was not frequently used, from the mid-1990s onward it has become a dominant aspect of collective (and individual) bargaining in the public sector. It has been used to strike down agreements after they are made and to control their signing beforehand. The head of the Wage and Labor Accord Department has become the central agent for all wage negotiations in the public sector, be it the State Service, municipalities, or other budget-supported institutions.

The justification for this arrangement is that it is necessary to remedy a negative externality. Public employers who want to attract good workers, keep their workers satisfied, or simply maintain industrial peace are willing to raise wages and benefits, knowing that the state must bail out the public employer in case of a deficit.[34] This negative externality is less acute when corporatist practices are functioning. As noted in chapter 1, one of the major advantages

33. The current arrangement is codified in the law from 1985, but similar arrangements appeared in the annual budget laws beginning in 1982.

34. Supreme Court HCJ 6231/92 Albert Zaguri v. National Labor Court, PDI 49(4):749; Supreme Court HCJ 539/85 General Histadrut v. National Labor Court, PDI 40(4):834; National Labor Court 54/4-16 Local Municipalities Authority—General Histadrut, PDA 32:1.

attributed to corporatism is that centralized and concentrated arrangements can overcome precisely such negative externalities. It is therefore possible to point to section 29 as a substitute for corporatist arrangements. However, to what extent is it a substitute? This can be answered by pointing to the advantages and disadvantages of the arrangement.

Since the statutory arrangement has become enforceable, it has strongly influenced bargaining with regard to all publicly funded undertakings. For example, in municipalities that encountered economic difficulties, recovery agreements were signed under the umbrella of a centralized collective agreement that was designed to provide a framework within the confines of section 29 (Davidov-Motola 2000). Thus, not only does this arrangement allow the Ministry of Finance to oversee agreements after the fact and void them, but it also encourages some centralized elements in a growingly decentralized bargaining regime.

However, section 29 has also been detrimental to collective bargaining by further weakening what remained of the corporatist regime. Because of the Finance Ministry's deep involvement in all wage and benefits agreements in the public sector, all negotiations are de facto with the ministry and not with the public employers. This has led to an intrusive regulatory regime, which has overtaken autonomous negotiations. In the industrial relations triangle, the state is no longer an employer-participant or a mediator but a regulator. Moreover, the central role that has been accorded to the Ministry of Finance in negotiations has made it both the agent responsible for setting the budget and the human-resources policies and the implementer of those policies. This is analogous to the role of management in a private enterprise without a union. The setting of the budget has been determined by the law to be "political" and therefore outside the domain of negotiations. The ministry's de facto veto power over all agreements, curtailed almost solely by judicial review and administrative law, has weakened the position of collective agreements considerably. What remains of the freedom of association under these circumstances is a relatively limited sphere of bargaining, one that resembles "effects bargaining" in the private sector (i.e., bargaining after management has made a decision regarding the effects of the decision—with regard to layoffs, for example). The legal power accorded to the Ministry of Finance has made it a virtually omnipotent player in the industrial relations system.

Thus, while corporatist bargaining and section 29 of the Budget Foundations Law are functionally similar, their effects are different. Both stem from the need to overcome inherent externalities in negotiations, particularly in the public sector. Yet corporatist bargaining places the emphasis on negotiations, with all the side effects that accompany such negotiations—most notably, industrial action. By contrast section 29 allows bargaining only within the limited sphere allowed by the Ministry of Finance and construes the boundaries of the sphere as a political matter that is subject to limited judicial scrutiny at most. The role of law in the governance of the public sector has therefore changed. It now prescribes power to the regulator and also provides checks and balances by means of judicial review. This proactive role contrasts sharply with its latent role in securing the centralized and concentrated nature of the corporatist regime in the past.

DIRECT REGULATORY INTERVENTION IN WAGE SETTING: THE 1985 AND 2003 BARGAINING ROUNDS

Despite the importance of section 29 of the Budget Foundations Law, it was assumed that the limits it set for negotiations were all within the confines of what the negotiating partners had determined to be "generally acceptable." However, events that took place in 2003 indicated that the new labor law even refused to view prevailing collective agreements as a constraining norm.

In 2003 the government decided to initiate an emergency economic plan. This was yet another among the many austerity measures taken since the end of 2002. Since then, every six months, the government has assembled a lengthy list of amendments to economic and social legislation. At the time of the budget's preparation, these measures are compiled into the Annual Law of Economic Arrangements, which has been prepared together with the Budget Law since 1985.[35] At first it was used only to pass temporary and urgent adjustments to legislation that were necessary to achieve the economic targets set by the budget. In 1985 this was part of the government's successful effort to halt hyperinflation. However, over time it has become a potent instrument in the hands of the Ministry of Finance, whereby many economic and social reforms have been introduced. The advantage of initiating legal reforms in this manner is that the Law of Economic Arrangements covers many aspects, which frequently have been posed at the political level as a "take it or leave it" package. Moreover, the Law of Arrangements is voted together with the annual Budget Law, and the two are tightly packaged together. Because a failure to pass the annual Budget Law carries severe political consequences for the government, a vote of confidence in the Law of Arrangements has often served as a politician's survival tactic. As was demonstrated at the outset of part 3, legislation has become a battlefield for competing interests. Until early in the present decade, the ease with which it was possible to pass legislation initiated privately by members of Parliament, even if it entailed grave economic implications and budget costs, was neutralized by the ease with which the Ministry of Finance could "freeze" such legislation in the Law of Economic Arrangements. This process has been publicly criticized for its weak democratic features (Nachmias and Klein 1999).

The extensive use of lengthy legislation to reform the socioeconomic map of Israel was therefore greatly helpful to the Ministry of Finance when it decided to launch a neoliberal reform of Israel's markets. Yet the pace of events made it necessary to expedite the legislative framework for reform, and in 2002 and

---

35. Law of Economic Arrangements (Legislative Reforms for Attaining Budgetary Targets and Economic Policy) (2003).

2003 midyear legislation of a similar nature was introduced.[36] One of the major challenges for the 2003 midyear economic legislation was to reform the public sector. Unlike previously unsuccessful attempts to instigate reform by means of a public committee (State of Israel 1989a, 1989b), this reform was crafted as a managerial restructuring of a private enterprise. The Minister of Finance announced his intention to cut wages in the public sector (broadly defined to include all undertakings funded at least in part by the state) by 4 percent, and to drastically reform the tenure system. Even more dramatic was the intention to reform the entire pensions market by raising the retirement age, equalizing retirement age for men and women, gradually removing the Histadrut from the governance of the old pension funds it owned prior to the pension reform in 1995, introducing "management participation payments" in all types of pension funds, and more. Moreover, the employees' contributions were raised and the formulas for determining the benefits were changed to the detriment of many beneficiaries.

Despite the fact that all these proposals had a considerable effect on collective agreements, the proposals were not negotiated but announced unilaterally. The Ministry of Finance agreed to negotiate with the unions but remained adamant that the law would be passed if negotiations did not materialize within a short period of time. Law was therefore used as a significant instrument of intimidation against the trade unions and as a means to almost completely bracket collective negotiations. While the reform was at first presented as a response to a severe actuarial crisis in pension funds and a budgetary deficit, it was later admitted that it extended beyond what was required to address the crisis. It was held by all to be a measure specifically designed to reduce the trade unions' power in the public sector and in the pensions market in favor of increasing managerialism, statism, and reliance on market mechanisms. That these were in fact the objectives of the legislation was hardly doubted, and whatever differences there were had mostly to do with the normative assessment of such reforms—whether they were desirable or not (Symposium 2004).

A simple analysis of these laws would have suggested that this was an unprecedented use of legislation to narrow the sphere of bargaining on wages and job security. As noted at the beginning of chapter 3, when the corporatist system was devised, it was agreed that some legislation was necessary but that law would not intervene in matters of wages and job security. Thus, the 2003 legislative proposal appears to have trespassed precisely into the two areas always deemed to be insulated from labor law.

It is important to note, however, that there had been previous incidents of wage legislation in Israel. The most notable example consists of two laws legislated in 1975–1976, temporarily reducing the benefits prescribed in collective agreements.[37] A second example is a law from 1985, which postponed

---

36. Economic Emergence Plan Law (2002); Economic Recovery Plan Law (2003).
37. Collective Agreements Law (temporary order no. 2) (1975); Collective Agreements Law (temporary order) (1976).

various payments that were required by the prevailing collective agreements.[38] However, these comparisons merely add weight to the implications of the 2003 legislation. Former uses of legislation to derogate rights that had been accorded in collective agreements were themselves based on collective agreements. That is, in both the aforementioned cases there had been agreement between the Histadrut and the state, which required statutory entrenchment in order to make the agreements stick. Statutory codification of the concession-bargaining round was intended to secure the concessions from judicial review (Mironi 2004). Legislation therefore served to support the social partners' negotiated objectives. By contrast, the 2003 legislation was a unilateral move that sought to defeat the other side rather than obtain its agreement. Mironi (2004) also points to two other examples of secondary legislation in the past that sought to amend the state of rights as determined in collective agreements. In both cases the government's efforts were deemed by the Labor Court to have encountered some legal difficulty.[39] However, in both cases the scope of action taken by the state was very limited and hardly as significant as an across-the-board wage reduction in the public sector.

The 2003 legislation is therefore unprecedented in its function and scope, and I argue that it is symptomatic of the transition away from corporatism. Not only does it derogate rights that were negotiated in collective bargaining, but it also avoids negotiations with the trade unions and at best gives them a chance for much reduced effects bargaining after the legislative proposal has already been put on the Knesset's table. Moreover, law is being used to break the other side and weaken collective bargaining, unlike past uses of law that were intended to serve the needs and interests of the bargaining partners.

THE RESULTS OF THE JURIDIFIED BATTLE OVER ECONOMIC REFORM IN 2003–2004

Despite the Ministry of Finance's grandiose plan to use the law to reform public-sector employment relations, the 2003 law was not passed as intended. Negotiations commenced under the threat of moving to the courtroom. Eventually, the wage cut was implemented in law with some amendments to the original plan, after an agreement was reached with the General Histadrut. For workers whose representative union was the General Histadrut, the wage cut was therefore based on a collective agreement. The law was necessary to extend this result also to workers whose representative trade union was not the General Histadrut. The changes regarding the tenure system were largely left out of the law and did not take place. Changes in the pension system did take

38. Law of Economic Arrangements (1985), sec. 8.

39. In one episode, the Ministry of Interior sought to equalize the wages of firefighters across the country after Tel-Aviv firefighters broke away from the previously uniform wages (National Labor Court 40/4-18 General Histadrut—Tel-Aviv Municipality, PDA 12:52). It should be noted that the Court's position against statutory interference in industrial relations, together with its nonintervention in this particular case, may be explained by the corporatist objectives of the state—that is, to promote the centralization and concentration of wage setting.

place and were the reason for a large strike several months later, and their constitutionality was challenged and left for the Labor Court to decide, in light of the freedom of association as constructed in domestic jurisprudence and the ILO's conventions 87 and 98.[40]

Regardless of the number of issues that have reached the legislative stage, the state's success, from its point of view, in reducing the strength of organized labor and marking the direction for future reforms cannot be contested. Yet a focus on the function of law in this process reveals several characteristic trends. The legislative process in 2003 may not have been simple, but it opened the way for future legislative interventions in the industrial relations system. Immediately after the law was passed and industrial action taken in response, further proposals to drastically curtail the right to strike were proposed.[41] Moreover, despite the growing critique of the Law of Economic Arrangements, it does not seem to be losing any strength or importance in the legislative arena. Further attempts to change by this statutory mechanism the rights and duties of employees in the public sector are constantly introduced. It will take time to assess the importance of the 2003 legislative process in perspective, but at the time of writing it seems to be an important landmark in the move away from corporatism.

At the same time, corporatism is not altogether a relic of the past. A social system is too "sticky" to be set aside wholesale. In fact, some of the more troubling elements of corporatism were important to the 2003 legislative process; most notably, restricting negotiations to the General Histadrut, without further consultation with the other unions, and the enforcement of the agreement on other unions by means of legislation are symptomatic of the corporatist past much more than the pluralist present. However, these features are only part of the package and do not undermine the move away from the consent-based design of the corporatist past to the power-breaking function of the pluralist present.

Regulating Individual Norms between Employees and Employers

The first section of this chapter was devoted wholly to the juridification of the collective bargaining relationship. The various components of the juridification process indicated the legal system's need to prescribe legal solutions to problems that had been formerly resolved within the autonomous corporatist

---

40. National Labor Court 323/03 General Histadrut—Israeli Industrialists Association (2003, unpublished).

41. Draft proposal for amendment to the Settlement of Industrial Disputes Law (2003). Law was proposed by MK Ruchama Avraham (Likud) but supported by the Ministry of Finance. Proposal on file with the author. The proposal and others that were raised at the time are documented in a memo prepared by the Knesset's Research Authority on the Right to Strike (January 19, 2004)

industrial relations system of the past. Yet juridification of the collective relationship was incomplete because, as was explained in the previous chapter, the importance of collective bargaining had declined to begin with, the coverage of collective agreements had shrunk, and the centrality of the collectively bargained norm was diminished as well. A growing segment of the working population no longer enjoyed the backing of a collective agreement.

With the declining coverage and density of collective bargaining, individual employees and employers found themselves in need of a substitute for the collective regime. This required the establishment of norms that traditionally had been relegated to collective bargaining—such as protection from dismissals. Second, norms that still prevailed in collective agreements were more difficult to enforce in a growing number of enterprises, mostly in the private sector, where the collective agreements continued to apply but the supportive mechanisms of enforcement, such as joint committees and workers' committees, had become either too weak or nonexistent. Third, with the decline of extralegal institutions for the resolution of disputes, a growing number of claims by both employers and employees, as well as by NGOs and extracorporatist associations who represented them, reached the legislature and the Labor Court, outside the confines of traditional collective labor law. Together these processes brought about an unprecedented juridification of the employment relationship, wholly outside the collective bargaining sphere.

In this section I will describe the intensive juridification of the employment relationship, the nature of the new regulatory regime, as distinguished from the collective regime of regulation, and the legal tools that were used to develop the new regulatory regime.

The Employees' Bill of Rights

The development of regulation pertaining to the employment relationship, but which is detached from the collective bargaining regime, extends over a broad range of issues, some of which were regulated by collective bargaining in the past, while others present new types of regulation. An inventory of the new regulatory regime might be useful.

First, the traditional aspects of statutory regulation—mainly health, safety, and "social benefits" such as working time, annual leave, and sick leave—have hardly developed since 1987. In these matters, the corporatist legislation of the early 1950s, with the subsequent amendments and additions to it (e.g., in the matter of sick pay), remained in effect. This standstill in classical labor regulation should not be overlooked because the reluctance to update these laws for such a long period of time, despite the fact that some of them have become outdated (most notably the Hours of Work and Rest Law [1951]), displays a preference for leaving these issues to market regulation and—to a lesser extent—collective regulation.

On the issue of wages, the process of juridification is best demonstrated by the minimum wage legislation from 1987, which was discussed in detail in the introduction to part 3. The Minimum Wage Law, it was argued, is the paradigmatic symptom of the transition from a corporatist labor law to a pluralist one. The state's intervention in the collective negotiations over wages in 2003 demonstrated that further intervention is conceivable, although mostly as a means to cap wages and not raise them.

While one pillar of collective relations—wagesetting—has remained for the most part outside the domain of mandatory legislation, the other pillar—protection from dismissals—has been extensively juridified. This process at first included the statutory protections against dismissals, in cases where dismissals are unlawfully discriminating or otherwise motivated by unlawful considerations. But the Labor Court has gone much further, gradually constructing a just-cause dismissals doctrine, which substitutes for the common-law rule of employment at will. This process was described in the previous chapter.[42] In a nutshell, the Labor Court developed an expanding list of circumstances according to which dismissals were deemed to be in bad faith. Over time some judges on the Labor Court have also suggested the total substitution of the employment-at-will rule with a state-regulated just-cause dismissals policy (Mundlak 1999a). In this process, the issue of dismissals has been completely taken over by the regulators (legislatures and courts), and the regulatory norm was presented as filling in not only for inadequate protection at the individual employment level but also for collective agreements that did not extend sufficient procedural or substantive protection to the workforce.[43]

The new process of juridification has also significantly increased the level of regulation on issues of equality and human rights in the workplace. As to the former, during the 1900s there was abundant legislation (but little adjudication) of measures to combat discrimination, broadly defined, in the workplace. In addition to the general prohibition of discrimination, legislation also adopted affirmative steps to address work-related discrimination, such as particular protections for women, affirmative action, and comparable worth.[44] Furthermore, while the initial legislation on discrimination in the workplace focused only on gender-based discrimination, during the 1990s the law extended the prohibited bases for classification into a long and rather comprehensive list—including origin, nationality, ethnicity, gender, parenthood, sexual orientation, age, disability, political preferences, association in trade unions,

---

42. See chapter 5.
43. See chapter 5.
44. Employment of Women's Law (1954), as amended sixteen times during what has been designated here as the postcorporatist phase (1987–2004), compared with seven amendments in the corporatist phase (1954–87) (mostly extending pregnancy and maternity-related protections); Employment (Equal Opportunities) Law (1988) (amendments expanded the list of prohibited bases for discrimination); Equal Opportunities for People with Disabilities (1998); Discharged Soldiers Law (1949), as amended in 2001; section 29 of the Genetic Information Law (2000) (further expansion of prohibited bases for discrimination); Women's Equal Rights Law (1951), as amended in 2000; section 15 of the Civil Service (Appointments) Law (1959) (requiring affirmative action); Equal Pay for Women and Men Law (1964) (comparable worth); Prevention of Sexual Harassment at Work Law (1998).

participation in military reserves duty and more. In addition to those generally familiar categories, the law has also extended particular protections against genetic-based discrimination (responding to the potential consequences of the Genome Project) and even for the benefit of women who were battered by their spouses or partners.

Statutes and case law on human rights in the workplace encompass various human rights. The courts have extensively discussed the problem of covenants not to compete, balancing the protection of employees' freedom of occupation with the employers' property rights and the freedom of contract.[45] Similarly, the courts extended some protection to employees whose employers restrict the workers' freedom of speech and privacy. For example, the Labor Court placed restrictions on the use of testing at work (as a violation of privacy),[46] and the legislature extended protection to whistle-blowers (as part of the need to protect free speech).[47] It should be emphasized that the recognition of human rights in the workplace has not been necessarily a one-sided tilting of the law in favor of employees (Raday 2000). Given that the right of property is explicitly protected by the Basic Law: Human Dignity and Liberty and the freedom of contract is derived from the explicit right to dignity, thus employers enjoy constitutional protection just as much as employees. Acknowledging the human rights of third parties (e.g., consumers and the public) has also been used to restrict the workers' right to strike. For example, the right of the workers in the Ministry of Internal Affairs to strike did not allow them to refuse to issue passports and visas because the Labor Court balanced the right to strike with the public's freedom of movement.[48]

The Developers' Tool Kit Revisited: The Constitutionalization of Labor Law

With some minor adaptation, the legal tools for the juridification of the individual employment contract are similar to those described in the previous section with regard to the collective labor relationship.

The statutory developments rely on the simple mechanism of regulation. The differences between the new statutes and the corporatist ones have been

45. National Labor Court 164/99 Dan Frummer and Checkpoint Technologies Inc.—Redguard Inc., PDA 34:294; this view was also endorsed by the Supreme Court in CA 6601/96 AES Systems Inc. v. Moshe Sa'ar, PDI 54(3):850.

46. Cf. National Labor Court 97/4-70 Tel-Aviv University—General Histadrut, PDA 30:385. For other examples of privacy-related litigation, see Goldberg (2002).

47. Protection of Workers Law (Exposure of Offences of Unethical Conduct and Improper Administration)(1996) (protection of whistle-blowers). For an example of free speech litigation, see Jerusalem District Labor Court 90/3-1000 Joanna Yechiel—Palestine Post (1993, unpublished); National Labor Court 93/3-223 Palestine Post—Joanna Yechiel, PDA 27:436 (controversy among the judges regarding the balancing of journalists' right to speech and publisher's right to property and to manage the newspaper).

48. Jerusalem District Labor Court 52/4-8 State of Israel—General Histadrut (2002, unpublished).

described in detail in previous chapters. Simply put, the differences lie mostly in the issues being regulated, the scope of regulation, and the gradual replacement of collective norms by statutes. The issues being regulated are centered mostly on individual rights and identity (mostly in the area of antidiscrimination and equal opportunities). The new statutory regime is more complex and more extensively interventionist. Finally, the new statutes display less caution in preserving the primacy of collective norms making than was the case in the corporatist regime.

More interesting is the method the Labor Court is using to develop the law. In the collective labor context, I have demonstrated that the Court is relying mostly on the freedom of association and the right to property. In the individual sphere, the freedom of association plays no role, and while the right to property has some significance, it is of lesser extent than in the collective sphere. However, the logic that guided the Labor Court in its reliance on these two human rights is applicable in full to the individual employment relationship as well. Generally, the Labor Court's method has been a piecemeal constitutionalization of labor law.

The general principle that guided the development of Israeli law (not limited to labor) during the 1990s was the infusion of the human rights discourse into the private employment relationship. In the context of employment, human rights penetrate the relationship in pairs. On the employer's side there is the right to property and often the freedom of contract. On the employees' side there are other rights—the freedom of occupation, freedom of speech, the right to privacy, and the right to equality. These are the four rights that have been discussed by the Labor Court thus far. Potentially, the Court may also look into the right to dignity, the freedom of movement, freedom of conscience, and others.[49]

Where no particular human rights can be applied, the Court draws on the general principle of good faith. The legal principle of good faith appears in the law of contracts, which holds that in negotiations and in the performance of a contract the parties must act in good faith.[50] Israeli law adopted the principle from European, most notably German, legislation and extended its breadth and depth to cover even noncontractual relationships and to suggest that its presence designates a notion of altruism in contractual relationships. Despite its appearance in the law of contracts, the principle of good faith is in tension, but not contradiction, with the freedom of contract because it serves as a valve through which public values infiltrate the contractual relationship.[51]

49. The right to dignity was referred to in National Labor Court 51/4-21 General Histadrut—Israeli Water Industries (Tahal), PDA 23:3 (discussing whether workers have a right to work at the time the employer decides to temporarily cease production in one of its undertakings). Freedom of movement was referred to in National Labor Court 1459/02 Dan Buchiman—Best Entrepreneurs Inc. PDA 38:824 (employers' confiscation of their migrant workers' passports is a violation of their freedom of movement).

50. Law of Contracts (General Part) (1973), secs. 12, 39.

51. This description of the relationship between the freedom of contract and good faith is extremely simplistic and merely serves to illustrate the importance and significance of the extensive use of good faith. The freedom of contract does not have to take on the liberal reading

(Sitkin and Bies 1994). The new juridification can be viewed as the postindustrial emancipation of workers. In the words of Spiros Simitis (1994, 183), "The employee finally steps out of the shadow of the bourgeois individual." The assumption that human rights and principles of fairness and justice apply only to the public sphere and are not affected by inequalities in the private sphere has been replaced by the acknowledgment that civil liberties in the public sphere are not equally accessible to all individuals.[54]

A more critical view might hold that the creeping expansion of juridification is a Pyrrhic victory. Most of the new rights, particularly in the field of collective labor law, are indicative of a weakening industrial relations system, rather than a triumph of one side or another. Protections to workers who try to organize are often granted too late and cannot rescue the organizing drive that has been trumped by the employer. Regulatory measures that are intended to protect some are then used to reduce the rights of others. For example, the power of the Ministry of Finance to cap wages has been used to prevent wage hikes of highly compensated workers, but more often it has been used to cap the wages of the least well-off. Moreover, the juridified response to labor disputes may undermine fragile trust relations, and pragmatic negotiations are replaced by intensively adversarial strategies instigated by lawyers who are trained and motivated by the notion of legal victory in court.

On my own dialectic view, the new juridification must be understood critically, that is, it must be understood to display both advantages and shortcomings (Mundlak 2001). Whether the norm is achieved through political exchange, market monitoring, or a corporatist exchange has an effect on its substance. Minimum wage that is upheld by a stable corporatist exchange can accommodate flexible market changes better than the slow process of political exchange. Moreover, when the norm is enforced by the corporatist partners, workers may fare better than if they seek to enforce their rights individually in the labor courts. More generally, corporatist exchange delivers not only the substantive norms but also the means to enforce them. In the transition to pluralist making of law, the problem of slack enforcement has become a fundamental obstacle in Israel (Davidov 2005). At the same time, the guarantee of minimum wage by political exchange serves as a better guarantee when corporatist negotiations no longer materialize. The calculus of gains and losses becomes all the more complicated when qualitative issues are at stake. Individual rights in terms of equal opportunities are more vulnerable to discriminatory majoritarian interests that are typical of corporatist and political exchange. However, it has also been demonstrated that the constitutionalization of labor law is not a panacea, and the promise for workers may remain unfulfilled (Raday 1993). Regardless of the benchmark, whether efficiency, distributive justice, protection of human rights at work, or the rationalization of management, the comparison of the corporatist and pluralist forms of law-

---

54. This line of analysis can be traced back to Karl Marx, "On the Jewish Question." Reprinted in Marx (1975, 16).

making does not provide a clear indication that one is consistently better than the other.

In this chapter I have focused on the rights and obligations of workers and employers. I therefore emphasized aspects that were mostly associated with the *relational* dimension of corporatism in the corporatist period. In the following chapter I will discuss yet another set of endnorms—those associated mainly with corporatism's *internal* dimension and the distribution of opportunities within the labor side.

7 The Changing Legal Construct of Dualism

Labor Market Segmentation

While the traditional focus of labor law has been on the relationship between employers and their employees, or capital and labor, the particular characteristics of the labor market render the distributive aspects of work and benefits among the workforce equally important. Unlike capital investment in workplaces, which may be liquidated and converted to other forms of capital, the supply of labor is mainly dependent on the labor market, and the market's limited opportunities and scarcity of resources place the workers in competition with one another. The third function of law is to govern the distribution of resources among the workers—that is, within the labor side.

The third function of labor law cannot be detached from its second function. Regulating the distribution of labor market opportunities among workers is often contingent on the labor market institutions and norms developed by employers and labor associations. The issues dealt with in this chapter can be characterized as covering matters in which there is an agreement between labor and employers to exclude some workers and promote others. The employers and trade unions therefore arrange for a consensus-driven agreement among the "insiders" of the workforce at the expense of those who are, at the time of signing of the agreement, still outsiders. Such an agreement eases the tension in exercising the second function of labor law, only to relocate the conflict in the exercise of its third function. The agreement is not necessarily formal and may be composed of varied norms, practices, and institutions.

The regulation of labor market resources and their distribution among workers is an important method of allowing, upholding, or entrenching labor market segmentation and dualism. Barriers to mobility and limitations on opportunities in some sectors, occupations, and workplaces that are reserved for majority groups and particular social networks are explained by different economic and sociological theories. A short survey of these theories reveals that while law is for the most part assigned only a secondary role in them, it is actually a necessary ingredient in segmentation. Otherwise stated, these are hardly "natural processes" that spontaneously occur in the labor market. They rely on legal institutions that actively or passively make segmentation possible.

Generally, segmentation of the workforce is explained by reference to several concepts, including the emergence of post-Fordism (Amin 1997; Boyer 1988; Hirst and Zeitlin 1991), dualism in the labor market (Doeringer and Piore 1979; Kalleberg 2000), and a distinction between core and periphery both in the labor market and at the enterprise level (Atkinson 1984; Osterman 1993; Belous 1989; Rodgers and Rodgers 1989). Common to all of these concepts is the observation of distinct segments in the workforce, one of relatively privileged workers (core) and the other of workers with few rights and low levels of economic security (periphery). At the same time, the various concepts differ from one another in several respects, including their theoretical, ideological, and disciplinary premises and the level of analysis.

In the studies of segmentation in the last decades there is a growing interest in the expanding debate on flexibility (Atkinson 1984; Pollert 1991). The discussion on the emergence of flexibility points to the move away from what is characterized as the Fordist employment model—secure, lifelong employment patterns, usually designed for full-time and indefinite employment contracts—toward atypical, contingent, or precarious employment arrangements. These are all characterized by various deviations from the Fordist arrangement—fixed duration contracts, temporary work, part-time work, outsourcing and subcontracting, self-employment, employment through temporary work agencies, and more (Stone 2004). The diffusion of these models is twofold. First, there is a growing peripheralization of employment arrangements across the board (Standing 1999; Standing 2002). Lifelong tenure is becoming rarer, and after layoffs have taken place in companies where lifelong employment commitments were an important part of the organizational culture, it has become clear that such commitments are always relative and contingent on various external circumstances. Second, there is a growing cleavage between workers with employment arrangements that still resemble the Fordist pillars of work, wage, and social security, and others who have none of these and are compelled to rely on precarious work arrangements (Pfeffer and Baron 1988).

From the perspective of the pluralist-corporatist axis, the two processes are not identical. A general growth in flexibility and relaxation of workers' security can be part of corporatist arrangements. This process can be observed in most countries, but there are differences in the way it develops. While market forces play a greater role in shaping flexible arrangements in the United States, elsewhere corporatist pacts are being used to negotiate a flexibility-security trade-off. By contrast, the second pattern of flexibility is based on a divide between core and periphery. This process of flexibility is much more difficult to square with corporatism because the gains of some are won at the expense of others. Thus, the externalities and behaviors that corporatism was designed to eliminate are the animating forces behind the split between core and periphery. This type of segmentation can be explained by economic needs (Atkinson 1984) but also by reference to theories of exploitation and subordination of minorities by stronger groups (Bonacich 1972; Piore 1979). These latter explanations underscore the gap between the substantive norms associated with corporatism—most notably, equality—and those that characterize the objectives and outcomes of segmentation.

The two trends of flexibility are nonexclusive, but there is a certain trade-off between them. Various options are available to an employer who must cut labor costs to compete with global low-cost competitors. For example, instead of increasing wage flexibility, the employer may decide to increase functional flexibility by providing cutting-edge technological training to the workers. More important in the present context is the choice between cutting costs equally among all workers employed—for example, by an across-the-board wage reduction—or distributing the gains and costs unevenly—for example, by outsourcing some production to subcontractors who lower labor costs by avoiding labor standards. Both options can be negotiated with a union, but only one reflects the values and principles of corporatism. In corporatist negotiations, we would expect the general wage-cut option to be preferred. In a more pluralist regime, by contrast, all options are feasible, contingent on the dynamic coalitions and power relations among the agents.

This chapter is concerned with flexibility solutions that are not universal (of the first type) but targeted and selective (of the second type). Moreover, I am particularly interested in those cases where exclusionary options were implemented through negotiations and not simply by the employers' unilateral use of their managerial prerogative. These situations are the most appropriate for crystallizing the third function of labor law and distinguishing it from the second. The major questions in these situations are why labor is willing to sell short some workers' rights and what the consequences of such choices are to all parties in the industrial relations system.

Segmentation and dualism have played an important role in the literature on Israel's corporatism (Shalev 1992; Grinberg 1991). The most significant argument against the corporatist characterization of the Israeli industrial relations system was that Israel's corporatism was split, its institutional structure fragmented between the public and private sectors and its nationalist objectives segmented between the opportunities available to Jewish citizens and those available to the Palestinians residing within Israel. The hegemonic position of the General Histadrut and its affiliation with the long-term ruling party favored the situation of workers who were members of the Histadrut and denied labor-market opportunities to workers who dissented from the Labor Party's politics or from trade unions in general, or who refused to be members for other reasons. This was not everyone's corporatism but rather a peak-level trilateral representation of the insiders' interests at the expense of the outsiders.

However, throughout this book the framework chosen to explain the transformation of the Israeli system has been that of corporatism. I argue that segmentation and dualism have always persisted in the system. The major difference is, therefore, not segmentation but the gradual erosion of corporatist institutions that prevailed until the early 1980s. I argue that the transformation from corporatist to pluralist institutions has also shaped the nature of segmentation and that the legal construct of labor-market dualism does matter. To demonstrate this claim, I will present two examples in this chapter. The first touches on the nationalist nature of the Israeli system, which emerges from a comparison between the entry of Palestinian workers from the Occupied Territories following the Six Day War in 1967 and the entry of migrant workers from around the world beginning in 1993. Although the two processes served similar functions in the Israeli labor market, and the latter in fact substituted for the former, the construct and outcomes of segmentation have been different. In the second part of this chapter I will discuss the peripheralization of a growing segment of the workforce, focusing on the politics of temporary work agencies. This relatively detailed discussion summarizes most of the trends discussed in part 3 of the book—the multiplicity of institutional agents, growing adversarialism between labor and capital and hence also between the various workers' organizations, and the juridification of norms governing the labor market. Both examples reveal that there are similarities in the institutional design of segmentation during the corporatist and postcorporatist phases. However, the institutional changes described in this book affect the nature of segmentation and determine the demographic nature of the periphery, as well as the political and economic opportunities that are available to those who wish to cross the border between core and periphery, between primary and secondary labor markets.

The National Boundaries of the System: Palestinian and Migrant Workers in Israel

The Historical Background of Foreign Workers in Israel

As described in chapter 2, the corporatist system in Israel was based on the nationalist objectives of the Histadrut and of the institutions that were developed to advance the interests of the Jewish population in Palestine under the British Mandate. Consequently, the boundaries of the industrial relations system were tailored to fit the borders of the newly founded state. Most employees and employers were organized within the industrial relations system. External investments were channeled into enterprises that were part of the domestic pact and there were no "foreign workers" as such. This scheme was designed to ensure a close fit between the contours of the comprehensive industrial relations system and the borders of the state. It was never a perfect fit, however, and always relied on a periphery of workers allowing for some flexibility. These included groups that were one step removed from the core of Israeli society—Palestinian citizens of Israel, and Jewish migrants (*olim*), most notably those from Arab, African, and Asian countries. They could be employed by the labor market when necessary, even at lower wages. When they were not needed, they were on their own (the Palestinian citizens of Israel) or on welfare (the Jewish migrants). Thus, despite the seemingly comprehensive appearance of the corporatist scheme that developed in Israel, it was based on some segmentation (Rosenhek 2003).

PALESTINIAN WORKERS IN ISRAEL: 1967–1993

Until 1967, the national character of the industrial relations system and the political system resisted the entry of workers who were twice removed from the core of Israeli society—that is, non-Jewish and nonresident. No migrant workers were allowed into Israel except under extraordinary circumstances.[1] The initial entry of "foreigners" into the Israeli labor market took place not as a direct result of economic necessity but because of geopolitical factors. Once the Six Day War ended, Israel found itself occupying, with no well-defined plan, new territories inhabited by many Palestinians. Shortly after the occupation began, when the borders were for the most part still common knowledge but physically unmarked in most areas, Palestinians started to cross them to work within Israel. At first their numbers were negligible, but as it became evident that the status of the territories was not likely to change in the very short term, they increased. Once the move had been made, a policy on foreign workers was required. This policy was shaped in 1970, combining economic and security considerations, and negotiated in a corporatist spirit (Grinberg 1993, 162–205).

As to the security considerations, the dominant position was that economic integration could be used as a means of controlling the population in the Occupied Territories. It was envisaged that employment opportunities in Israel would provide some legitimacy to the political situation and prevent a revolt. The hawkish security stance also dovetailed with some pressing economic interests. Prior to the Six Day War, the Israeli economy had been facing escalating wage demands by the General Histadrut. Unable to control the wage escalation, the economy plummeted into a recession. The Minister of Finance saw the influx of additional workers into the Israeli labor market as a means of breaking the Histadrut's monopoly over the labor market and therefore as an instrument for economic recovery.

---

1. This was controlled by two measures—the Employment Service Law (1959), which required most recruitments for work to be conducted through the employment bureaus, to which nonresidents had no access, and the Law on Entry to Israel (1952), which places restrictions on visas for work or for other purposes in Israel.

Despite the strong security and economic considerations that justified the policy permitting the entry of Palestinian workers into Israel, there were objections to it as well. Some were ideological, based on the premise of Zionist constructive-socialism, which viewed Jewish work as a value in itself. Others saw the entry of Palestinian workers as the token of a long-term occupation and the beginning of a de facto annexation of the Territories. Yet the most challenging objection was voiced by the Histadrut, which was concerned with wage undercutting (Margalit 1994, 297–310). The Histadrut's objection was part of a nationalist agenda that sought to ensure high wages for domestic labor. The economy in the Territories was unorganized, and wages there were drastically lower than those prevailing in Israel. It was clear that the Palestinians would be willing to work for wages that would undermine all the Histadrut's efforts to escalate wages.

The final political compromise was expressed in a cabinet decision in October 1970. This decision established the basic principles, which are still in force, regarding the employment of Palestinian workers in Israel.[2] The central provision of the decision was that Palestinians who held a work permit would be entitled to work in Israel, and their wages would be equal to those of domestic workers. To ensure compliance, the cabinet decision further stipulated that all work permits would be obtained from bureaus to be established by the Israeli Employment Service in the Territories. In practice, this has been the basis for holding that work permits are not general in nature but attached to a specified employer. The Employment Service's payments division would also collect the wages and benefits from the employers and remit them to the workers, this to ensure that employers would not underpay their Palestinian workers. It further ensured that the employment of Palestinian workers would not be part of the informal economy. All wages would be reported, and the payments division would be able to make all the necessary deductions from the workers' wages. Despite the importance of the 1970 cabinet decision, it was enacted into law only in 1994, as part of the statutory arrangements implementing the Israeli-Palestinian peace process.[3]

The Palestinian workers admitted into Israel found an existing niche waiting to employ them: manual labor jobs requiring low levels of skill and offering low levels of pay and social status. The period of rapid growth after the Six Day War ensured that the Palestinians' entry into the Israeli labor market would not be accompanied by internal displacement and unemployment, as those who comprised the lower segments of the labor force, especially the Jewish population, moved upward to more secure and better-paying jobs (Semyonov and Epstein 1987, 43–64). The ongoing state of occupation created a new and complex reality in Israel. The borders between Israel and the Territories were

2. The Ministers' Committee on Security number 1/B, from October 8, 1970. The cabinet decision matches an earlier agreement between the Histadrut and representatives of the cabinet on October 24, 1968 (Grinberg 1993, 198).

3. The Law Implementing the Agreement on the Gaza Strip and Jericho Area (1994).

clear but lost some of their significance. Jewish settlements were erected in the Territories in tandem with the growing use of military force to suppress sporadic revolts against the occupation. The economic borders were even more fluid. The Territories relied on Israel for necessary commodities and Palestinian workers continued to stream into Israel (Tamari 1980). During this period, the number of permitholders gainfully employed in Israel was steadily on the rise, yet almost the same number of workers worked in Israel without holding a permit. It is estimated that at times almost a third of the workforce in the Territories was employed in Israel (Farjoun 1984). Although Palestinian workers accounted for only a small share of the workforce in Israel (5 to 10 percent, depending on the period of time and whether undocumented workers are included), they secured a few niches in which they dominated. These included menial, low-wage work and temporary (seasonal) work, most notably in construction and agriculture, and to a lesser extent in traditional industries and services.

The 1970 cabinet decision was generally carried out, at least at the level of formal policy, and to a large extent also at the level of formal administrative implementation. In reality, however, the large number of undocumented workers and the disorder that accompanied the administration of Palestinian work in Israel suggest a more diverse picture. Some workers experienced the humiliation of selling their labor on a daily basis in informal venues located at major highway junctions. By contrast, some permit holders, especially from East Jerusalem, enjoyed the right to vote and the right to get elected in workers' committees that were established at their workplaces, and they were promoted according to rules established by collective bargaining agreements.

The political climate changed drastically during the Palestinian uprising (intifada) that began in November 1987. The spontaneous, widespread revolt against the occupation was not the result of a well-organized nationalistic agenda. The active participants in it were for the most part workers whose motivation was to exact vengeance for the daily humiliation they experienced at work and at checkpoints in the course of searches and confiscation of their identity cards (Gilbar 1992; Schiff and Yaari 1990). Surprisingly, throughout the first intifada the number of Palestinians working in Israel remained relatively stable as a result of the mutual economic dependency of the Palestinians and the Israeli economy. Neither side could separate from the other. By 1993 the mutual dependency of the Palestinians and the Israelis came to an end, ironically just as the alleged peace process was launched. This came about because of the employers' successful lobbying of the Minister of Labor to admit workers from other countries to fill in for the Palestinians, mostly in agriculture and construction.

MIGRANT WORKERS IN ISRAEL: 1993 TO THE PRESENT

While the number of permits allowed for migrant workers from abroad was at first very limited, the decision to overcome the traditional objection to these workers was in itself highly significant. Within a very short period the number of permits issued to employers multiplied rapidly. At the same time the number of permits for Palestinians was gradually reduced, allegedly for security reasons but also as a means of exerting economic pressure on the Palestinians at a time of political negotiations. The unique combination of economic and geopolitical considerations, which had been the basis for the Palestinians' admittance in 1970, also served the process of rapidly replacing the Palestinian day workers with migrant workers from around the world (Bartram 1998; Rosenhek 2000). Throughout the transition, Palestinian workers and migrant workers together accounted for roughly 10 percent of the workforce, and the only difference was in the share of each group, as the latter gradually substituted for the former.

The new and unprecedented influx of migrant workers into Israel resembled the entry of Palestinian workers after the Six Day War in one significant respect—it was neither planned nor carefully thought out. Unlike the Palestinian workers, migrant workers had a much stronger presence, as they were not frontier workers who commuted back and forth to their homes. Toward the end of the 1990s, more than 10 percent of Tel Aviv's population consisted of migrant workers. They had become much more than mere workers, as their condition began to resemble that of residency (Schnell 1999). Yet this is also what made them a threat to the Israeli state. While the state's concern with the Palestinian workers was related to security and the political relationship between Israel and the Palestinians, the concern raised with regard to migrant workers was that they threatened the Jewish nature of the Israeli state and the very little that remained of constructive Zionism. Nevertheless, for the industrial relations system they were deemed necessary because they catered to the interests of the primary workforce. Despite growing levels of unemployment, the migrant workers were considered necessary to perform the "black" (or "Arab") jobs, at prices and working conditions (mostly Jewish) Israeli workers would have rejected out of hand.

As in 1970, the approval of permits to employers who wanted to employ migrant workers was made possible because of a conjuncture of political interests. However, the agents whose interests were taken into consideration were very different from those of 1970.

The General Histadrut and other trade unions were almost silent on the issue of migrant workers. In the spirit of postcorporatism, the argument of wage undercutting no longer played a role as an important consideration in the political process, and the Histadrut did not view the matter as one of its priorities. The Industrialists Association, the largest employers' association, which was a key player in the early 1970s, was also not an avid supporter of allowing migrant workers in. It was the employers in agriculture and construction who led the lobbying to give employers permits to employ migrant workers. Later, agencies dealing with care workers also added their pressure. The Industrialists Association was not an active or vocal agent, mostly because industry did not rely on migrant workers, especially when labor-intensive sectors moved out of Israel to neighboring countries (e.g., Jordan) or outsourced some of their production to developing countries. Thus, unlike the labor side, the employers' position was active but very fragmented, and it harbored conflicting interests, as well as competition over permits.

As demonstrated at the outset of part 3, the state has also become more fragmented. The Knesset was almost idle at the time the original decision was made but has become more active over time. It has even established a subcommittee to deal with the "problem of migrant workers." But on the whole its position in the matter of migrant workers has been split according to political lines. The more dominant branch has been the executive, but frequent changes in government since the entry of migrant workers have led to an erratic course of policymaking, which is very vulnerable to pressure groups and factions (Asiskovitch 2004). Policy changes have resulted from frequently changing ministers, rapid coalition changes, and conflicts between the ministries of labor and finance. Each of these ministries has pushed in different stages for expanding or retracting the employment of migrant workers.

As explained in chapter 5, the fourth side in the new politics of labor law consists of NGOs. On the side of both the employers and the employees, NGOs have been leading policy changes by means of active lobbying and adjudication (Kemp and Raijman 2001; Raijman and Kemp 2002). These associations are not part of the trilateral industrial relations system, but in the area of migrant workers they have dominated policymaking beyond what the classic social partners have attempted.

Despite some similarities in the function played by Palestinian workers in the past and by migrant workers today, the politics of rights have been different for the two groups. The changes fit well with the framework presented in chapter 5 regarding the changing rules of interests representation. Corresponding to this change there has been a change in the level of juridification, described in chapter 6. While law played a marginal role, at most, with regard to the Palestinian workers, it has been a central arena of policymaking regarding the position and rights of migrant workers. In both legislation and adjudication, migrant workers have a growing presence and visibility in the law. The almost complete withdrawal of the Histadrut from the regulation of foreign employment in Israel, together with the continuous juridification of the migrant workers' presence on the basis of competition between interest groups and factions, stands therefore at the center of the distinction between corporatist and postcorporatist segmentation.

Labor Law and Segmentation

LABOR LAW IN THE SERVICE OF CORPORATISM: THE LEGAL STATUS OF PALESTINIAN WORKERS

The formative policy regarding the status of Palestinian workers in Israel was the government's cabinet decision from 1970, which was described in the previous section. Technically this is law. However, the decision was the output of a compromise among the social partners that was not formalized in statute until many years later (in 1994, when the Palestinians were already being gradually expelled from the Israeli labor market). A cabinet decision is low-visibility law: it is difficult to trace, little known, and has the status of a government policy that cannot be reviewed except by administrative law and is relatively difficult to enforce. These were not deemed to be problems at a time when litigation over rights was not a significant mode of operation. In the corporatist phase, what mattered most was the actual corporatist agreement. In the absence of active NGOs at the time, the workers were dependent on the goodwill of the employers and the Histadrut, and the common legal venues were not deemed important to the workers, employers, the associations, or the state.

The 1970 executive decision appeared to take an exceptionally favorable position toward the Palestinian dayworkers. It provided them with rights equal to those of Israeli workers and put in place a system of wage and benefits collection to ensure that these rights were enforced. This appearance might be taken to indicate that the corporatist nature of decision making was coupled with substantive corporatist results, characterized by a tendency toward equality and inclusiveness.[4] There was, however, a gap between the appearance and the reality of the legal status enjoyed by the day workers. The gap can be described as two-tiered. First, as is typical in regard to peripheral workers, the promise of equality was difficult to administer, lending itself in fact to only a very partial equality. Second, the promise of equality was not designed to reflect the view that Israeli and Palestinian guest workers were equal. It was an instrumental strategy aimed at ensuring the rights of the insiders (Israeli workers), and equality was extended to the outsiders only to the extent that it benefited the insiders (Mundlak, 1999b).

With regard to the problem of administration, documented guest workers from the Occupied Territories encountered problems that typically make claiming rights so difficult (Felstiner, Abel, and Sarat 1980). Significant informational barriers regarding rights and a hazy division of labor between the payments division in the employment bureau and the employers made it unclear who was responsible for which benefits.[5] There was also slack enforcement, which is typical of the Israeli labor market generally but the impact of which is much graver for exceptionally vulnerable groups.[6] These problems were even more acute for the undocumented workers. Admittedly, in later stages the Labor Court clarified that employment rights are not contingent on having a lawful status and are therefore applicable to undocumented workers

---

4. On whether corporatist procedures are necessarily related to corporatist outcomes, see chapter 1.

5. For documentation of these problems see Kav La-Oved (The Workers Hotline), Bulletins (March 1993, July 1993).

6. For documentation of these problems see Kav La-Oved (The Workers Hotline), Bulletins (March 1993, May 1994, September 1994).

2003). First, there were problems directly connected with the employment relationship, mostly the denial of wages and benefits that were lower than the statutory minimum. More fundamental was the problem created by the binding arrangement that denied the migrant workers their market power. A second category of problems was related to the new dimension that had been added to the employment of foreigners in Israel, which included all the aspects of residency that migrant workers, unlike daily frontier workers, brought with them. These included the protection of civil liberties and social rights, such as the rights to health, education, and housing. The problems associated with the employment of migrant workers were no longer confined to the employment relationship but reached deep into the core of immigration policy in Israel, which has traditionally denied all immigration except for *aliyah*—the immigration of Jewish people to the Jewish homeland. Industrial relations, which were shown to have emerged from a nationalist pact in Israel, intertwined again with the fundamental questions of Zionism and the relationship between the desire to maintain an exclusive state for the Jewish people and to provide an inclusive state for all its inhabitants.

An extensive discussion of the legal developments with regard to the migrant workers lies outside the scope of the current analysis (Mundlak 2003, 2007). There are, however, several indicia that aptly demonstrate the different reaction to the entry of migrant workers and that, on the basis of the previous analysis, can be attributed to the shift away from corporatism. A few years after the entry of migrant workers, NGOs and public-cause lawyers started representing them in individual claims in the courtroom. The beginning may have been hesitant, but within several years the number of NGOs dealing with migrant workers increased (Rosenhek 1999; Kemp and Raijman 2001). Since then, litigation has covered more ground and legislative changes are on the rise.

The most fundamental legal problem for migrant workers was the structural arrangement put in place to ensure segmentation. This consisted, first and foremost, of the binding arrangement. Because the employment permit was given to the employer, the employee had no leverage in negotiations. If she would not accept her employer's conditions, she would lose not only her workplace but also her visa. Consequently, almost any abuse of rights could go unnoticed. The binding arrangement was the most potent instrument of segmentation. It was aimed at ensuring that migrant workers would be confined to where the state wanted them to work but removed from the labor market. Because a "market" assumes that an employee can choose from among more than one employer, binding the employee to a single employer does away with almost all the characteristics of market transactions.

The efforts of human-rights NGOs were therefore directed at eliminating the binding arrangement. Despite the very slow and sometimes unsuccessful legal challenge, the system's external agents had one advantage on their side that made their claim at least feasible. As noted above, the major problem in challenging the infrastructure of segmentation is that the insiders have a common incentive to protect themselves from the outsiders. As has been demonstrated, the social pact that allowed the entry of Palestinian day workers was a compromise among the interests of the insiders but took little account of those of the outsiders as an end in itself. This arrangement endured for many years because it was designed in a manner that was perceived to continuously benefit all the insiders. Under these circumstances, there was little tolerance for claims by agents within the social pact in favor of the outsiders' rights. By contrast, changes over time in the binding arrangement, slight as they were, were made possible because there was no longer a social pact of insiders; the binding arrangement was not the product of prior political or social negotiations. The changes in the binding arrangement came about not because of any change of heart in favor of the outsiders' rights but as a result of the revelation that some insiders were advancing their position at the expense of others.

There were several reasons for the insiders' internal conflict: the binding arrangement encouraged more undocumented workers, it had little success in securing segmentation and state control over the migrant workers, and it lowered the wages of the insiders; it was also argued that it increased unemployment (and hence also the social expenditures of the state for welfare) among low-wage workers. Some of these arguments are controversial and require further empirical support. However, they unified voices on the left (e.g., NGOs) who were interested in advancing human rights, and those on the right (e.g., the Ministry of Finance, the Bank of Israel) who were interested in reducing unemployment and social expenditures.[15] The binding arrangement was criticized by the state's comptroller, the Ministry of Labor, and academics in all the social sciences, and eventually its adverse consequences for the insiders became apparent. Despite these outcomes, the arrangement did not disappear because its major beneficiaries—the employers themselves—succeeded in preserving it, just as they succeeded in their lobbying for permits to employ migrant workers to begin with (Asiskovitch 2004). Absent a general agreement on segmentation, like the one in 1970, each of the parties has used its political power to maximize its gains.

Beyond political power, law has also come into play. Litigation by NGOs, which hardly existed in the corporatist phase, brought the binding arrangement to the Supreme Court. The NGOs petitioned to declare it void because it infringes human rights.[16] This type of litigation is in line with other trends of constitutional juridification described in the previous chapter. After several

15. The Central Bank of Israel, A Message to the Press: Foreign Workers in Israel (December 18, 2000); Inter-Ministerial Report on Foreign Workers and the Establishment of an Immigration Authority (2002) (committee was chaired by a representative of the Ministry of Finance).

16. The first petition against the binding arrangement was Supreme Court 6883/00 Baktita Diva and others v. Minister of Interiors (petition was canceled at the agreement of the parties); a similar petition was filed later: Supreme Court 4542/02 Kav la-Oved v. Government of Israel (2006, yet unpublished).

years, in 2006, the Supreme Court decided the binding arrangement is unconstitutional and must be abolished. While the state received a grace period before it must devise a new regulatory scheme, this process has been slow. Because the interests of NGOs and governmental ministries in doing away with the binding arrangement are very different, there is no agreement on the desirable alternative. Yet it is clear that the postcorporatist effort to institutionalize segmentation in favor of all the insiders' interests has failed for two complementary reasons. First, there was no effort to coordinate the conflicting interests of the insiders from the outset. Second, there was no longer a way to stifle the interests of dissenting insiders and outsiders or to keep them away from the courtroom. The corporatist pact is no longer existent, and pluralist interests have turned the institutional arrangement into a competitive and strategic game.

Similar processes can be observed in other legal areas governing the rights of migrant workers. These can be roughly divided into those concerned with employment rights and those concerned with the social rights associated with the migrants' ongoing presence in Israel. With regard to employment rights, unlike the Palestinian workers, migrant workers found their way into the courtroom relatively quickly with the help of NGOs. The most fundamental problems have been related to access to justice. In this matter the Labor Court has been responsive, and despite its corporatist heritage it has acknowledged the migrant workers' disadvantageous position in the labor market.[17] In addition it has acknowledged the strong affinity between employment rights, access to justice and human rights and has brought in NGOs as active participants in the case law determining future rights in the courtroom.[18] Despite various challenges, the Court has rarely deviated from the premise of equal application of the law.[19]

As opposed to the situation in the Labor Court, little attention has been paid to employment rights in the legislative arena. The more important legislative amendment to the Foreign Workers Law (1991) was enacted in 1999, ensuring, inter alia, a minimum standard for private health insurance

17. This has been most extensively demonstrated in National labor Court 1218/02 Xue Bin—A. Dori PDA, 38:650.

18. National labor Court 1127/00 Orsetz—Denia Sybus Inc., PDA 37:305; National Labor Court 1064/00 Daniel Kinyanjui Mwangi—Olitski Roadworks Inc., PDA 35:625; National Labor Court 1155/00 Jonjono—MECS Manpower, Engineering and Constructions (2000, unpublished); National Labor Court 1218/02 Xue Bin—A. Dori, PDA 38:650.

19. One exception held that migrant workers are not entitled to prior notice before dismissals because they are bound to their employer and thus do not need the time to look for a new employer. Jerusalem District Labor Court 300214/95 Dias—Popovtzer (2002, unpublished). A second exception is in fact occupation-based, but given that the occupation is staffed predominantly by migrant workers it is difficult to distinguish the two. In National Labor Court 1113/02 Todroangan—Moshe Maayan, PDA 39:409, the National Labor Court held that overtime payments do not apply to live-in domestic workers. This holding has been contested by some of the judges in the Labor Court itself since then. See, for example, National Labor Court 405/05 Elba Sorieno—Margareta Kalfon (2006, unpublished).

and housing requirements. Yet with regard to employment rights it had little impact.

The Histadrut has remained almost completely outside the employment sphere with regard to migrant workers. While its collective agreements apply to migrant workers as well, it has done little to help them enforce their rights. Furthermore, the Histadrut negotiated a collective agreement in the construction industry in which special deductions from the migrant workers' wages were bargained.[20] In what might have been a clear example of corporatist exclusion, the Minister of Labor extended this agreement to the whole industry, except for the section dealing with migrant workers, which he found to be discriminatory.[21] Again, comprehensive exclusion, as had been practiced with regard to the Palestinians, was no longer feasible.

Similar outcomes can be observed with regard to the other social rights of migrant workers, but the road taken was significantly more difficult to navigate. Because Palestinian workers had very limited claims, if any, in the social sphere, and because security considerations were considered to override their civil liberties—such as free speech and rights at time of arrest—there was no rights jurisprudence in place at the time migrant workers started substituting for Palestinian workers. Unlike the premise of equality that served as the starting point for the legal development of employment rights, the implicit starting point for human rights was that they were nonexistent.

The juridification of relationships also applied to the rights of migrant workers. As a result of extensive lawsuits and lobbying, some changes have come about regarding rights at time of arrest and deportation, freedom of speech, freedom of association, health, education, and the physical conditions of residence. As a result of these changes rights have been granted, but they have also legitimized practices of denying rights to outsiders. The right to private heath-care insurance for all migrant workers was secured in law, but at the same time the categorical exclusion of all migrant workers from the national health-care system was legitimized.[22] The changes have guaranteed judicial review of detention before deportation, but the review is not independent of the government's interests, as is the case in criminal litigation, nor is it as swift or fond of due process as is the general standard of the law when applied

20. Supplement 7032/2000 to the collective agreement from April 9, 1968 (No. 1255/68) that was signed (December 21, 1999) by the General Histadrut and the Central Association of Constructors in Israel.

21. Extension order to the agreement was published in YP (official publications) 5011, p. 3782 (2001).

22. Initially a petition was filed requesting an injunction ordering the state to issue a regulation extending the National Health Care Law (1994) to migrant workers: High Court of Justice 6433/01 Maria Emily Filora v. Minister of Health (2001, unpublished). As it was clear this strategy would not succeed in the courts, after the Foreign Workers Law was amended, NGOs turned to litigate the new framework of regulated private insurance for migrant workers. High Court of Justice 82/04 Physicians for Human Rights v. Insurance Commissioner (petition filed on January 5, 2004 and dismissed with the consent of the petitioner, 2004).

first emphasized the formal employment contract and therefore considered the temporary work agency to be the employer, for which reason the workers were not legally entitled to the same wages, benefits, and working conditions as their peers who were hired directly by the users.[32] The second approach emphasized the substantive relationship: on the factual presumption that the users of labor power are the real employers, it held that the workers hired through temporary work agencies were entitled to the same rights as those accorded to workers who were hired directly.[33]

While there were only a handful of cases on temporary work agencies, a growing number of agencies were concerned with the possibility that their status might be juridified.[34] The employer-users were equally concerned that juridification would result in the forced equalization of the wages and employment conditions accorded to those hired directly by the users with the wages and conditions of those hired through temporary work agencies. The Histadrut was also ambivalent, even establishing an agency of its own to recruit workers to Histadrut-owned enterprises, such as the Histadrut-managed health-care provider. Moreover, the Histadrut acknowledged that while the use of temporary work agencies could be a threat to collective bargaining, it could also be seen as a concession that made collective bargaining possible. To avoid the threat of juridification, all the agents of the industrial relations system sought to promote the use of collective agreements between the Histadrut and the temporary work agencies themselves, as a means of mainstreaming the temp industry. By the mid-1990s a few dozen such agreements had been concluded (Raday 1998).

Despite the emergence of collective agreements, the growth of temporary work agencies brought to the attention of the public and policymakers the fundamental problem regarding this practice. Whereas in most countries hiring through temporary agencies is only for the purpose of filling temporary tasks or temporary replacements (EIRO 1999; Blanpain and Graham 2003), the objective of these agencies in Israel was to permanently bypass collective agreements. Hiring through agencies was often meant to artificially disguise the true relationship between the worker and the real employer so as to allow the employer to evade the coverage of collective agreements and extension orders with their relatively generous wage scales, protection from dismissals, and fringe benefits such as pension schemes.

With the maturation and entry of temporary work agencies into the mainstream, and their consequent growth, the legal questions became more pressing. In the early stages the question was, Who is the employer, the user or the agency? On the one hand, it was clear that if the agencies were held to be the

32. See the cases cited supra at note 28.

33. The leading case to demonstrate this approach is National Labor Court 52/3-142 Chassan Aliaha El-Harinath—Kfar Ruth, PDA 24:535.

34. The concern about juridification was not unfounded. As early as 1986 there was an attempt to regulate temporary work agencies in a statute. See Proposal: Amendment to the Employment Service Law (1986 *Legislative Proposals* 1810).

legal employers, then the use of temporary work agencies for short-term temporary hiring would be more attractive and make it possible to reduce un-employment. This was thought to be an important consideration because tem-porary work agencies had become a substitute for the state-run employment bureaus. These corporatist "dinosaurs" could no longer provide adequate ser-vice in a growingly volatile, versatile, and pluralist market.

At the same time, a clear rule holding temporary work agencies to be the employers would have also allowed opportunistic hiring through agencies as a way of avoiding the costs of collective bargaining and some aspects of protec-tive labor law.[35] If employers bargain with the trade union and then avoid the agreement by hiring workers from agencies, the agreement no longer has any significance. The fear that hiring through agencies might undermine collective arrangements was not remote because by the early 1990s there were already workers, especially in the public sector, who had been employed for several years as "second-class" workers because they had been hired through tempo-rary work agencies (Yizraeli and Benjamin 2000).[36]

The legislature was not eager to provide a solution to the dilemma since it would have led to a loud outcry from both the temporary work agencies and the employer-users. The market in general, and the employers in particular, had just started realizing the versatile potential in the use of temporary work agencies, and they certainly had no desire to relinquish it right at the outset. By contrast, the Labor Court was bound by the plaintiffs' agenda. Despite the slow pace of juridification, the Court gradually identified a way of avoiding the either-or determination of who the employer was; this was to place the so-lution in a changing context. For example, the court held that *for the purpose* of determining the coverage of extension orders, the workers hired through temporary work agencies deserved the same rights accorded to workers who were employed directly,[37] and that *for the purpose* of unemployment insurance—and later severance pay—remitting a worker to the agency was

35. This was particularly acute in the mid-1990s, when the legal responsibilities of tempo-rary work agencies and employer-users in a triangular relationship were not clearly demarcated. In later years, many statutory labor standards were amended, and now the division of obliga-tions and responsibilities is more specifically defined. See The Municipalities Law (1964, as amended in 2000), sec. 174A; Women's Work Law (1954, as amended in 1998), sec. 9; Preven-tion of Sexual Harassment Law (1998), sec. 2; Genetic Information Law (2000), sec. 29; Mini-mum Wage Law (1987, as amended in 2002), sec. 6A; Employment (Equal Opportunities) Law (1988, as amended in 2002), sec. 2; Workplace Safety Bylaws (Personal Safety Equipment) (1997).

36. See, for example, the facts in National Labor Court 1189/00 Ilana Levinger—State of Is-rael (2000, unpublished). In that case, Ilana Levinger was employed as an independent contrac-tor for almost a decade and then continued to do the same work while employed by temporary work agencies. From time to time the agencies were replaced by other agencies to avoid a long-term relationship of the employee with any one employer. As the Labor Court noted, the only temporary characteristic of this allegedly short-term employment was the ever-changing com-panies, not the job itself.

37. Haifa Regional Labor Court 49/6-16 Construction Workers' Pension Fund—Zamir Manpower Services, PDA 24:4 (regional cases).

akin to a dismissal by the employer-user.[38] Consequently, the court started to gradually equalize the rights of workers who were registered as workers of a temporary work agency with those of workers hired directly.

The Regulation of Temporary Work Agencies: 1996–2000

As the use of temporary work agencies increased and the state of the law became more complex, the legislature decided to take matters into its own hands. The initiative came mostly from the professional civil servants in the Ministry of Labor, not from the legislature itself, the Histadrut, the employers, or the state. This in itself was an indication that the legislative process would be modeled on the pluralist rather than the corporatist variant of labor legislation. As described in chapter 5, the pluralist model does not emerge from consensus among the elements of the tripartite structure of interests representation but from multiple institutions that view law as a means of advancing the interests of one group at the expense of another.

The Employment of Employees by Manpower Contractors Law (1996) sought to regulate, for the first time, the operation of temporary work agencies in Israel. On the face of it, this law seemed to defeat the effort to bring temporary work agencies into the mainstream, singling them out from all other employers and instituting regulation based on two principles. The first was the requirement that temporary work agencies must register and post a warranty to ensure that they would be able to pay their workers' wages.[39] In a constitutional attack on this part of the law, instigated by the agencies' association shortly after the law was passed, the association argued that this was a discriminatory approach that infringed on the agencies' freedom of occupation. The Supreme Court rejected the argument, holding that while the law did indeed infringe on their freedom of occupation, this was for a valid purpose and proportionate to the risk posed by this mode of employment.[40]

In the second part of the statute, the legislature sought to regulate the trilateral relationship among the workers, the agencies, and the employer-users. Just like the labor courts, the legislature sought to avoid the need to provide a dichotomous response to the question of who the employer was. What the law provided instead was the following arrangement:

Section 13:
(a) The terms of a collective agreement that applies to the workers who are employed in a workplace where there are also manpower contractors' employees, will apply to the manpower contractors' employees who are employed in the

38. National Labor Court 55/2-109 Osnat Dafna Levin—National Insurance Institute, PDA 29:10; National Labor Court 57/3-56 Tzvi Shafir—Nativ Industry and Others, PDA 32:241.
39. The Employment of Employees by Manpower Contractors Law (1996), sec. 2–10.
40. Supreme Court HCJ 450/97 Tnufa Manpower and Holdings Services v. Minister of Labor and Welfare, PDI 52(2):433.

same workplace for more than three years, except for terms that deal with tenure.

(b) [Omitted here]

(c) The provisions of subsection (a) shall not apply in relation to an employee whose terms of employment with a manpower contractor are regulated by a collective bargaining agreement. . . .

In my view, section 13 embodies the whole of Israeli labor law's move away from corporatism. It relied on corporatist institutions as a means of compromise between conflicting interests, but at the same time these measures were used for the objective of advancing the interests of some against those of others, thereby concealing the fact that the solutions were conflictual rather than consensus-driven. Simply put, section 13 was corporatist and compromising on the outside but pluralist and adversarial on the inside.

Section 13(a) sought to distinguish between workers employed for a long time through temporary work agencies and those hired to fill temporary needs. Only the former were expected to receive equal or partially equal rights. In a manner similar to the judicial strategy of focusing on a particular context described earlier,[41] the legislature avoided the question, determining instead that workers employed in the same workplace for more than three years would enjoy the collective agreement prevailing in the user's workplace. The compromise was very partial, however, and very convenient to the employers and the agencies despite appearing to offer protection to the workers. First, by any standard a three-year employment period is considerable. Second, even the requirement to match the rights of the workers employed by the agencies to those of workers hired directly did not extend protection from dismissals, leaving them with only the slim protection of the employment-at-will doctrine.[42]

However, the more important compromise was concealed in subsection (c). In it the legislature relied on the idea of derogation, which had been more commonly used in the corporatist legislative phase.[43] According to subsection (c), even if a worker was employed through a temporary work agency for more than three years, if the agency had a collective agreement with a representative trade union, the worker would not be entitled to the rights accorded to the workers hired directly by the employer-user.

On the face of it, the purpose of section 13(c) was to encourage the continuation of collective agreements between temporary work agencies and the Histadrut. The simple explanation for this is that it was a relic of patterns and institutions left over from the corporatist phase. It revealed a preference for ordering by collective bargaining rather than statute, and the legislature in fact structured a penalty (subsection [a]) that could be avoided only by a derogatory collective agreement. This preserved the superiority of the collectively

41. See supra notes 37–38.

42. However, see chapter 5 for a description of the gradual transition from the at-will doctrine to a policy of mandatory good faith.

43. On derogation arrangements in the corporatist phase, see chapter 4.

status of the National Histadrut, arguing that the National Histadrut recruited members on the basis of fraudulent practices. The law on collective bargaining provides no institutionalized response to this type of problem, since it was written mostly in the late 1950s when the problem of interunion rivalry was almost theoretical and practically nonexistent. Consequently, the Supreme Court remanded the case to the Labor Court, and the Minister of Labor and Welfare simply let the hot potato cool with no particular response to the problem, other than a few attempts at mediation and investigation. As the problem continued to develop, there was mostly a sense that everyone just wished it would somehow go away (Ben-Israel 2002a).

Instead of relying merely on legal arguments to dispute the National Histadrut's collective agreement, the General Histadrut also continued to negotiate secretly with some temporary work agencies. Consequently, the five largest agencies abandoned the original Temporary Work Employers Association and established another employers' association, which concluded a collective agreement with the General Histadrut.[53] This agreement was somewhat more generous to the workers, but it was also expected to drive some of the small agencies out of the competition and therefore to compensate the large agencies for their higher costs. The agreement was submitted to the Minister of Labor and Welfare with a request to extend it so that it could comply with the requirement for derogation in the law. Consequently, at this stage there were two competing agreements pending before the Ministry of Labor and Welfare, with no agreement as to which was the representative union; which procedure was to determine the representative union; whether there were two separate bargaining units, one in the public sector and one in the private sector, or one encompassing unit that included all the temporary work agencies and their workers; and how and where the decisions regarding these questions should be made (Ben-Israel 2002a).

The outcome of the conundrum was that, against all expectations, the equality principle, as prescribed by section 13(a) to the amended law, came into effect. The lesson to be learned from this turn of events reaffirms the conclusion drawn from the Palestinian/migrant workers comparison earlier in this chapter. As long as the agents taking part in the collective ordering and politics of labor market regulation succeed in coordinating their moves, they can achieve a high level of segmentation, even within the group traditionally taken to be the insiders. For better or worse, corporatist arrangements are unqualified and impermeable. When they include, they are characterized as being all-inclusive. When they exclude, they leave little recourse to those excluded. By contrast, pluralist arrangements are dynamic, have a problem in reaching inclusive coverage, and cannot adequately respond to broad problems of collective action. When they seek to enhance the

---

53. Collective agreement between the Association of Human Resource Providers and the General Histadrut, concluded on December 14, 2001.

rights of one side, that side cannot take their stability for granted. Yet when they seek to exclude, they may not succeed in achieving exclusion as neatly as corporatist arrangements.

From Corporatism to Pluralism—and Back?

The two components of the 2000 amendment to the Employment of Employees by Manpower Contractors Law (1996)—the nine-month rule and the equality principle—have yet to make a difference to the workers who are employed through temporary work agencies. The nine-month rule has been consistently stalled by the government and as of this writing has not come into effect. The equality principle came into effect but has not been observed very faithfully because of problems in implementation and enforcement, as well as a gradual shift from employment through temporary work agencies to the use of subcontractors who are not similarly governed by law. These outcomes reveal the fragile protection offered by pluralist arrangements because they are not backed by sufficient agreement and consensus. Absent the necessary legitimacy of the legal arrangements, the multiple agents who are involved in this matter have acted to stall the law and, when such a strategy was impossible, have tried to bypass it, litigate it, avoid it (the state and employers and their associations), and enforce it (workers and their associations, and to a much lesser extent, the state as well). This could have marked the end of the transition from corporatist agreements to pluralist juridification.

Yet the concluding section of this case study points to what may seem to be yet another revival of corporatist measures, and one which tries to compensate for the deficiencies in the corporatist measures used in 1996. At the same time that the General and the National histadruts were litigating, competing and fighting each other over who would win zero-sum control over the temporary work sector, they were also conducting discreet talks, leading to a general pact that was signed in February 2004 by the two associations of temporary work agencies that had previously signed the separate collective agreements and, in an unprecedented fashion, by the two histadruts themselves with the involvement of the Federation of Israeli Economic Organizations, which represented the employer-users of temporary work agencies. This unprecedented multiparty agreement prescribed the rights and duties of the temporary work agencies and the workers employed by them in the private sector. Like the previous agreements, it was contingent on the issuance of an extension order by the Minister of Labor to render it a proper derogation agreement as prescribed by section 13(c) of the law. For this agreement, unlike the previous rival agreements, an extension order was duly issued.[54]

---

54. The extension order was issued in August 2004.

Does this new development in the twisted story of the regulation of temporary work agencies in Israel make it necessary rethink our position on the fading of corporatism? What we see is multiple parties joining in a general collective agreement that resembles the idea of a social pact, despite its application only to the private sector. The collective agreement becomes the central regulatory mechanism for temporary work agencies and their workers through the two mechanisms highlighted in the presentation of the corporatist paradigm of labor law: the derogation arrangement and the extension order. Has, then, the departure of corporatism been prematurely announced?

The 2004 pact does not suffer from some of the problems that were highlighted with regard to the 1996 arrangement and its outcomes. The pact pulls together fragmented agents instead of encouraging competition among them. It is, in my view, an indication that the corporatist heritage is not just a long-forgotten lesson in history. The pact shows that strategies still remain open even after the massive shift in labor law and industrial relations. It defeats the argument that a move from corporatism to pluralism is inevitable and can be measured and pointed to on a linear continuum. For example, this solution could not have developed in the United States, where the institutions of corporatism are not part of the repertoire of available options.

At the same time, this outcome does not negate the general transformation that has taken place—and a decade of legal intervention in the governance of the temporary work agencies has also led to developments that are less common in countries that have sustained sectoral or national regulation by means of autonomous collective bargaining. For example, the Israeli story can hardly match that of Belgium, where for many years the regulation of temporary work agencies was in the sphere of ongoing sectoral collective bargaining.

This conclusion extends to other events that have taken place in Israel. For example, in 2005, the secretary of the General Histadrut was elected to head the Labor Party in the 2006 elections for the Parliament. Again, this would hardly seem feasible in the United States. At the same time, it would be difficult to make an inference that this is the sign of a corporatist revival. Even the newly elected leader of the General Histadrut campaigned for raising the minimum wage in statute and not for relegating negotiations over wages back to collective bargaining. Singular and discrete episodes of pluralism or corporatism must not be taken out of the more general context.

The ongoing transformation of temporary work agencies' regulation is illustrative both of the slide towards pluralism and of the corporatist "noise" the system still carries. Taken together, the cases of the foreign workers and the workers employed through temporary work agencies illustrate the difference between corporatist and pluralist labor law. The lesson to be drawn from both examples is that excluded workers are not necessarily better off in a corporatist regime, nor do they enjoy the corporatist tendency toward equality. Even if less common, once exclusion does take place, it is more difficult to challenge. This therefore indicates that future developments in the area of temporary work agencies will not necessarily be favorable to temporary workers. The equality principle, although difficult to enforce, at least provided a strategic valve that individuals and associations could try to manipulate. The corporatist-like agreement that was signed in 2004 provides the workers employed through temporary work agencies more rights but takes away equality and shuts that valve for future contestation of rights.

Part IV

CORPORATIST LABOR LAW IN CONTEXT

Now that we have completed our journey through more than eighty years of labor law in Israel, it is time to return to the original questions posed at the end of the first chapter, namely:

1. What are the legal enabling conditions of corporatism, and what are those of pluralism?
2. How do these legal institutions come about and how do they interrelate with the industrial relations system?

Chapter 8 summarizes the findings of the Israeli case study, describing the distinction between different types of labor law. This is where the study of Israel is particularly instructive, in that a far-reaching, yet gradual, transformation of the legal system took place in a relatively short period of time. The comparison between the two phases is based on a distinction among labor law's functions, objectives, and institutions. It is argued that the emphasis must be on law's objectives as the appropriate level of analysis for comparison. A comparison of labor law's objectives in corporatist and pluralist regimes reveals the fundamental differences between the two types of law.

Chapter 9 responds to the second question by describing the relationship between the legal and the industrial relations system. It is argued that the dynamic relationship between law and industrial relations is different in the two regimes. The Israeli experience suggests that many of the norms developed in corporatist law originate in bi- and tripartite negotiations among the social partners and therefore reflect prior agreements. By contrast, pluralist law evolves from competition and disagreements and seeks to resolve disputes over power in the industrial relations system.

demonstrated to include the use of incentives, and occasionally even coercion, for membership in the corporatist associations. The most notable example in many corporatist countries is the Ghent system, which in Israel was improved by relegating health care and pensions to the jurisdiction of the trade unions.[3] Another feature is the singling out of the trade unions and employers associations from other associations—for example, by granting consultation status in political processes and legislation, establishing bi- and tripartite institutions, and by securing an autonomous sphere for the associations.[4] Third, there are rules that seek to promote centralized bargaining over local agreements. In some countries such rules may be explicit, while in Israel it was demonstrated that the endorsement of centralized bargaining was, for example, by means of relaxed rules on the representative nature of the trade unions.[5] A fourth type of legal rule is that which elevates the collective norm above contract and statute—for example, by means of derogation clauses in legislation and extension orders.[6]

By contrast, in pluralist regimes, demonstrated by Israel after 1987 as well as in other pluralist states, such as the United States, labor law is composed of legal doctrines that seek to assimilate trade unions to other associations, most notably by treating them as private voluntary associations, or political lobbyists, and by removing them from the public sphere of decision making. Decentralization is reflected in the legal emphasis on workplace bargaining, and avoidance of concentration is most obvious in legal doctrines that abstain from favoring some associations over others. Strongly related are legal doctrines that seek to advance individual rights, even if these may weaken the collective.[7] These can include fragmentation of bargaining units, the duty of fair representation that secures the rights of individuals over the interests of the group, and an opposition to union security clauses in collective agreements.[8] More generally, pluralist systems are characterized by a much stronger

3. For examples of the Ghent system in other corporatist countries see: Vilrokx and Van Leemput (1998) (Belgium); Kjellberg 1998, 101 (Sweden).

4. This method is dominant in the Netherlands (Visser and Hemerijk 1997; chapter 5); Germany (Jacobi, Keller, and Muller-Jentsch 1998, 19–20); Belgium (Blanpain 2004, pars. 742–44, 730).

5. For example, in Belgium the law provides a hierarchy of norms that places centralized agreement over decentralized ones (Blanpain 2004; Vilrokx and Van Leemput 1998, 316–18). Different institutions that serve similar objectives can be viewed in Sweden (Aldercreutz 1998, pars. 109, 474, 496, 649).

6. Derogation clauses are common in corporatist regulation. Cf. Aldercreutz (1998, par. 109) (Sweden); Jacobi, Keller, and Muller-Jentsch (1998) (Netherlands). There are also "opening clauses" in centralized collective agreements that are similar to statutory derogation clauses (Visser and Van Russeveldt 1996, 153; Thelen 2001) (Germany).

Extension orders are similarly characteristic of corporatist states. For a comparative study see EIRO (2002). It is also possible to observe voluntary extensions by employers (Weiss 2000, pars. 363–65; Kjellberg 1998, 75) (Germany). There are, however, countries in which extension orders exist but are rarely used (Austria) or do not exist at all (Sweden). In both countries there are functional equivalents that ensure a very high level of coverage.

7. Compare with the United States (Abraham 1988).

8. The law in Israel is following, with delay, a host of American doctrines, described by Colvin (1998), Rogers (1999), and Hyde (1984).

Instead, law responds to individual choice and hence prefers to accommodate individual choices over collective means. For example, in Israel, like the United States, the courts have become more lenient regarding the possibility of fragmenting bargaining units. In this, law's objective has been reversed.[12] For corporatism, a broad bargaining base is considered necessary to construct social solidarity. In pluralism, the union must maintain the ongoing, homogenous interests of its membership by nonlegal means because otherwise it will be vulnerable to lawsuits. Law does not encourage the trade unions' role in constituting the identity of the labor force.[13] It views identity as a matter of exogenous individual preferences, which unions are allowed only to accommodate and respond to.

Relational Characteristics: The Centrality of the Collectively Negotiated Norm

Corporatist law must promote the idea of self-regulation as the preferred method of regulation. Corporatism favors labor market ordering by collectively negotiated norms not merely because a group of individuals prefers it but because it is a good in itself. This good may be justified in terms of economics (e.g., demonstrating a positive link between corporatist ordering and macroeconomic measures of restraint), equality (e.g., demonstrating the relationship between corporatism and lower levels of inequality), or democracy (e.g., on the basis of deliberative democracy as a method preferred over representative democracy). Consequently, the legitimacy of corporatism rests on the state's endorsement of negotiated policymaking as the prominent method of ordering. This requires an active endorsement of corporatist structures, not merely treating the issue as an output of individuals' use of their liberties. It further requires the application of the outcomes of negotiated change to the population as a whole, for otherwise individual choices may undercut the corporatist pact.

The centrality of the collective norm is strongly linked to the objectives of centralization and concentration. The corporatist regime may prioritize some agreements—namely, the centralized ones—over others. In Israel this was done by according more relaxed rules for recognition of sectorwide bargaining. In other countries—for example, Belgium and Sweden—similar objectives are achieved by giving more weight to broad over local bargaining and to unions that are affiliated with national unions over ones that are not.[14]

By contrast, pluralist systems provide relatively simplified solutions that are based on individual liberties and voluntary choices. In a pluralist system, collective bargaining is viewed as merely an extension of individual choice,

12. On the law of bargaining units in the United States, see Colvin (1998).

13. Compare with the American dispersive nature of interests representation as described by Crain and Matheny (2001).

14. See, in Sweden, Aldercreutz (1998, pars. 109, 474, 496, 649), and in Belgium, Vilrokx and Van Leemput (1998, 316–18).

and statutory law is also perceived as the output of processes that can be understood as displaying individual preferences ("public choice"). The belief that the competition between different forms of labor market ordering is merely a matter of aggregating exogenous individual preferences eliminates much of the complexity from the law.

The distinct characteristics of collective bargaining are therefore strongly linked to the fundamental differences among the perceived nature of associations, their authority over individuals, and their relationship with the state. Corporatist law develops institutions that actively elevate the collectively negotiated norm above other types of norms. The institutions used to advance this objective are, for example, derogation clauses and extension orders. By contrast, the bottom-up, individual-oriented design of pluralist labor law precludes adopting these corporatist measures. The gradual disappearance of extension orders and derogation clauses in the new legislation brings contemporary Israeli labor law much close to American labor law and removes it from its European origins.

The Problem of Juridification in Corporatist and Pluralist Labor Laws

The various objectives of corporatist law complement one another. The first and second objectives deal with the institutional structure in which corporatist associations operate, while the third deals with the output of their interaction. Moreover, the three tasks are subject to the same internal tension. The legal enabling conditions of corporatism are, by the nature of law, a form of the sovereign's use of power to mandate, regulate, and direct private and public agents. Yet corporatist law also requires the withdrawal of the state's sovereign power in favor of self-regulation by associations within civil society. This clearly worries the state. At the same time, legislation and the recourse to legal instruments are a threat to the social partners. Legislation substitutes for their own function and can be used as a threat against recalcitrant associations. Thus, although the logic of corporatism requires the law, it also resists legalization.

Given the nature of corporatist law and its need to maneuver between the conflicting needs of the corporatist system, it is not surprising to find that the literature on corporatist systems often refers to legal intervention as an indication of the system's weakness. For example, Belgian employers' reliance on litigation to reduce strike activity during the 1980s has been described as a resort to statism (Vilrokx and Van Leemput 1998). The Swedish unions' achievements in passing far-reaching laws in the 1970s have been described as an important reason for the withdrawal of the classical Swedish system (Kjellberg 1998). Dutch reforms were often conducted under the threat of legislation (Visser and Hemerijck 1997). In the earlier chapters of this book numerous references were provided for the use of law as a threat in Israel. For example, the state used legislation to freeze wages, restrict industrial action, and intervene in the use of temporary work agencies.[15]

Juridification explains why the corporatist literature often depicts law as a villain. At the same time, all corporatist countries have relied on legal provisions to stabilize and construct the corporatist system. While centralized systems of bargaining began to appear from the end of the nineteenth century—at different periods and in different countries—all have become, at some stage, reliant on particular institutional configurations, embedded in law, which helped the corporatist project endure over time. Similarly, at the present time, the renewed strength backing corporatist structures in some European countries is the result of governance schemes that are developed at the European level and that accord corporatist tripartite institutions a formal role in policymaking (Zeitlin and Trubek 2003).

The question is therefore not, as sometimes phrased, whether there should be more law or less law. This is not a quantitative issue but rather a qualitative one—what kind of law is beneficial and what kind destructive. Some legal provisions can enhance the autonomy of the industrial relations system, while others infringe on its autonomous position.

Autonomy and juridification are the two fundamental elements of corporatism's ambivalence regarding law. Autonomy is displayed by the withdrawal of intervention in the associations' internal affairs and in the norms developed by the bargaining partners. Direct intervention in the associations' internal affairs, as occurred in the United Kingdom in the 1980s (Davies and Freedland 1993), is uncommon in corporatist regimes. Respect for the associations' autonomy is sometimes formally recognized in the law (e.g., the German constitutional principle of *Tarifautonomie*), and at other times, as was the case in Israel, it is simply an inherited tradition of passive nonintervention. Intervention in the content of bargaining does occur, even with regard to core issues such as wage determination (e.g., Belgium, Netherlands, and Sweden—at different periods), but it is regarded as a retreat from corporatist premises. Autonomy is also displayed in processes of consultation prior to lawmaking. Corporatist lawmaking is characterized by prior consultation with the social partners and avoidance of legislation against the interests of one or more of the bargaining parties. Again, prior consultation may appear as a formal requirement in legislation or as a matter of practice and custom.[16]

By contrast, the flourishing industry of writing statutory labor standards is the cornerstone of pluralist legal systems. In contemporary Israeli labor law, as in the United States, law has become immensely juridified. On the basis of the analysis of juridification offered in chapter 6, this means more than merely having a legal rule in place. The full meaning of juridification assumes a detailed

15. See chapter 6.
16. The clearest example of a formal requirement for prior consultation can be seen in the Swiss constitution.

legal doctrine, frequent use and reliance on legal strategies, and the legal rule's priority over alternative industrial norms. It should also be reemphasized that the substantive norm itself can be in favor of one party or the other, but that in itself is not a characteristic of pluralist labor law. The essence of juridification is the belief that a correct prescription of rights and obligations, and the ongoing supervision of these legal rights' implementation, can create the necessary balance of powers between workers and their employers. It is all about "getting the legal rule right." The argument is therefore that pluralism is associated with juridification as a social phenomenon and not with any one particular end norm.

9 The Rule and Role of Law in Industrial Relations

What makes labor law corporatist law or pluralist law? In chapter 8, the different objectives of the two types were outlined, and the corresponding legal institutions were demonstrated. However, are these enabling conditions of an industrial relations system (corporatist or pluralist) or the outcomes of the system? Is law necessary to create and construct industrial relations or merely its output?

The literature that compares corporatism and pluralism, as well as related bodies of literature that distinguish between centrally managed economies and liberal market economies (Soskice 1999), repeatedly emphasizes that *institutions matter*. Among these institutions, legal institutions play an important role. The rule of law may inhibit economic transformation, as various institutional designs are constitutionally entrenched, morally and politically protected, or simply difficult to legislate (or litigate) away. Law is therefore an important institutional factor that determines the range of options open for interaction between and within the social and economic systems. Law is also an institution that is being constantly changed and designed to accommodate transformation. Big or small, desired changes eventually require adjustments in the law. It therefore stands at both ends of transformation: it governs the process and is the outcome of the process.

There is, however, too little discussion of law in itself in the industrial relations literature. At times it is considered merely a reflection of political processes or of the bargaining between the parties to collective bargaining. According to this view, law may be nothing more than a mirror of the electoral processes that shape the political economy, or of the bargaining parties' relative bargaining power. At other times, law is treated as an exogenous factor that defines the contours of the bargaining partners' strategies: a "background condition." It is particularly useful for explaining behavior, and in a simplistic analysis it can be assumed that social processes mirror the law. Whichever view the writer adheres to, law tends to be a black box that is not sufficiently open to analysis, despite the trivial assumption that it is there, and that legal variations are probably important.

Despite the intrinsic limitations of a case study in providing a broad picture of trends and influences, it nevertheless has an advantage when one needs to answer questions of causality. A case study can obviate the need to determine whether legal arrangements are a dependent or independent variable to be fitted into a regression analysis. They can be both a cause and an outcome. This was clearly observed throughout this book. In some stages, laws originated from prior deliberations by the trade unions and employers' associations. Other times, legislation was used to empower one side against the others or even to increase the state's control over labor and employers. Similarly, the Labor Court was shown to be an institution that evolved from the bargaining parties, and its structure was intended to reflect that of the industrial relation system. It sought to devise active methods to entrench the corporatist system. However, at later stages, the Labor Court became more independent and autonomous and was expected to resolve the disputes that could no longer find their resolution outside the courtroom. The Israeli experience suggests the ongoing process of dual causality, in which law and society intermesh.

To make the relationship between law and industrial relations more explicit, this chapter ties together several bodies of literature. The first consists of the classical industrial relations literature. A discussion of John Dunlop's basic model, which constituted much of the modern literature on industrial relations, demonstrates the multiple roles that law plays in the study of industrial relations. In the second part of the chapter, the ambiguity of law's position in the industrial relations schema is compared with diverse bodies of thought in the "law and society" writings. The discussion demonstrates how the sociolegal analysis supports both the constitutive and the reflective roles of law that appear in Dunlop's model of the industrial relations system. To refute the notion that either the legal or the industrial relations system serves as a natural point of departure for this complex relationship, particular attention is paid to the literature on reflexive labor law. Like Dunlop's model, this is fundamentally a systems approach, yet it has the advantage of placing law and industrial relations side by side on an equal footing, without hierarchy. To complete the discussion yet a third element must be added. While the jurisprudential writings and the systems analyses try to abstract the system model from the local nature of politics, society, and economy, in the third part of this chapter I argue that the two roles of law play out differently in corporatist and pluralist regimes. The different weight assigned to law's roles in the two types of regime is actually part of the fundamental difference between corporatist and pluralist labor law. That is, not only are corporatist and pluralist labor laws different in *content*, but they are also different in *role*. The reflective role of law is more dominant in corporatist regimes, while the constitutive role of law is more important for pluralist regimes.

The Legal and Industrial Relations Systems

The basic, albeit often challenged, conceptual framework of industrial relations is still the model provided by John Dunlop in *Industrial Relations Systems* (1993).[1] The model holds that the industrial relations system is a distinct social-economic system that is composed of dynamic interactions among three groups of agents—workers and their associations, employers and their associations, and the state. These agents produce norms and rules that govern employment. Their interaction takes place against a background of several variables—technology, the design of markets, and power relations in society at large. The system is kept intact by ideology and shared norms.

What is the role of law in Dunlop's industrial relations system framework? Law seems to be everywhere: it is part of the rules the system manufactures, it is part of the dynamic interplay between the parties, and it is also part of the background norms. Despite its multiple positions in the system, its precise role in the overall scheme is fuzzy. This perhaps can be attributed to Dunlop's view that "[d]ifferences in form, private or public, may be of concern to students of law, but they cannot be the primary interest of attempts to treat industrial relations more analytically" (Dunlop 109–10).

In Dunlop's account, the legal system is not really viewed as a distinct social system. It is intertwined in the industrial relations system. He aptly notes (15–17, 51–53) that negotiations and bargaining in the industrial relations system take place not only between the employers' and workers' sides of the triangle but also at the state level—whether in the process of legislation, executive action, or even in the courtroom. Throughout the book, Dunlop supports this view with examples; thus he notes the social partners' role in establishing a specialized industrial tribunal (109) and points out that the legislation that was devised for the railroad sector in the United States was influenced by the employers' and unions' involvement in the legislative process (55–56). Dunlop's theory presents two central premises: (1) law is the output of negotiations among the participants in the industrial relations system, and (2) law is one type of rule the system produces, others being a range of written and unwritten norms of practice, routines, systems of pay and compensation, and the like. While these two premises are in my view important, and are very realistic in their portrayal of law, they also require further clarification.

First, it is true that law is not the sole institutional arrangement for codifying binding and semibinding norms. This point has been well developed in the

1. Accounts of industrial relations, even with a specific focus on law, were already in print when Dunlop wrote, starting with the pioneering work of Beatrice and Sidney Web, as well as studies by scholars who were identified with the Wisconsin school (cf. Commons and Andrews 1936). However, many of the early writings in industrial relations were strongly tilted towards praxis.

institutional legal writing as well (cf. Ellickson 1991). At the same time, there is still a need to distinguish between law and other forms of norms making. Take, for example, Dunlop's discussion of the British industrial relations system, where he states that "rule-making is determined in some industries by voluntary private collective bargaining, in other industries by publicly established wage councils, and in all others by joint industrial councils. . . . While these institutional variants are of interest for some administrative and historical purposes, they tend to obscure the unity of the British industrial relations system" (60). Again, this is an important point in the sense that it indicates that similar objectives can be reached by different types of institutions. However, conflating the various institutions into one because they are all designed to advance the same function is also very limiting. Consider, for example, the transformation in the minimum wage legislation in Israel that has been studied here. While minimum wage has existed for many years, it was regulated until 1987 in collective agreements and after 1987 in statute. This change was chosen here as a landmark that designates the transformation of the Israeli industrial relations system and labor law. The seemingly similar outcome conceals considerable difference in the method according to which the norm is made. Dunlop's statement implies that the relevant question is whether wages are regulated. An important dimension that gets lost in this focus is, who regulates the wage norm, and how? In my view, a system in which the norm is established in industrial negotiations and a system in which it is established in political negotiations are very different systems.

Second, it is an important observation that the various agents of the industrial relations system are engaged in the process of making law. Again, this is a progressive reading of law in its social context and one that defies notions of legal positivism. At the same time, Dunlop also views law as an exogenous variable and part of the given background conditions for the understanding of the industrial relations system. Dunlop explains that, like all systems-oriented explanations, his too takes some elements as given. "Public policy" is part of the elements he holds to be exogenous. For example, in an anecdotal reference to the situation in Israel, Dunlop notes that

> the status of workers' organizations in respect to management in different national industrial-relations systems is also reflected in the functions described for the union. . . . In some countries these functions are very narrow, while in others they constitute a very wide range of duties. Among those countries with the widest functions for workers' organizations is Israel, where they developed activities which affect nearly every phase of the social and working life of the people. (1993, 112)

Yet, on the basis of the study presented in this book, is it fair to describe the Histadrut's function and position in society as a "public policy" that helps to explain the industrial relations system? Or is it an output of continuous negotiations, which ensured that the legislation of labor law would help to entrench and expand the role of the Histadrut in public policy?

A related issue emerges from Dunlop's later works with several colleagues (Kerr et al. 1960). In their book the authors suggest that over time we should expect to see a convergence of industrial relations systems. This point is somewhat downplayed in later writings—for example, in Dunlop's opening comments to the 1993 edition of his *Industrial Relations Systems*. Yet there are others who not only predict convergence but also argue that they have seen it. These claims are usually made by those who observe the triumph of a growing market economy and of the decentralization, privatization, and increased flexibility of the labor market. Superficially, the Israeli system may seem to fit in with this diagnosis. The decline of unions and growing liberal thrust of public policy in a country that was once presented as an idiosyncratic model of social-democratic corporatist policy is an obvious demonstration of convergence. However, on closer examination the Israeli experience cannot be explained by a simple theory of convergence. In fact, it demonstrates how important historical legacies, traditions, and norms are to the development of law and hence also of the industrial relations system. The study of the peculiarities of the Israeli legal system actually demonstrates responses that diverge from the "typical" corporatist and pluralist systems. This was aptly demonstrated in the discussion of temporary work agencies in chapter 7. The importance of law, the differences in legal institutions, and the fact that these differences both reflect distinct industrial relations systems and constitute different strategies for adaptation and change all suggest that the working hypothesis should actually be divergence.

What useful components, then, can be taken over from Dunlop's system theory? Despite the many critiques leveled at his practical systems approach, I consider many of his model's components to be highly useful, in line with American legal realism and its predecessors, and view some of its internal tensions as an open-code waiting for development rather than a fixed testament. Dunlop's model has the advantage of demonstrating law's multiple relationships with industrial relations—where law is both the cause of industrial transformation and strategies and an outcome.

While subsequent developments in the core literature of industrial relations have made significant advances in adding the layers missing from Dunlop's basic model, the role of law has made little progress into the theoretical scholarship of industrial relations. For example, Kochan, Katz, and McKersie (1986) emphasize the need to study the strategic choices made by the agents taking part in the industrial relations system. They also formally acknowledge that outputs become background conditions in a dynamic process that is part of the parties' strategic decision making (11). They therefore insert an important dynamic component that was missing from Dunlop's model. However, while they devote a chapter to workers' interests and refer throughout their book to unions' choices, public policy and state agencies are generally set aside. Moreover, the authors hold that "while we have explicitly noted that the legal environment has an important effect on management and union strategies, we have not sought to analyze in detail the . . . status of labor law

to seek a bridge between the two. Similarly, the recognition of a particular group in one legal context may lead other groups to seek recognition in other legal contexts. The development of new legal instruments can also encourage groups to mobilize around law. Legal action can be a high-visibility activity that attracts members, supporters, and, at the least, media attention. This can be used to raise consciousness among the public in general, but more particularly among the individuals who may want to identify with the group and support it.

The various questions dealt with in social jurisprudence maintain the dual role of law—as a reflection of social processes and as a factor that constitutes these very same processes. As McCann (1998, 98) notes:

> The many connections between law and social movements suggest a decentered, conflict oriented approach that emphasizes how legal conventions at once construct and, in turn, are reconstructed by the political struggles of social movements. In this view, law is understood as distinctive forms of intersubjective knowledge whose relative power and meaning varies among differently situated groups in different institutional contexts.

The dual causation in the study of social jurisprudence seems to sustain the schizophrenic relationship between law and industrial relations that emerged from Dunlop's model. It can be argued that the change in the subject of study, from industrial relations to law, simply reverses the causation, suggesting that industrial relations are reflective (in the study of law's impact) and constitutive (in the study of the way in which legal norms have developed) as well. However, this similarity merely underlines the existence of the dual causation and further suggests that to hold that one field simply mirrors the other because of the reflective/constitutive concepts is a misguided notion. The intricate dynamics on both sides of the equation suggest that both reflection and constitution are very different from "mirroring." In both fields of study, authors question how and when the processes take place. There are too many active agents in both spheres, refuting the idea that there is an active sphere and a passive—mirroring—sphere.

There are several ways to move beyond the issue of dual causality. For example, one way is to limit the scope of the study, that is, to choose one causal direction and mention the other in an apologetic footnote. Looking back at the study of Israel's transition, I would hesitate to dismiss one causal direction or the other. This study tells its own story and provides sufficient evidence to support both causal directions. This point is highlighted by Hunt (1993, chap. 3), who designates the dual position of law in the sociology of law as a "problematic"—that is, the framing of the problem also presents a potential solution to the problem itself. Thus, any a priori choice that singles out one system as explaining the other, or one causal direction as dominating the other, will simply determine the appropriate answers in advance. The avoidance of disciplinary barriers and bracketing of some causal directions are made possible by an extensive case study that can inform very different perspectives simultaneously.

Consider, for example, the simplicity and beauty of the assumption that labor law mirrors the industrial relations system. If we were to adopt such an explanatory framework, the story would state that labor law developed in a manner that mirrored the Histadrut's strong position in society and its ties to the governing party. As the Histadrut lost its power and the Labor Party lost its role as the leading party in government, employers' interests as well as those of the center-right wing governing party took over and shifted law away from corporatist bargaining. This is indeed a compelling story, but for the fact that it does not conform to the various examples outlined throughout this book. Labor law did not simply shift from a prolabor to a probusiness stance. Significant parts of the new labor law were actually prolabor. More generally, the shift from the old to the new labor law indicates that it is wrong to assume that prolabor and probusiness are merely two sides of a unidimensional continuum. Sometimes law has been more protective of one group and downplayed its protection of another; sometimes law has compensated for labor's declining power; quite rarely the protections of labor law have been removed because labor could no longer secure the legitimacy and support for prolabor rules; sometimes the norm remained the same (as in the law of minimum wage and the law of dismissals), but the process that led to the norm changed dramatically, thus suggesting future differences in the norm and in its implementation.

Even if law reflects the industrial relations system or any other set of social interactions one deems relevant, it certainly does not mirror a simple balance of power. This has been demonstrated most clearly, for example, with regard to law's role in exacerbating the emergence of pluralist structures of interests representation. As demonstrated, the dwindling promise of corporatism and the recognition of discrimination have opened up efforts to further generate gains for marginalized groups in labor law. The spillover effects of the emerging constitutional bill of rights in Israel have all had an impact on the emergence of pluralist associations and a growing awareness of social movements. Legal strategies have also been used as a way of displaying activism and generating self-awareness among individuals and communities. They have therefore been useful, when successful, not only for the group's cause but also for its self-identity. Leaving out half of this evolutionary cycle by subscribing only to "reflection" is a choice that assumes the priority of one over the other. Observing the Israeli study as a whole, I believe the evidence defies such choices.

To resolve the problem concerning the multiple roles law and industrial relations play in explaining each other's development, it is necessary to place them on an equal footing in terms of importance. Toward this end it is useful to incorporate yet another perspective—namely, that of reflexive labor law.

Reflexive Labor Law

Perhaps the most explicit reference to the relationship between law and industrial relations within the framework of a systems analysis, or even generally perhaps, is in the literature on autopoiesis and reflexive law. Based on Niklas Luhmann's (1985, 1995) work, followed most notably by that of Gunther Teubner (1993) in legal scholarship, the theory of autopoiesis develops the systems theory in a manner that provides a framework for broadly analyzing the relationship among social and economic systems and, for our purpose in particular, between the legal system and other systems (Přibáň and Nelken 2001). This view holds that social, economic, and legal systems are separate and self-reproducing.

In a strict sense, a self-regulating system is one that seeks closure from other systems. It is engaged in self-reference, uninterested in its effects on other systems, and receives no input from others. Such a view of closure would contrast strongly with Dunlop's analysis, which sees law intertwining with the industrial relations system in numerous ways. However, a strict closure of systems is also complemented by a cognitive openness. Moreover, systems, even if separate, seek their own autonomy from others. Autonomy may imply not strict separation but also recognition and support from other systems. Closure is therefore associated with both independence and relatedeness. Systems are not detached one from the other but coexist with each other, although the emphasis of the literature on autopoiesis is on the internal self-constitution of each system.

In a more general context, Teubner (1993, 2001b) further explains the relationship between law and other systems by the term "structural coupling." In his view, legal and economic systems are separate, and although they interact it is wrong to assume either one or the other as a dependent or independent variable:

> Binding arrangements do not create a new unity of law and society, unified socio-legal operations, or common socio-legal structures. While their events happen simultaneously, they remain distinct parts of their specific discourse with a different past and a different future. The only condition for their synchronization is that they need to be compatible one with the other. . . . [T]here is no unilateral determination of the direction in which the change of the other side will take place. Their interrelation cannot be described as institutional identity. It is equally wrong to describe it as causal dependency between an independent and dependent variable. . . . [A] binding arrangement, tying law to a social discourse, does not develop in one single historical trajectory but in two separate and qualitatively different evolutionary paths of the two sides which are reconnected via co-evolution. (2001b, 435–36)

The coexistence of closure and openness is of particular significance for the legal system, which is not only self-regulating but also formally entrusted with regulating other systems. The legal system, like others, seeks to advance its own legitimacy. To that end, it must also respect the autonomy and power of other systems. The extent of regulation is therefore an outcome of the balance of legitimacy and autonomy (ends) and the choice of legal instruments (means).

When observing the implications of autopoiesis with regard to the coupling of labor law and industrial relations, it is important to bring in an extension of the general theory—namely, the concept of reflexive labor law (Rogowski and Wilthagen 1994; Rogoswski 2001). The literature presenting the concept of reflexive labor law points out, for example, the unique characteristic of collective labor law, which must respect the collective agreement as an independent instrument of social regulation. Law on collective bargaining must be aware that industrial relations constitute a "full blown societal system" (Rogowski 2001, 183). Porcher (1994) notes the unique nature of the labor courts and other measures used for labor-dispute resolution that are derived from the particularities of labor disputes themselves. These writers not only indicate the tension between juridification and reflexivity but also demonstrate how deregulation fits within the general legitimacy-autonomy framework. This framework aids in highlighting necessary trade-offs in regulatory trends—whether between the need to provide security to employees and flexibility to employers or between finely crafted rules and legal simplicity.

It seems to me that other than the leading framework chosen to understand the Israeli system—that of the transition from corporatism to pluralism—the reflexive labor law framework is the most helpful for analyzing the changes that have taken place in Israeli labor law. The latter framework introduces the law into the changes in a political economy in a manner that recognizes law as a separate system but not as isolated as legal positivists would assume. For analysis that focuses on the legal rule, the reflexive labor law framework extends beyond legal positivism, which assumes that law is merely a closed system of communication. The legal system is aware of other systems around it, and the needs of the legal system are defined much more broadly than the positivist quest for internal legal coherence. For analysis that focuses on industrial relations, the reflexive labor law succeeds in breaking the assumption that law is an exogenous factor or a "black box."

Despite its advantages, the notion of reflexive labor law still requires the juxtaposition of one additional framework. While the various systems analyses are general in their observation of the relationship between the systems, and hence comply with the jurisprudential effort to abstract and universalize, the Israeli study suggests that different levels of insularity, reflexivity, and respect for autonomy can be matched to different types of industrial relations systems. In essence, what is still missing is a distinction that matches different types of law and law's different roles to different types of industrial relations systems (Teubner 2001a, 29–30).

How can the concepts of autopoiesis and reflexive labor law be helpful in identifying differences between production regimes? Before I turn to the literature on production regimes, it is useful to review the relevant evidence from the previous chapters. The legal system in Israel was always tied to the industrial relations system, but in the corporatist phase the needs and interests of the two systems were more aligned than they were in the later pluralist phase. The legal system reflected prior agreements between the agents of the industrial relations system and refrained from lawmaking that was not consistent with those agreements. This ensured that the law was supportive of, and even actively maintained, the separate and autonomous existence of an industrial relations system. The legal system resisted the legalization of norms that were not derived from collective norms. It developed measures, most notably extension orders, that kept a strong link between the industrial origin of the norm and its legal appearance. The legal system preserved the rhetoric of the industrial relations system instead of disputing it. Legal arrangements were kept to a minimum, derogation by collective agreements was made possible, and policy disputes were transferred to the Labor Court, which was entrusted with the task of speaking with a different voice than the rest of the judicial system. Thus, during the corporatist phase, the reflective role of labor law was relatively strong. The constitutive role, or the "enabling conditions of corporatism," was primarily to be found in the legal infrastructure for collective bargaining (the metalevel of labor law), but even this role was mostly based on prior agreements concluded outside the Parliament.

By contrast, since the inception of the pluralist phase, the law's reflective role has been suppressed. The industrial relations system gradually lost its internal cohesion and set of shared communications. To the extent that law was reflective, it reflected only the process of strategic and adversarial attempts made by multiple parties to conquer the legal terrain. Given the relatively intensive, erratic, and uncoordinated efforts to influence the law, this reflection was imperfect. Legal "achievements" multiplied, interacted with one another, and over time shifted the center of action from industrial relations to law. There was no well-ordered agenda for transformation. The separation between the legal and industrial relations systems grew larger over time, and the legal life developed an independent existence. This has been seen most clearly in the fact that constitutional discourse has surpassed other frames of reference and become one of the dominant social schemes. Law has become much more explicit about what should be done, more reliant on the basis of its own values, and more constitutional (and hence, seeking to govern), and its outcomes have become less expected. Generally, law no longer seeks to preserve the modes of communication that were typical of the extralegal industrial relations system. On the contrary, the process of juridification has colonialized other spheres, including that of industrial relations. The legal system has grown in importance at the expense of the industrial relations system. Thus, in the pluralist phase the law has had a stronger constitutive role. As will be argued in the following section, these differences between the two phases are not coincidental but reflect two different clusters of the law/society coupling.

Distinguishing the Role of Law in Different Political Economies

The Corporatist and Pluralist Equilibriums

The discussion thus far has treated the relationship between law and industrial relations in general terms, abstracting from the particular features of one regime or another. At the same time, the transition that has taken place in Israel and the far-reaching implications it has had for the country's labor law suggest that the relationship between law and industrial relations must be sensitive to the prevailing regime of production. Moreover, these changes must also account for the process of transition itself. Is law being "moved" from one position to another, or is law the "moving force"?

The current literature clearly distinguishes two distinct clusters. These can be designated as centrally managed economies and liberal market economies (Soskice 1999), liberal and nonliberal economies (Streeck and Yamamura 2001), different regimes of regulation (Boyer 1990), and the related typology for welfare regimes (Esping-Anderson 1990). These distinctions have evolved from different disciplines, respond to different questions, and may sometimes be at odds with one another on theoretical grounds. There is, however, a great deal of overlap among them, particularly when the distinction maintains only two clusters. In general, the clustering corresponds to that used throughout this book, that is, on the basis of the distinction between corporatist and pluralist systems of interests representation.

These distinctions tend to be based on the institutional design of the political economy. It is also emphasized throughout the literature that institutions are socially embedded in history, culture, and social norms (Granovetter 1985; Holingsworth and Boyer 1997). While there is a separation between different branches of government, and within society, the evolution of institutions is path-dependent. Thus, new institutions encompass within their design (form), and in the norms they produce (substance), much information on the past and on the society within which they are embedded. Moreover, the reference to production regimes continues to place emphasis on the fact that institutions in each regime cannot be treated in isolation, as they are all mutually reinforcing ("institutional complementarities").

Just as in industrial relations, while legal institutions are mentioned throughout the literature discussing the "varieties of capitalism," the study of law is often left out. This may be a result of the continued disciplinary division of labor suggested by Dunlop, whereby legal matters are best left to law students. It may also be a result of the growing emphasis on the firm (Hall and Soskice 2001) as the major unit of study. Yet other segments of the literature fill this gap by asking explicit questions about the evolution of capitalism's varieties (Streeck and Yamamura 2001; Thelen 2004), integrating history, culture, and social norms into the understanding of institutional diversity.

How does law fit into the analysis of diverse models of capitalism? As noted earlier, differences are the most clear when comparing the law's objectives rather than its functions or particular institutions. In liberal regimes, where more legal emphasis is placed on statutory regulation and the courts, there is a greater need for individual-based explanatory frameworks. Public choice theory can account for electoral influence on the legislature, and similar modeling of judicial preferences may also apply to the study of judicial decisions. These tools in themselves, however, are not sufficient to help us understand the legal design of corporatism (Kitschelt et al. 1999). The rules that govern the corporatist relationship are more enduring and more deeply embedded in social institutions. This may not require abandoning rational choice theory, but it does require integrating it into a more extensive understanding of social and historical norms (March and Olsen 1989; Hall and Soskice 2001). Whether such integration is sufficient to capture differences is a contested issue, and in this book I have taken a more historical view of how change came about.

To understand the different role of law in relationship to the industrial relations system, it is important to emphasize the evolution of legal norms and institutions and how these affect or are affected by changes in the industrial relations system. Clearly, in both pluralist and corporatist (centrally managed/ liberal) regimes some observations are similar. It seems that law in itself can hardly suffice to explain the evolution of the systems to begin with. Corporatist regimes are traditionally associated with the historical evolution of states of war or other periods of surging national spirit. The Israeli case is merely another variation, as there the corporatist institutions rest on the foundations of the Zionist state-building project prior to statehood. After the social institutions have gathered power, a competition for hegemony usually takes place among several discourses and social ideologies (Lehmbruch 2001). Into this process law may be invited, but law is more generally required when the competition is decided and the winners' gains have to be secured. Law is therefore not the trigger of events but a more developed stage in social competition. On the basis of the literature surveyed here, it can also be argued that changes in law and changes in industrial relations are interrelated but not one and the same, and certainly do not mirror each other (Teubner 2001a). Both sides are actively and dynamically changing, and neither corresponds to the passive image of a mirror. However, between evolution and change, it is possible to describe two states of equilibrium.

In a *corporatist equilibrium*, the initial quest for corporatist solutions is based on preexisting social structures (e.g., professional guilds) and social incentives that support centralization and concentration in interests representation (e.g., the need for national unity in the face of war). As was demonstrated throughout this book, in Israel the pooling of interests and the creation of a centralized, highly coordinated system of social bargaining are not things that can be sustained over time merely by voluntarism. It is necessary to overcome individual interests and those of factions or small groups, as well as to occasionally compromise the interests of large groups in the process of national-level negotiations. The Israeli case demonstrates that corporatist stability requires legal support. This is one of the enabling conditions of corporatism, with which this book began. The legal response must target labor law's metalevel first and foremost. It impacts the identity of the social partners (playing gatekeeper), grants autonomy to the bargaining agents, and aids in alleviating the position of the collective norm. In addition it delineates processes for making further legal norms (legislates on how to legislate) and makes decisions that affect the resolution of labor disputes (legislates on how to adjudicate).[3] It establishes or formalizes the bi- and tripartite institutions necessary for the smooth functioning of the corporatist pact (legislates on how to formulate labor market policies). The formative legal response is part of the constitutive role of law. However, this role is limited in scope. Law is mostly structural (concerned with designing institutions). It may be minimal in size, but its rules are of crucial importance. At the outset, the metalevel of labor law must engage in the internal contradictions of law in relationship to corporatist industrial relations. Law is necessary, but it must secure the autonomy of the social agents from legal intervention. The autonomy expected from law is also in tension with law's gatekeeper objective (reducing competition and friction among representatives of social interests) and the active extension of collective norms to the labor market as a whole.

Once the metalevel of labor law has been adjusted to uphold the institutional design of the corporatist system, equilibrium emerges. The social partners are accorded a generous autonomy; they devise their own norms, which are then applied to a broad segment of the population; and they also decide, or at least influence, the decision as to when broadly applicable norms should be translated into law. As long as the industrial relations system sustains its autonomy and succeeds in generating solutions to its internal conflicts by reference to its own terms, the legal system remains for the most part reflective of industrial relations. On balance, in the corporatist equilibrium the reflective role of law is more dominant than its constitutive role. This should be viewed as one of the characteristics of corporatist labor law. It is a reflection on the role of law that is derived from outside the legal system, yet it is also tightly linked with the legal discourse of corporatist labor law as viewed from within that system.

The evolutionary story of the corporatist and pluralist systems begins with the same competition over a discursive hegemony. In a *pluralist equilibrium,* the competition does not result in the granting of priority to centralized, concentrated, or coordinated solutions. There are many reasons for this, including even legal disincentives or discouraging legal responses toward coordinated attempts. However, even if the law plays a role, it seems difficult to account for

---

3. As has been demonstrated in this study of the Israeli experience, the legal system itself should not be viewed as a monolithic entity, as there are also interactions between the legislature and the judiciary, including acts of mutual recognition, assertions of autonomy and independence, and rivalry over spheres of competence.

the competition over meaning solely in terms of legal rules. The fact that a corporatist discourse cannot prevail in the competition for shared social meaning necessarily leads to the fragmentation of ideas and interests representation. As in the corporatist equilibrium, law has a constitutive role. It must erect a system of interests representation and collective bargaining. As in corporatist labor law, the most important aspects of the newly founded law lie at labor law's metalevel. Here, too, labor law must face internal contradictions, although these are different from those that pervade corporatist labor law. In a pluralist system, the law must deal with the pressure of a pluralist system to place the individual at the center. Hence, individuals are represented by unions, by other associations, or as individuals—according to their personal preference. Given problems of collective action that pervade the labor market, particularly the labor side of the labor market, labor law must move beyond the negative liberty of the freedom to associate and constitute the necessary institutions for collective bargaining, but the collective and the individual remain in tension. The solutions here seek to mediate between the individual, as the central moral agent, and the various collectives. ·

Once solutions to the internal tensions of the pluralist system are devised, an equilibrium emerges. The pluralist system is agnostic (at least on paper) with regard to any association that individuals may wish to join. Yet the refusal to pool interests and the equal treatment accorded to all associations, as well as to substantive claims of the groups they represent, leave open a less expected path, in which the legal rule is something over which associations compete. Labor law is relatively weak at the metalevel. However, at the level of end norms—whether these distribute between labor and employers or among the workers themselves—labor law can be weak or strong, intensive or loose, protective of labor or of employers. Strategic lobbying and adjudication are therefore more developed and play a more important role in the process of affecting the content of the law. Law therefore doesn't mirror any single set of power relations, and it is generally weaker in its reflective capacity. By contrast, legal rules, once established, often have a greater effect on the agents in the industrial relations system. Because they have not emerged out of prior agreements, they allow new agents to emerge in response to the changes in the legal rule, and new agendas to develop. In contrast to corporatist labor law, pluralist labor law is therefore composed of a more significant constitutive element that persists also after the initial establishment of the system(s).

The centrality of law at the corporatist metalevel of labor law further accounts for why law is more entrenched in these regimes and norms tend to be more stable and foreseeable (or "sticky," others might say). First, the law is developed in part outside the conventional legislative and adjudicative processes. Second, it takes more than a simple change in elections to initiate the rewriting of labor law at the metalevel. Both the formation and stability of norms in the corporatist regime are influenced by the social institutions, not merely by voting and contracting individuals. Both of these claims are extrapolated from the study of the Israeli experience. As to the first, corporatist labor law was designed by the social partners and the state but had begun to develop even before the state was founded. Similar arguments have been made, for example, with regard to the Japanese and German systems, in which nonliberal industrial relations developed at times of postwar political instability. The social regime developed institutions that influenced the political system, which in turn provided the rules that were necessary for the social regime. Second, it is noteworthy that the dramatic political turn of events in the 1977 elections was not, in itself, sufficient to cause a major overhaul of the law. At the metalevel, corporatist labor law was too well entrenched to allow such a change. To generalize—in corporatism institutions, including associations and the norms of collective agreements, seem to precede the law, but law is then influenced by the very same institutions to ensure their reproduction and stability. By contrast, in liberal regimes law is more sensitive to electoral outcomes and labor market conditions, and there are therefore more nodes of strategic interplay and political veto points between numerous uncoordinated agents, who can pitch and toss the legal system back and forth between competing policies and interests.

Moving between Equilibriums: The Israeli Case in Comparative Context

In describing the two equilibriums, I have focused so far on the evolution of legal norms with regard to labor market regulation. The final question that should be posed pertains to the assumption of convergence: To what extent are the two systems open to transformation from one to the other? What is the likelihood that we shall yet see the corporatist equilibrium become a historic relic?

Major political transformations or incremental ones are often the result of destabilization of the production regime, caused by external factors (the global economy), internal factors (political developments), or both internal and external factors, as is usually the case with war. Often a regime will sustain its fundamental features in response to a shock, changing particular regulations without pulling the mat from under its fundamental institutions. That is, when systems are in equilibrium, both within each system and between systems, there are methods for resolving disputes, whether they are concrete industrial disputes or disputes over social policy. When shocks become too great and the system cannot adapt to the change, the fundamental institutions may change as well, in which case a change of regime is observed.

The Israeli case, for example, demonstrates what is in my view a clear tilt toward a liberal economy and away from the country's corporatist heritage, despite the absence of any single shock that can account for the change. In this, it is similar to processes that have taken place in the United Kingdom, New Zealand, and in a later stage, Australia. The systems view suggests that in order to understand the transition that has taken place in Israel, labor law clearly must be studied in tandem with industrial relations. At the same time, it should be emphasized that law also played a constitutive role in the transformation. Some have argued that, as in the United States, law had a discouraging effect on collective bargaining (Raday 2004). I would like to propose a milder version of this argument. Because a corporatist equilibrium of law and industrial relations was maintained in Israel, the dominant role of the law was reflective. The norms that developed throughout the corporatist phase were shown to have been favorable toward the active agents in the industrial relations system. I believe that the set of norms that developed was probably as good as the social partners could have wished for. Clearly it was not the ideal wish list of any one of the partners but a sustainable compromise that reflected prior agreements in a generally turbulent industrial relations system.

While it is difficult to prove the expected outcomes of a counterfactual situation, it nevertheless seems to me that one of the weaknesses of corporatist labor law was that it was paradoxically too well matched with the corporatist industrial relations system. In other words, the state was not sufficiently autonomous and removed to assess the ability of the industrial relations system to adapt to potentially changing circumstances. One example that was described in detail in part 2 was the strict adherence to the principle that the Histadrut was for all practical matters the (almost) sole representative of workers and the working class. There were hardly any unions outside it, and there were no works councils to strengthen its position in bargaining at the enterprise level. The responsiveness of the legal system to the insularity of the industrial relations system was so great that when circumstances changed and the legally entrenched agents were no longer able to respond to these changes by means of agreements, there was no longer any way to resolve disputes other than by pluralist means of law. The corporatist equilibrium became progressively distorted as incremental changes took place on the industrial relations side and pluralist measures were developed on the legal side. The law that developed from the late 1980s onward indicated a shift from the more reflective labor law typical of corporatism to the more constitutive labor law typical of pluralism. The changeover from one system to another can therefore be accounted for by change not only in the content but in the role of law as well. This is of particular importance in those instances where the content changed only slightly (e.g., the minimum wage), but the significance of the shift is better understood by the less visible change in law's role and objectives.

By their nature, case studies highlight the idiosyncratic and very local events that have taken place in the studied context. However, the Israeli situation is one that can be enriched and explained by the contrast between corporatism and pluralism, although not one that can be simplistically summarized as an inevitable product of convergence. In fact, asking what went wrong (in the institutional, not the normative sense) in the Israeli case is necessary because a host of studies argue against convergence (Ferner and Hyman 1998; Berger and Dore 1996; Wallerstein, Golden, and Lange 1997; Hall and Soskice 2001; Zeitlin and Trubek 2003). Despite the similar challenges faced by developed economies, the responses have differed in many respects—law, industrial relations, training, monetary policy, as well as matters at the margins of this study such as foreign affairs. Models today no longer look as clear as they were in the past, and perhaps they were never as clear as has been suggested by some schools of institutional comparison (including the early literature on corporatism). Depending on the level of resolution of study, it is possible to conceal such differences. Indeed, all systems today face employers' demands for greater flexibility. There is a difference, however, between the American (and now Israeli as well) method of trying to "bust the union" to remove barriers to the free use of managerial prerogatives and the pressure to include more derogation clauses in legislation and in collective agreements. The latter is not an interim step on the way to the former, and evidence of persisting institutional divergence remains. So how do we conclude our discussion of the Israeli system and its relationship to the convergence thesis? Let me propose two endings.

The first conclusion is that in low resolution the Israeli story fits in with the neoliberal convergence thesis. However, despite the short time elapsed since the transition—which makes any understanding of the present and prediction of the future tenuous at best—it seems that the history and heritage of the older system simply refuse to disappear. The repertoire of institutions that is being used still consists largely of corporatist means, such as extension orders (even if sometimes for perverse reasons). As this book nears completion, the Labor Court is weathering a governmental inquiry on its future with a large measure of success (State of Israel 2006). While it may expected to be integrated more fully into the general judiciary and lose some of its corporatist trademarks, it will remain an all-encompassing social court. The political seesaw in Israeli politics also places a question mark as to what paths will be taken in the future. Patterns that are typical of liberal systems, such as union busting (and the corresponding developments in law on the freedom of association), are matched by institutions that are typical of corporatist systems (regulation of industry by collective agreements). The corporatist-pluralist dichotomy offered here does not indicate an either/or story but two polar narratives that help in identifying institutional movement over time and comparing one system with the other.

The alternative conclusion may be that Israel did walk an all-too-long road down the pluralist path, and that for better or worse it is gradually laying its corporatist heritage to rest. Time will tell whether the Labor Court is losing what remains of the ideology that constructed it with each attack upon it. Sectorwide collective bargaining and the use of extension orders to extend employees' concessions rather than their gains are merely corporatist crumbs soon to be brushed off the table. In that case, instead of raising the convergence flag, I think it would be advisable to ask why Israel was so persistent in its shift from one system to the other, while other countries were much more successful in preserving their corporatist institutions, and some states (Ireland, Italy, Spain) have in fact adopted mechanisms of coordination and centralization that were not part of their institutional repertoire in the past. There are several answers that can be helpful in this context. For one thing, most of the

Barak, Aharon. 1989. "Judicial Review and National Responsibility—The Scope of the Supreme Court's Review over the National Labor Court's Judgments." *Hapraklit* 38:245–62. [Hebrew]

Barenberg, Mark. 1993. "The Political Economy of the Wagner Act: Power, Symbol and Workplace Cooperation." *Harvard Law Review* 106:1379–1496.

Bar-Niv, Zvi. 1974. "The Labor Courts and Their Place in the Legal and Labor Relations System of Israel." *Israel Law Review* 9:558–67.

Bar-On, Shany, and David De-Vries. 2002. "The Limits of Professionalism: Lawyers and the Shaping of the Histadrut's Commorades Tribunal in the Twenties and Thirties." *Labor, Society and Law* 8:15–42. [Hebrew]

Bar-Shira, Israel. 1929. *Labor and Employment Laws in Eretz Israel*. Jerusalem: Council of Jerusalem Workers. [Hebrew]

——. 1948. "Labor Legislation in the State of Israel." *Chikrei Avodah (Labor Research)* 2:59–78. [Hebrew]

Bar-Tsuri, Roni. 1995. "Strikes in Israel 1983–1992." *Economy and Work* 9:132–55. [Hebrew]

Barnard, Catherine. 2002. "The Social Partners and the Governance Agenda." *European Law Journal* 8(1): 80–101.

Bartram, David. 1998. "Foreign Workers in Israel: History and Theory." *International Migration Review* 32(2): 303–25.

Belous, Richard S. 1989. *The Contingent Economy: The Growth of the Temporary, Part Time and Subcontracted Workforce*. Washington, DC: National Planning Association.

Ben-Israel, Ruth. 1977. *The Collective Agreement*. Tel Aviv: Sadan Press. [Hebrew]

——. 1986a. "The Parties to a Collective Agreement." *Tel Aviv University Law Review (Iyunei Mishpat)* 12:29–76. [Hebrew]

——. 1986b. "The Political Strike." *Tel Aviv University Law Review (Iyunei Mishpat)* 11:609–24. [Hebrew]

——. 1990. "The Juridification of Labor Relations in Israel." *Labor Law Yearbook* 1:9–36. [Hebrew]

——. 1997. "Outsourcing: Employment of Workers by Temporary Work Agencies." *Labor Law Yearbook* 7:5–42. [Hebrew]

——. 2001. "The Fundamental Right to the Freedom of Association: The Legitimacy of Funding a Trade Union by Means of Agency Fees Collected from Nonmembers." In *The Goldberg Book*, edited by A. Barak et al., 141–71. Tel Aviv: Sadan. [Hebrew]

——. 2002a. "Employing Workers through Temporary Work Agencies: Questions on Bargaining Units and Representativeness in the Aftermath of the Law's Amendment." *Moznei Mishpat* 2:9–52. [Hebrew]

——. 2002b. "Israel." In *International Encyclopaedia for Labour Law and Industrial Relations*, edited by R. Blanpain. Deventer, Neth.: Kluwer.

Ben-Israel, Ruth, and Gideon Ben-Israel. 2002. "Senior Citizens: Social Dignity, Status and Representative Association." *Labor, Society and Law* 9:229–63.

Ben-Israel, Ruth, and Mordehai Mironi. 1987. "The Role of Neutrals in the Resolution of Shop Floor Disputes (Israel)." *Comparative Labor Law and Policy Journal* 9:99–111.

——. 1988. "The Role of Neutrals in the Resolution of Interest Disputes in Israel." *Comparative Labor Law and Policy Journal* 10:356–73.

Berenson, Tsvi. 1958. "A Special Tribunal for Labor Issues." *Labor and National Insurance (Avodah Ve-Bituach Leumi)* 10:30–35.[Hebrew]

Berger, Suzanne, and Ronald Dore, eds. 1996. *National Diversity and Global Capitalism*. Ithaca: Cornell University Press.

Blanchflower, David, and Richard Freeman. 1992. "Going Different Ways: Unionism in the United States and Other Advanced OECD Countries." *Industrial Relations* 31(1): 56–79.

Blanpain, Roger. 2004. "Belgium." In *International Encyclopaedia for Labour Law and Industrial Relations*, edited by R. Blanpain. Deventer, Neth.: Kluwer.

Blanpain, Roger, and Ronnie Graham. 2003. *Temporary Agency Work and the Information Society.* Deventer, Neth.: Kluwer.

Blau, Francine D., and Lawrence M. Kahn. 1995. "The Gender Earnings Gap: Some International Evidence." In *Differences and Changes in Wage Structures*, edited by R. Freeman and L. Katz, 106–44. Chicago: University of Chicago Press.

Blyth, Conrad A. 1979. "The Interaction between Collective Bargaining and Government Policies in Selected Member Countries." In *Collective Bargaining and Government Policies in Ten OECD Countries.* Paris: OECD.

Bobacka, Roger. 2001. *Corporatism and the Myth of Consensus: Working Hours Legislation in Finland in the 1990's.* Aldershot, UK: Ashgate.

Bonacich, Edna. 1972. "A Theory of Ethnic Antagonism: The Split Labor Market." *American Sociological Review* 37:547–59.

Boyer, Robert. 1990. *The Regulation School: A Critical Introduction.* New York: Columbia University Press.

Boyer, Robert, ed. 1988. *The Search for Labour Market Flexibility: The European Countries in Transition.* Oxford: Clarendon Press.

Brauer, David. 1990. "Does Centralized Collective Bargaining Promote Wage Restraint? The Case of Israel." *Industrial and Labor Relations Review* 43:636–49.

Bruno, Michael, and Sachs, Jeffrey. 1985. *The Economics of Worldwide Stagflation.* Oxford: Blackwell.

Calmfors, Lars. 1993. "Centralisation of Wage Bargaining and Macroeconomic Performance—A Survey." *OECD Economic Studies* 21:161–91.

Calmfors, Lars, and John Driffil. 1988. "Centralization of Wage Bargaining and Macroeconomic Performance." *Economic Policy* 6:14–61.

Cameron, David. 1984. "Social Democracy, Corporatism, Labor Quiescence and the Representation of Economic Interest in Advanced Capitalist Society." In *Order and Conflict in Contemporary Capitalism*, edited by J. Goldthorpe, 143–78. Oxford: Oxford University Press.

Chermesh, Ran. 1993. *A State within a State: Industrial Relations in Israel 1965–1987.* Westport, CT: Greenwood Press.

Chou, Yuan K. 2000. "The Effect of Collective Bargaining and Central Bank Independence on Inflation and Unemployment: Evidence from the OECD." University of Melbourne Department of Economics Research Paper No. 770.

Clark, Jon. 1985. "The Juridification of Industrial Relations." *Industrial Relations Journal* 14:69–90.

Cohen, Yinon, Yitchak Haberfeld, Guy Mundlak, and Ishak Saporta. 2003. "Unpacking Union Density: Membership and Coverage in the Transformation of the Israeli Industrial Relations System." *Industrial Relations* 42(4): 692–711.

———. 2004. Membership and Coverage Rates in Trade Unions: Past, Present and Future. *Labor, Society and Law* 10:15–49. [Hebrew]

———. 2005. "Employers' Membership in Employers' Association. Facts and attitudes." Ministry of Commerce, Industry, and Labor: Department of Development, Planning, and Research.

Collins, Hugh. 1989. "Labour Law as a Vocation." *Law Quarterly Review* 10:468–84.

Colvin, Alexander. 1998. "Rethinking Bargaining Unit Determination: Labor Law and the Structure of Collective Representation in a Changing Workplace." *Hofstra Labor and Employment Law Journal* 15:419–90.

Commons, John R., and John B. Andrews. 1936. *Principles of Labor Legislation.* New York: Harper & Collins.

Cox, Andrew. 1988. "The Old and the New Testament of Corporatism: Is It a Political Form or a Method of Policy Making?" *Political Studies* 36:294–308.

Crain, Marion, and Ken Matheny. 2001. "Labor's Identity Crisis." *California Law Review* 89:1767–1846.

Crouch, Collin. 1985. "Conditions for Trade Union Restraint." In *The Politics of Inflation and Economic Stagnation: Theoretical Approaches and International Case Studies* edited by L. Lindberg and D. Maier, 105–39. Washington, DC: Brookings Institution.

Danziger, Leif, and Shoshana Neuman. 2005. "Delays in Renewal of Labor Contracts: Theory and Evidence." *Journal of Labor Economics* 23:341–71.

Davidov, Guy. 2002. "Three Axes of Employment Relationships: A Characterization of Workers in Need of Protection." *University of Toronto Law Journal* 52:357–418.

——. 2005. "Enforcement Problems in 'Informal' Labor Markets: A View from Israel." *Comparative Labour Law and Policy Journal* 27:3–26.

Davidov-Motola, Sigal. 2000. "Labor Law: Annual Review." *Labor, Society and Law* 8:69–101. [Hebrew]

Davies, Paul, and Mark Freedland. 1993. *Labour Legislation and Public Policy: A Contemporary History*. Oxford: Clarendon Press.

De-Vries, David. 1999. *Idealism and Bureaucracy—the Origins of "Red Haifa."* Tel Aviv: Hakibbutz Hameuchad. [Hebrew]

——. 2000. "The Making of Labor Zionism as a Moral Community—Workers' Tribunals in 1920s Palestine." *Labor History Review* 65(2): 139–65.

Doeringer, Peter, and Michael Piore. 1971. *Internal Labor Markets and Manpower Analysis*. Lexington, MA: Heath Lexington Books.

Doron, Avraham. 2002. "Fifty Years to the Kanev Commission's Report on Social Security in Israel." *Labor, Society and Law* 8:43–65.

——. 2003. "Labor and Social Insurance Legislation: The Policies of the Palestine Mandate Government." In *Economy and Society in Mandatory Palestine: 1918–1948*, edited by A. Bar-Eli and N. Karlinski, 519–52. Beer-Sheva: Ben Gurion University Press. [Hebrew]

Doron, Avraham, and Ralph Kramer. 1991. *The Welfare State in Israel: The Evolution of Social Security Policy and Practice*. Boulder, CO: Westview Press. [Hebrew]

Dror, David, and Aryeh Shirom. 1983. *Employers Associations in Israel*. Tel Aviv: Institute for the Advancement of Industrial Relations. [Hebrew]

Dunlop, John. 1993. *Industrial Relations Systems*. Rev. ed. Cambridge, MA: Harvard Business School Press.

Ebbinghaus, Bernhard. 2004. "The Changing Union and Bargaining Landscape: Union Concentration and Collective Bargaining Trends." *Industrial Relations Journal* 35(6): 574–87.

EIRO. 1999. *Temporary Agency Work in Europe*, http://www.eiro.eurofound.ie/1999/01/study/tn9901201s.html.

——. 2002. *Collective Bargaining Coverage and Extension Procedures*, http://www.eiro.eurofound.eu.int/2002/12/study/index.html.

——. 2004. *Individual Labor/Employment Disputes and the Courts*, http://www.eiro.eurofound.eu.int/thematicfeature7.html.

Ellickson, Robert. 1991. *Order without Law: How Neighbors Settle Disputes*. Cambridge, MA: Harvard University Press.

Eshet, Ido. 2005. "On the Virtue of the Virtual Strike." *Labor, Society and Law* 11:29–51. [Hebrew]

Esping-Andersen, Gosta. 1990. *The Three Worlds of Welfare Capitalism*. Princeton, NJ: Princeton University Press.

Esping-Andersen, Gosta, and Marino Regini, eds. 2000. *Why Deregulate Labour Markets?* Oxford: Oxford University Press.

Fahlbeck, Reinhold. 2003. "Comparative Labor Law—Quo Vadis." *Comparative Labor Law and Policy Journal* 25(1): 7–20.

Farjoun, Emannuel. 1984. "Palestinian Workers in Israel: A Reserve Army of Labor." In *Forbidden Agendas*, edited by J. Rothschild, 107–43. London: Al Saqi Books.

Felstiner, William, Richard Abel, and Austin Sarat. 1981. "The Emergence and Transformation of Disputes: Naming, Blaming, Claiming." *Law and Society Review* 15:631–54.

Ferner, Anthony, and Richard Hyman. 1998. *Changing Industrial Relations in the New Europe*. 2nd ed. Oxford: Blackwell.

Finkelstein, Karen. 2003. *A Solution to Public Sector Strikes in Israel*. The Institute for Advanced Strategic and Political Studies. Policy Studies (new series) 1. [Hebrew]

Flanagan, Robert J. 1999. "Macroeconomic Performance and Collective Bargaining: An International Perspective." *Journal of Economic Literature* 37:1150–75.

Flanagan, Robert. J., David W. Soskice, and Lloyd Ulman. 1983. *Unionism, Economic Stabilization, and Income Policies: European Experience*. Washington, DC: Brookings Institution.

Forbath, William. 1991. *Law and the Shaping of the American Labor Movement*. Cambridge, MA: Harvard University Press.

Fraser, Nancy, and Axel Honneth. 2003. *Redistribution or Recognition?: A Political-Philosophical Exchange*. London: Verso.

Freed, Mayer, Daniel Polsby, and Matthew Spitzer. 1983. "Unions: Fairness and the Conundrums of Collective Choice." *South California Law Review* 56:461–525.

Freeman, Richard. 1988. "Labour Market Institutions and Economic Performance." *Economic Policy* 3:63–80.

Freeman, Richard, and Robert S. Gibbons. 1995. "Getting Together and Breaking Apart: The Decline of Centralized Collective Bargaining." In *Difference and Changes in Wage Structures*, edited by R. Freeman and L. F. Katz, 345–70. Chicago: University of Chicago Press.

Freeman, Richard, Joni Hersch, and Lawrence Mishel, eds. 2005. *Emerging Labor Market Institutions for the Twenty-First Century*. Chicago: University of Chicago Press.

Gal, John. 1994. "The Development of Unemployment Insurance in Israel." *Social Security* (Israel, English ed.) 3:117–36.

———. 1997. "Unemployment Insurance, Trade Unions and the Strange Case of the Israeli Labour Movement." *International Review of Social History* 42:357–96.

———. 2002. *A Burden by Choice? Policy Toward the Unemployed in Pre-State Palestine and Israel, 1920–1995*. Tel Aviv: Byalik. [Hebrew]

Galin, Amira. 2001. "On the Amendment to the Employment of Employees by Manpower Contractors Law: Losses and Gains." *Labor, Society and Law* 8:103. [Hebrew]

Galin, Amira, and Aryeh Shirom. 1978. *Assessment of the Labour Courts' Impact on Collective Disputes*. Tel Aviv: Faculty of Business. [Hebrew]

Galin, Amira, and Yanai Tab. 1971. "The Package Deal—A Turning Point in the Israeli Industrial Relations System." *Economic Quarterly* 18(69–70): 106–13. [Hebrew]

Garrett, Geoffrey, and Peter Lange. 1986. "Performance in a Hostile World: Domestic and International Determinants of Economic Growth in the Advanced Capitalist Democracies." *World Politics* 38:517–45.

Gavison, Ruth. 1999. "A Constitutional Revolution?" In *Towards a New European Ius Commune*, edited by A. Gambaro and A. Rabello, 517–26. Jerusalem: Hebrew University of Jerusalem.

Getenyu, Yossi. 1990. "The Legislation of the Minimum Wage Law (1987)—Important Development for Advancing Welfare Policy, or Blunt Intervention in Wages and Industrial Relations?" *Labor Law Yearbook* 1:55–65. [Hebrew]

Gidron, Benjamin, Michal Bar, and Hagi Katz, eds., 2003. *The Third Sector in Israel: Between the Welfare State and Civil Society*. Tel Aviv: Ha-Kibbutz Ha-Me'uchad. [Hebrew]

Gilbar, Gad. 1992. "The Demographic and Economic Origins of the Intifada." In *At the Core of the Conflict: The Intifada*, edited by G. Gilbar and A. Susser. Tel Aviv: Hotsaat Ha-Kibbuts Ha-Meuhad. [Hebrew]

Gladstone, Alan. 1997. Rapporteur's Report, "Legal Perspectives—The Juridification of the Employment Relationship." Proceedings of the 5th International Industrial Relations Association (IIRA), European Regional Industrial Relations Congress.

Goldberg, Menachem. 1989. "On the Scope of the Supreme Court's Judicial Review over the National Labor Court." *Hapraklit* 38:263–80. [Hebrew]

———. 1992. "The Characteristics of Employers' Associations in Labor Law." *Hapraklit* 40(3): 372–94. [Hebrew]

———. 2002. "The Protection of Employees' Privacy and the Employers' Duty of Disclosure." *Labor, Society and Law* 9:89–111. [Hebrew]

Golden, Miriam. 1993. "The Dynamics of Trade Unions and National Economic Performance." *American Political Science Review* 87:439–54.

Gorni, Yossef. 1973. *The Labor Unity, 1919–1930*. Tel Aviv: Hakibbutz Hameuchad. [Hebrew]

Gorni, Yossef, Avi Bareli, and Yizhak Greenberg, eds. 2000. *The Histadrut: From Workers' Society to Trade Union, Selected Essays on the Histadrut 1920–1994*. Sede Boker: Ben-Gurion University of the Negev. [Hebrew]

Granovetter, Mark. 1985. "Economic Action and Social Structure: The Problem of Embeddedness." *American Journal of Sociology* 91:481–510.

Greenberg, Yitzhak. 2004. *Anatomy of a Crisis Foretold: The Collapse of Labor Owned Enterprises*. Tel Aviv: Am Oved.

Grinberg, Lev L. 1991. *Split Corporatism in Israel*. Albany, NY: SUNY Press.

———. 1993. *The Histadrut Above All*. Jerusalem: Nevo. [Hebrew]

Gutwein, Dan. 2004. "Changes in the Economic Policy of the Israeli Right 1977–2003: From National Privatization to Oligarchic Privatization." *Labor Society and Law* 10:221–40. [Hebrew]

Haberfeld, Yitchak. 1995. "Why Do Workers Join Unions? The Case of Israel." *Industrial and Labor Relations Review* 48(4): 656–70.

Hall, Peter A., and David Soskice, eds. 2001. *Varieties of Capitalism: The Institutional Foundations of Comparative Advantage*. Oxford: Oxford University Press.

Harel, Gedaliahu, Shay Tzafrir, and Peter Bamberger. 2000. "Institutional Change and Union Membership: A Longitudinal Analysis of Union Membership Determinants in Israel." *Industrial Relations* 39:460–85.

Hernes, Gudmund. 1991. "The Dilemmas of Social Democracies: The Case of Norway and Sweden." *Acta Sociologica* 34:329–60.

Hicks, Alexander, and Lane Kenworthy. 1998. "Cooperation and Political Economic Performance in Affluent Democratic Capitalism." *American Journal of Sociology* 103(6): 1631–72.

Hirschl, Ran. 1998. "Israel's Constitutional Revolution: The Legal Interpretation of Entrenched Civil Liberties in an Emerging Neo-Liberal Economic Order." *The American Journal of Comparative Law* 46:427–52.

Hirst, Paul, and Jonathan Zeitlin. 1991. "Flexible Specialization versus Post-Fordism: Theory, Evidence and Policy Implications." *Economy and Society* 20(1): 1–56.

Hofnung, Menachem. 1996. "The Unintended Consequences of Unplanned Constitutional Reform: Constitutional Politics in Israel." *American Journal of Comparative Law* 44(4): 585–604.

Hollingsworth, Rogers J., and Robert Boyer, eds. 1997. *Contemporary Capitalism: The Embeddedness of Institutions*. Cambridge: Cambridge University Press.

Horovitz, Dan, and Moshe Lissak. 1977. *From Yishuv to State*. Tel Aviv: Am Oved. [Hebrew]

Howell, Chris. 1992. *Regulating Labor*. Princeton, NJ: Princeton University Press.

Hunt, Alan. 1993. *Explorations in Law and Society: Towards a Constitutive Theory of Law*. London: Routledge.

Hyde, Alan. 1984. "Can Judges Identify Fair Bargaining Procedures?" *South California Law Review* 57:415–24.

Hyman, Richard. 2001. "Trade Union Research and Cross-National Comparison." *European Journal of Industrial Relations* 7:203–32.

ILO. 1992. Report of the Director General, Appendices: Report on the Situation of Workers in the Occupied Arab Territories. Geneva: ILO.

Iversen, Torben. 1999. *Contested Economic Institutions: The Politics of Macroeconomics and Wage Bargaining in Advanced Democracies*. Cambridge: Cambridge University Press.

Iversen, Torben, Jonas Pontusson, and David Soskice. 2000. *Unions, Employers and Central Banks: Macroeconomic Coordination and Institutional Change in Social Market Economies*. New York: Cambridge University Press.

Jacobi, Otto, Berndt Keller, and Walther Muller-Jentsch. 1998. "Germany: Facing New Challenges." In *Changing Industrial Relations in the New Europe*, edited by A. Ferner and R. Hyman, 190–238. Oxford: Blackwell.

Kahn-Freund, Otto. 1974. "On Uses and Misuses of Comparative Law." *Modern Law Review* 37:1–27.

Kalleberg, Arne L. 2000. "Non-Standard Employment Relationship: Part time, Temporary and Contract Work." *Annual Review of Sociology* 26:341–65.

Kamir, Orit. 1998. "What Kind of Harassment? Is Sexual Harassment a Violation of Equality or Dignity?" *Mishpatim* 29:317–88. [Hebrew]

Kanev (Kanevski), Yitzhak. 1942. *Social Security in the Land of Israel: Accomplishments and Problems*. Tel Aviv: Workers' Health Publishers. [Hebrew]

Kaspi, Amnon, and Batya Ben-Hador. 2005. "The Virtual Strike." *Labor, Society and Law* 11:9–27. [Hebrew]

Katz, Harry C. 1993. "The Decentralization of Collective Bargaining: A Literature Review and Comparative Analysis." *Industrial and Labor Relations Review* 47(1): 3–22.

Katzenstein, Peter J. 1984. *Corporatism and Change: Austria, Switzerland, and the Politics of Industry*. Ithaca: Cornell University Press.

Kemp, Adriana, and Rebecca Raijman. 2001. "Non-State Actors and the New Politics of Labor Migration in Israel." *Israeli Sociology* 3(1): 79–127. [Hebrew]

——. 2003. "Labor Migrants in Israel." *Adva Institute Reports on Inequality*. Tel Aviv: Adva. [Hebrew]

Kerr, Clark, John T. Dunlop, Frederick H. Harbison, and Charles A. Myers. 1960. *Industrialism and Industrial Man*. Cambridge, MA: Harvard University Press.

Kitschelt, Herbert, Peter Lange, Gary Marks, and John D. Stephens. 1999. "Convergence and Divergence in Advanced Capitalist Democracies." In *Continuity and Change in Contemporary Capitalism*, edited by H. Kitschelt et al., 427–60. Cambridge: Cambridge University Press.

Kjellberg, Anders. 1998. "Restoring the Swedish Model?" In *Changing Industrial Relations in the New Europe*, edited by A. Ferner and R. Hyman, 74–117. Oxford: Blackwell.

Klare, Karl. 1978. "Judicial Deradicalization of the Wagner Act and the Origins of Modern Legal Consciousness." *Minnesota Law Review* 62:265–339.

Kochan, Thomas, Harry C. Katz, and Robert McKersie. 1986. *The Transformation of American Industrial Relations*. New York: Basic Books.

Korpi, Walter, and Michael Shalev. 1979. "Strikes, Industrial Relations, and Class Conflict in Industrial Societies." *British Journal of Sociology* 30:164–87.

Kriesi, Hanspeter. 1999. "Movements of the Left, Movements of the Right: Putting the Mobilization of Two New Types of Social Movements into Political Context." In *Continuity and Change in Contemporary Capitalism*, edited by H. Kitschelt et al., 398–423. Cambridge: Cambridge University Press.

Kristal, Tali. 2004. "The Decentralization of Collective Wage Agreements 1957–1998." *Labor, Society and Law* 9:17–42. [Hebrew]

——. 2007. "Labor's Share of National Income and the Diversification in Workers' Sources of Income." Doctoral diss., Tel-Aviv University.

Kristal, Tali, and Yinon Cohen. 2007. "Decentralization of Collective Agreements and Rising Wage Inequality in Israel." In *Industrial Relations* (forthcoming).

Lange, Peter, Michael Wallerstein, and Miriam Golden. 1995. "The End of Corporatism? Wage Setting in the Nordic and Germanic Countries." In *The Workers of Nations: Industrial Relations in a Global Economy*, edited by S. M. Jacoby, 76–100. Oxford: Oxford University Press.

Lash, Scott, and John Urry. 1987. *The End of Organized Capitalism*. Cambridge: Polity Press.

Layard, Richard, Stephen Nickell, and Richard Jackman. 1991. *The Unemployment Crisis*. Oxford: Oxford University Press.

Leader, Sheldon. 1992. *Freedom of Association: A Study in Labor Law and Political Theory*. New Haven, CT: Yale University Press.

Leary, Virginia A. 1996. "The Paradox of Workers' Rights as Human Rights." In *Human Rights, Labor Rights and International Trade*, edited by L. Compa and S. Diamond, 25–36. Philadelphia: University of Pennsylvania Press.

Leertouwer, Erik, and Jakob De Haan. 2002. "How to Use Indicators for Corporatism in Empirical Applications." CESifo Working Paper 728(4).

Lehmbruch, Gerhard. 1984."Concentration and the Structure of Corporatist Networks." In *Order and Conflict in Contemporary Capitalism*, edited by J. H. Goldthorpe, 60–80. Oxford: Oxford University Press.

——. 2001. "The Institutional Embedding of Market Economies: The German "Model" and Its Impact on Japan." In *The Origins of Nonliberal Capitalism*, edited by W. Streeck and K. Yamamura, 39–93. Ithaca: Cornell University Press.

Lewinthal, J. 1954. *Labor Law in Israel*. Tel Aviv: Joshua Chachik. [Hebrew]

Lijphart, Arend, and Markus Crepaz. 1991. "Corporatism and Consensus Democracy in Eighteen Countries: Conceptual and Empirical Images." *British Journal of Political Science* 21:235–46.

Likhovski, Assaf. 1998. "Between 'Mandate' and 'State': Rethinking the Periodization of Israeli Legal History." *Mishpatim* 29:689–721. [Hebrew]

Lindbeck, Assar, and Dennis J. Snower. 1988. *The Insider-Outsider Theory of Employment and Unemployment*. Cambridge, MA: MIT Press.

——. 2001. "Centralized Bargaining and Reorganized Work: Are They Compatible?" *European Economic Review* 45:1851–75.

Locke, Richard. 1992. "The Decline of National Unions in Italy: Lessons for Comparative Industrial Relations." *International Labor Relations Review* 45(2): 229–49.

Locke, Richard, and Kathleen Thelen. 1995. "Apples and Oranges Revisited: Contextualized Comparisons and the Study of Comparative Labor Politics" *Politics and Society* 23(3): 337–67.

Lockwood, Graeme. 2005. "Trade Union Governance: The Development of British Conservative Thought" *Journal of Political Ideologies* 10(3): 355–71.

Lotan, Giora. 1964. *Ten Years of National Insurance: An Idea and its Implementation*. Tel Aviv: Tel Aviv University. [Hebrew]

Luhmann, Niklas. 1985. *A Sociological Theory of Law*. London: Routledge.

——. 1995. *Social Systems*. Stanford: Stanford University Press.

March, James G., and Johan P. Olsen. 1989. *Rediscovering Institutions: The Organizational Basis of Politics*. New York: Free Press.

Margaliot, Sharon R. 2001. "What's Left of Our Protective Labor and Employment Law System?" In *The Goldberg Book*, edited by A. Barak. et al., 463–84. Tel Aviv: Sadan. [Hebrew]

Margalit, Elkana. 1994. *The Trade Union in Israel—Past and Present*. Tel Aviv: Ramot. [Hebrew]

Marks, Gary. 1986. "Neocorporatism and Incomes Policy in Western Europe and North America." *Comparative Politics* 18:253–77.

Marx, Karl. 1975. *Early Writings*. New York: Vintage Books.

Mautner, Menachem, Avi Sagie, and Ronen Shamir, eds. 1998. *Multiculturalism in a Jewish and Democratic State*. Tel Aviv: Ramot. [Hebrew]

McCallum, John. 1986. "Unemployment in the OECD Countries in the 1980s." *Economic Journal* 96:942—60.

McCann, Michael W. 1998. "How Does Law Matter for Social Movements?" In *How Does Law Matter?* edited by B. Garth and A. Sarat, 76–108. Evanston, IL: Northwestern University Press.

Michelman, Frank. 1981. "Property as Constitutional Right." *Washington and Lee Law Review* 38:1097–1114.

Mironi, Mordehay. 1981. "The Duty of Fair Representation." *Tel Aviv University Law Review (Iyunei Mishpat)* 8:183–223. [Hebrew]

———. 1983. "Who Is the Employer? Defining Employee-Employer Relations in Modular Employment Relations." *Tel Aviv University Law Review (Iyunei Mishpat)* 9:505–42. [Hebrew]

———. 1986. *Arbitration in Industrial Disputes*. Jerusalem: Hebrew University, Faculty of Law. [Hebrew]

———. 1990–91. "Compulsory Arbitration—Eighty Years of Controversy." *Labor Law Yearbook* (pt. 1) 1:119–42; (pt. 2) 2:129–52. [Hebrew]

———. 2004. "The Use of Legislation to Derogate Rights and Achieve Organizational Change: Aspects of Labor Law and Industrial Relations." *Labor, Society and Law* 10:269–83. [Hebrew]

Mitchell, R., ed. 1995. *Redefining Labour Law: New Pespectives on the Future of Teaching and Research*. Melbourne: Melbourne University.

———. 1998. "Juridification and Labour Law: A Legal Response to the Flexibility Debate in Australia." *International Journal of Comparative Labor Law and Industrial Relations* 14:113–35.

Moene, Karl O., and Michael Wallerstein. 1993. "What's Wrong with Social Democracy." In *Market Socialism: The Current Debate*, edited by P. Bardhan and J. Roemer. Cambridge: Cambridge University Press.

———. 1995. "How Social Democracy Worked: Labor-Market Institutions." *Politics and Society*, 123(2): 185–211.

Moene, Karl O., Michael Wallerstein, and Michael Hoel. 1993. "Bargaining Structure and Economic Performance." In *Trade Union Behavior, Pay Bargaining and Economic Performance*, edited by R. Flanagan, K. O. Moene, and M. Wallerstein, 63–154. Oxford: Oxford University Press.

Mundlak, Guy. 1996. "Inter-Union Rivalry: On the Decentralization of the Industrial Relations System in Israel." *Labor Law Yearbook* 6:219–85. [Hebrew]

———. 1999a. "Information Forcing and Cooperation-Inducing Rules: Rethinking the Building Blocks of Labour Law." In *Law and Economics and the Labour Market*, edited by G. De Geest, J. Siegers, and R. Van den Bergh, 55–91. Cheltenham, UK: Edward Elgar Press.

———. 1999b. "Power-Breaking or Power-Entrenching Law? The Regulation of Palestinian Workers in Israel." *Comparative Labor Law and Policy Journal* 20:569–620.

———. 1999c. "Social and Economic Rights in the New Constitutional Discourse: From Social Rights to the Social Dimension of Human Rights." *Labor Law Yearbook* 7: 65–108. [Hebrew]

———. 2001. "Occupational Health and Safety: The Function of Law." In *The Goldberg Book*, edited by A. Barak et al. Tel Aviv: Sadan. [Hebrew]

———. 2002. "Quasi-Political Strikes, Quasi-Political Pedagogy." *Tel Aviv University Law Review (Iyunei Mishpat)* 11:609–24. [Hebrew]

———. 2003. "Neither Insiders nor Outsiders: The Contractual Construction of Migrant Workers' Rights and the Democratic Deficit." *Tel Aviv University Law Review (Iyunei Mishpat)* 27(2): 423–87. [Hebrew]

———. 2004. *Industrial Relations in Times of Transition*. Jerusalem: Israeli Democracy Institute. [Hebrew]

———. 2007. "Litigating Citizenship beyond the Law of Return." In *Transnational Migra-tion to Israel in Global Comparative Context*, edited by Sarah Willen. Lexington Books: forthcoming.

Mundlak, Guy, and Itzhak Harpaz. 2002. "Determinants of Israeli Judicial Discretion in Issuing Injunctions Against Strikers." *British Journal of Industrial Relations* 40(4): 753–77.

———. 2003. "Between the Systems: Judicial Discretion in Issuing Injunctions Against Striking Workers." *Tel Aviv University Law Review (Iuneiy Mishpat)* 26:145–95. [He-brew]

Nachmias, David, and Eran Klein. 1999. *The Economic Arrangements Bill: Between Eco-nomics and Politics.* Jerusalem: Israeli Democracy Institute. [Hebrew]

Nadiv, Ronit. 2004. "Diversified Employment: The Internal Labor Market of External Workers." Doctoral diss., Tel Aviv University. [Hebrew]

Neuman, Shlomo. 1996. *Funding Trade Unions.* Tel Aviv: Bursi. [Hebrew]

O'Donnell, Rory. 2001. "Towards Post-Corporatist Concentration in Europe." In *Inter-locking Dimensions of European Integration*, edited by H. Wallace, 305–22. London: Pintor.

OECD. 1997. *Employment Outlook.* Paris: OECD.

Offe, Claus, and Helmut Wiesenthal. 1985. "Two Logics of Collective Action." In *Disor-ganized Capitalism*, edited by Claus Offe, 170—220. Cambridge, MA: MIT Press.

Osterman, Paul. 1993. "Internal Labor Markets in a Changing Environment: Models and Evidence." In *Research Frontiers in Industrial Relations and Human Resources*, edited by D. Lewin, O. Mitchell, and P. Sherer. Madison, WI: IRRA.

Peleg, Dov. 1997. "Reform in the Pensions System." *Social Security (Bitachon Sotsiali)* 49:97–129. [Hebrew]

———. 1999. "Organization and Control in the Social Security Institutions in Israel and Around the World (Health, Pensions and Social Security)." *Social Security (Bitachon Sotsiali)* 55:40–64. [Hebrew]

Pestoff, Victor. 1994. *Employer Organizations and Collective Bargaining.* Paris: OECD Report.

Pfeffer, Jeffrey, and James N. Baron. 1988. "Taking the Workers Back: Recent Trends in the Structuring of Employment." *Research in Organizational Behavior* 10:257–303.

Pierson, Paul. 2000. "Increasing Returns, Path Dependence and the Study of Politics." *American Political Science Review* 94(2): 251–67.

Piore, Michael. 1979. *Birds of Passage: Migrant Labor and industrial Societies.* Cam-bridge: Cambridge University Press.

Plasman, Robert, and Francoise Rycx. 2001. "Collective Bargaining and Poverty: A Cross-National Perspective." *European Journal of Industrial Relations* 7:175–202.

Pollert, Anna. 1991. *Farewell Flexibility?* Oxford: Blackwell.

Pontusson, Jonas, and Peter Swenson. 1996. "Labor Markets, Production Strategies, and Wage Bargaining Institutions." *Comparative Political Studies* 29:223–50.

Porcher, Pascale. 1994. "The Changing Role of the French Labour Courts in Employ-ment Relations." In *Reflexive Labour Law*, edited by R. Rogowski and T. Wilthagen, 249–61. Deventer, Neth.: Kluwer.

Přibáň, Jiri, and David Nelken, eds. 2001. *Law's New Boundaries: The Consequences of Legal Autopoiesis.* Aldershot, UK: Ashgate.

Raday, Frances. 1971. "A Cooling-Off Period for Israel." *Israel Law Review* 6:569–94.

———. 1983a. *Adjudication of Interest Disputes.* Jerusalem: Saker Institute.

———. 1983b. "Trade Unions—Privileges and Supervision." Tel Aviv University Law Re-view *(Iunei Mishpat)* 9:543–68. [Hebrew]

———. 1993. "The Constitutionalization of Labour Law?" In *The Changing Face of Labour Law and Industrial Relations, Liber Amicorum for Clyde W. Summers*, edited by R. Blanpain and M. Weiss, 83–108. Baden Baden: Nomos Vesl. Gel.

——. 1995. "Political Strikes and the Fundamental Change in the Organization of the Workplace." *Hamishpat* 2:159–75. [Hebrew]

——. 1998. *The Policy on Employment of Workers by Manpower Companies: The Legislature, the Courts and the Histadrut.* Jerusalem: Institute for Economic and Social Research, the General Histadrut. [Hebrew]

——. 1999. "The Insider-Outsider Position of Labor Only Contracting." *Comparative Labor Law and Policy Journal* 20(3): 413–45.

——. 2000. "Privatizing Human Rights and the Abuse of Power." *Canadian Journal of Law and Jurisprudence* 13(1): 103–34.

——. 2002. "The Decline of Union Power—Structural Inevitability or Policy Choice?" In *Labour Law in an Era of Globalization*, edited by J. Conaghan, M. Fischl, and K. Klare, 353–77. Oxford: Oxford University Press.

——. 2004. "Trade Unions and Collective Bargaining in Israel: A Look to the 21st Century." *Mishpatim* 34(1–2): 39–90. [Hebrew]

Radin, Margaret J. 1996. *Reinterpreting Property.* Chicago: Chicago University Press.

Raijman, Rebecca, and Adriana Kemp. 2002. "State and Non-State Actors: A Multi-Layered Analysis of Labor Migration Policy in Israel." In *Public Policy in Israel: Perspectives and Practices*, edited by D. Korn, 155–73. Lanham, MD: Rowman and Littlefield.

Reale, Annalisa. 2003. "Representation of Interests, Participatory Democracy, and Lawmaking in the European Union: Which Role and Which Rules for the Social Partners." NYU School of Law Jean Monnet Working Papers 15/03.

Reder, Melvin, and Lloyd Ulman. 1993. "Unionism and Unification." In *Labor and an Integrated Europe*, edited by L. Ulman, B. Eichengreen, and W. T. Dickens, 13–44. Washington, DC: Brookings Institution.

Reshef, Yonatan. 1986. "Political Exchange in Israel: Histadrut-State Relations." *Industrial Relations* 25:303–319.

Rhodes, Martin. 2001. "The Political Economy of Social Pacts: Competitive Corporatism and European Welfare Reform." In *The New Politics of Welfare*, edited by P. Pierson, 165–94. Oxford, Oxford University Press.

——. 2003. "National 'Pacts' and EU Governance in Social Policy and the Labor Market." In *Governing Work and Welfare in a New Economy: European and American Experiments*, edited by J. Zeitlin and D. Trubek, 129–57. Oxford: Oxford University Press.

Rodgers, Gerry, and Janine Rodgers, eds. 1989. *Precarious Jobs in Labor Market Regulation: The Growth of Atypical Employment in Western Europe.* Brussels: International Institute for Labor Studies at the Free University of Brussels.

Rogers, Joel. 1999. "Divide and Conquer: Further Reflections on the Distinctive Character of American Labor Laws." *Wisconsin Law Review* 1990:1–147.

Rogowski, Ralf. 1994. "Industrial Relations, Labour Conflict Resolution and Reflexive Labour Law." In *Reflexive Labour Law*, edited by R. Rogowski and T. Wilthagen, 53–94. Deventer, Neth.: Kluwer.

——. 2000. "Industrial Relations as a Social System." *Industrielle Beziehungen* 7(1): 97–126.

——. 2001. "The Concept of Reflexive Labour Law: Its Theoretical Background and Possible Applications." In *Law's New Boundaries: The Consequences of Legal Autopoiesis*, edited by J. Přibáň and D. Nelken, 179–95. Aldershot, UK: Ashgate.

Rogowski, Ralf, and Ton Wilthagen, eds. 1994. *Reflexive Labour Law.* Deventer, Neth.: Kluwer.

Rosenhek, Zeev. 1999. "The Politics of Claims Making by Labor Migrants in Israel." *Journal of Ethnic and Migration Studies* 25(4): 575–95.

——. 2000. "Migration Regimes, Intra-state Conflicts, and the Politics of Exclusion and Inclusion: Migrant Workers in the Israeli Welfare State." *Social Problems* 47(1): 49–67.

——. 2003. "The Political Dynamics of a Segmented Labour Market: Palestinian Citizens, Palestinians from the Occupied Territories and Migrant Workers in Israel." *Acta Sociologica* 46(3): 231–49.

Rowthorn, Robert E. 1992. "Centralization, Employment and Wage Dispersion." *Economic Journal* 102:506–23.

Royo, Sebastian. 2002. *A New Century of Corporatism? Corporatism in Southern Europe—Spain and Portugal in Comparative Perspective.* Westport, CT: Praeger.

Sabel, Charles. 1996. *Ireland: Local Partnership and Social Innovation.* Dublin: OECD.

Sakamoto, Takayuki. 2005. "Economic Performance of 'Weak' Governments and Their Interaction with Central Banks and Labour: Deficits, Economic Growth, Unemployment and Inflation, 1961—1998." *European Journal of Political Research* 44(6): 801–36.

Schiff, Zeev, and Ehud Yaari. 1990. *Intifada.* Tel Aviv: Schocken. [Hebrew]

Schmitter, Philippe C. 1974. "Still the Century of Corporatism?" *Review of Politics* 36(1): 85–131.

——. 1977. "Modes of Interest Intermediation and Models of Societal Change in Western Europe." *Comparative Political Studies* 10:7–38.

——. 1981. "Interest Intermediation and Regime Governability in Contemporary Western Europe and North America." In *Organizing Interests in Western Europe: Pluralism, Corporatism and the Transformation of Politics*, edited by S. Berger, 285–327. Cambridge: Cambridge University Press.

——. 1989. "Corporatism is Dead! Long Live Corporatism." *Government and Opposition* 24(1): 54–73.

Schmitter, Philippe C., and Jürgen Grote. 1997. "The Corporatist Sisyphus: Past, Present and Future." European University Institute Working Paper SPS No. 97/4.

Schnell, Itzhak. 1999. *Foreign Workers in Southern Tel Aviv-Yafo.* Jerusalem: Florsheimer Institute for Policy Studies. [Hebrew]

Schwab, Stewart J. 1993. "Life-Cycle Justice: Accommodating Just Cause and Employment at Will." *Michigan Law Review* 92:8–62.

Semyonov, Moshe, and Noah L. Epstein. 1987. *Hewers of Wood and Drawers of Water.* Ithaca: ILR Press.

Shafir, Gershon, and Yoav Peled. 2002. *Being Israeli: Dynamics of Multiple Citizenship.* Cambridge: Cambridge University Press.

Shaked, Michal. 1999. "A Theory of Prohibition of Political Strikes." *Labor Yearbook* 7:185–219. [Hebrew]

——. 2003. "Freedom of Association in Israel: Workers and the Histadrut in the Law." Doctoral diss., Tel Aviv University. [Hebrew]

Shalev, Michael. 1992. *Labour and the Political Economy in Israel.* Oxford: Oxford University Press.

Shamir, Ronen. 2000. *The Colonies of Law: Colonialism, Zionism, and Law in Early Mandate Palestine.* Cambridge: Cambridge University Press.

——. 2002. "The Comrades Law of Hebrew Workers in Palestine: A Study in Socialist Justice." *Law and History Review* 2(2): 279–305.

Shapira, Anita. 1997. "Sternhell's Accusation." In *New Jews, Old Jews*, edited by A. Shapira, 298–317. Tel Aviv: Am Oved. [Hebrew]

Sharabi, Moshe, and Itzhak Harpaz. 2002. "An Over Time Analysis of the Importance of Work Goals." *Labor Society and Law* 9:43–64. [Hebrew]

Shirom, Aryeh. 1970. "A Comparative Analysis of Strikes in Ten Industrialized Countries from 1960–1969." *Labor and National Insurance* 1970(October): 427–31. [Hebrew]

——. 1983. *Introduction to Labor Relations in Israel.* Tel Aviv: Am Oved. [Hebrew]

——. 1995. "The Israeli Health Care Reform: A Study of an Evolutionary Major Change." *International Journal of Health Planning and Management* 10:5–23.

Shirom, Aryeh, and Dan Jacobson. 1975. "The Structure and Function of Israeli Employers' Associations." *Relations Industrielles* 30:452–77.

Siaroff, Alan. 1999. "Corporatism in 24 Industrial Democracies: Meaning and Measurement." *European Journal of Political Research* 36:175–205.

Siegel, Nico. 2005. "Social Pacts Revisited: 'Competitive Concentration' and Complex Causality in Negotiated Welfare State Reforms." *European Journal of Industrial Relations* 11:107–26.

Simitis, Spiros. 1987. "Juridification of Labor Relations." In *Juridification of Social Spheres,* edited by G. Teubner, 62–113. Berlin: Walter de Gruyter.

——. 1994. "The Rediscovery of the Individual in Labour Law." In *Reflexive Labour Law,* edited by R. Rogowski and T. Wilthagen, 183–206. Deventer, Neth.: Kluwer.

Simon, William. 1991. "Social Republican Property." *UCLA Law Review* 38: 1335–1413.

Singer, Joseph W. 1988. "The Reliance Interest in Property." *Stanford Law Review* 40:611–751.

Sitkin, Sim B., and Robert J. Bies. 1994. "The Legalization of Organizations: A Multi-Theory Perspective." In *The Legalistic Organization,* edited by S. Sitkin and R. Bies, 19–49. Thousand Oaks, CA: Sage.

Soskice, David W. 1990. "Wage Determination: The Changing Role of Institutions in Advanced Industrialized Countries." *Oxford Review of Economic Policy* 6(4): 36–61.

——. 1999. "Divergent Production Regimes: Coordinated and Uncoordinated Market Economies in the 1980s and 1990s." In *Continuity and Change in Contemporary Capitalism,* edited by H. Kitschelt et al., 101–34. Cambridge: Cambridge University Press.

Standing, Guy. 1999. *Global Labour Flexibility: Seeking Distributive Justice.* Hampshire, UK: Palgrave Macmillan.

——. 2002. *Beyond the New Paternalism: Basic Security as Equality.* New York: Norton.

State of Israel. 1950. *The Commission's Report on the Planning of a Social Security System* (Kanev Commission's report). Jerusalem: Official Publication. [Hebrew]

——. 1989a. *The Report of the Committee on the Assessment of the Public Service and State Budgeted Entites* (Kuversky Committee). Jerusalem: Official Publication. [Hebrew]

——. 1989b. *The Report of the Committee on the Wage System in the Public Sector* (Zussman Committee). Jerusalem: Official Publication. [Hebrew]

——. 1991. *The Report of the Committee on the Employment of Contractors.* Jersualem: Official Publication. [Hebrew]

——. 2000. *Labour Laws.* Jerusalem: Official Publication.

——. 2006. *The Report of the Committee on Labor Courts System* (Zamir Committee). Jerusaelm: Official Publications. [Hebrew]

Sternhell, Zeev. 1995. *Nation Building or a New Society? The Zionist Labor Movement (1904–1940) and the Origins of Israel.* Tel Aviv: Am Oved. [Hebrew]

Stone, Deborah. 1989. "Causal Stories and the Formation of Policy Agendas." *Political Science Quarterly* 104:281–300.

Stone, Katherine V. W. 1981. "The Post-War Paradigm in American Labor Law." *Yale Law Journal* 90:1509–80.

——. 2004. *From Widgets to Digits: Employment Regulation for the Changing Workplace.* Cambridge, NY: Cambridge University Press.

Strasser, Rudolf, and Johannes Kepler. 1992. "Labour Law and Industrial Relations in Austria." In *Encyclopaedia for Labour Law and Industrial Relations,* edited by R. Blanpain. Deventer, Neth.: Kluwer.

Streeck, Wolfgang. 1993. "The Rise and Decline of Neocorporatism." In *Labor and an Integrated Europe,* edited by L. Ulman, B. Eichengreen, and W. T. Dickens, 80–101. Washington, DC: Brookings Institution.

——. 1995. "Neo-voluntarism: A New European Social Policy Regime?" *European Law Journal* 1(1): 31–59.

——. 1998. "The Internationalization of Industrial Relations in Europe: Prospects and Problems." *Politics and Society* 26(4): 429–59.

Streeck, Wolfgang, and Philippe C. Schmitter. 1985. "Community, Market, State—and Associations? The Prospective Contribution of Interest Governance to Social Order." *European Sociological Review* 1(2): 119–38.

——. 1991. "From National Corporatism to Transnational Pluralism: Organized Interests in the Single European Market." *Politics and Society* 19:133–64.

Streeck, Wolfgang, and Kozo Yamamura, eds. 2001. *The Origins of Nonliberal Capitalism: Germany and Japan in Comparison.* Ithaca: Cornell University Press.

Summers, Clyde. 2003. "Comparative Labor Law in America: Its Foibles, Functions and Future." *Comparative Labor Law and Policy Journal* 25(1): 115–28.

Supiot, Alain. 2001. *Beyond Employment: Changes in Work and the Future of Labour Law in Europe.* Oxford: Oxford University Press.

Sussman, Zvi. 1969. "From National to Branch Level Wage Policy." *Economic Quarterly* 64:331–41. [Hebrew]

——. 1995. "From Collective Agreements to Individual Contracts: Wages, Industrial Relations and the Histadrut." *Economic Quarterly* 42(1): 17–35. [Hebrew]

Sussman, Zvi, and Dan Zakai. 1996. "The Decentralization of Collective Bargaining and Changes in the Compensation Structure in Israel's Public Sector." Bank of Israel Discussion Papers 96.04. [Hebrew]

Symposium. 2004. "The Social-Economic Reform 2002–2003: An Interdisciplinary Perspective." *Labor, Society and Law* 10:209–361. [Hebrew]

Tamanaha, Brian. 2001. *A General Jurisprudence of Law and Society.* Oxford: Oxford University Press.

Tamari, Salim. 1980. The Palestinians in the West Bank and Gaza: The Sociology of Dependency. In *The Sociology of the Palestinians,* edited by N. Nakhleh and E. Zureik, 84–111. London: Croom Helm.

Tarantelli, Ezio. 1986. "The Regulation of Inflation and Unemployment." *Industrial Relations* 25:1–15.

Teague, Paul. 1995. "Pay Determination in the Republic of Ireland: Towards Social Corporatism." *British Journal of Industrial Relations* 33(2): 253–73.

Teubner, Gunther. 1993. *Law as an Autopoietic System.* Oxford: Blackwell.

——. 2001a. "Alienating Justice: On the Surplus Value of the Twelfth Camel." In *Law's New Boundaries: The Consequences of Legal Autopoiesis,* edited by J. Přibáň and D. Nelken, 21–44. Aldershot, UK: Ashgate.

——. 2001b. "Legal Irritants: How Unifying Law Ends in New Divergences." In *Varieties of Capitalism,* edited by P. Hall and D. Soskice, 417–41. Oxford: Oxford University Press.

Teulings, Coen, and Joop Hartog. 1998. *Corporatism or Competition: Labour Contracts, Institutions and Wage Structures in International Comparison.* Cambridge: Cambridge University Press.

Thelen, Kathleen. 2001. "Varieties of Labor Politics in the Developed Democracies." In *Varieties of Capitalism,* edited by P. Hall and D. Soskice, 71–103. Oxford: Oxford University Press.

——. 2004. *How Institutions Evolve: The Political Economy of Skills in Germany, Britain, United States and Japan.* Cambridge: Cambridge University Press.

Tomlins, Christopher L. 1985. *The State and the Unions: Labor Relations, Law and the Organized Labor Movement in America, 1880–1960.* Cambridge: Cambridge University Press.

Traxler, Franz. 1993. "Business Associations and Labor Unions in Comparison: Theoretical Perspectives and Empirical Findings on Social Class, Collective Action and Associational Organizability." *British Journal of Sociology* 44(4): 673–91.

——. 2000. "Employers and Employers Organizations in Europe: Membership Strength, Density and Representativeness." *Industrial Relations Journal* 31(4): 308–16.

Vatta, Alessia. 1999. "Employers' Organizations and Concentration: Internal Dynamics and Institutional Influence." *European Journal of Industrial Relations* 5:245–64.

Vilrokx, Jacques, and Jim Van Leemput. 1998. "Belgium: The Great Transformation." In *Changing Industrial Relations in the New Europe*, edited by A. Ferner and R. Hyman, 315–47. Oxford: Blackwell.

Visser, Jelle, and Anton Hemerijck. 1997. *A Dutch Miracle: Job Growth, Welfare Reform and Corporatism in the Netherlands*. Amsterdam: Amsterdam University Press.

Visser, Jelle, and Joris Van Ruysseveldt. 1996. "Robust Corporatism, Still? Industrial Relations in Germany?" In *Industrial Relations in Europe: Traditions and Transitions*, edited by J. Van Russeveldt and J. Visser, 124–74. London: Sage.

Wallerstein, Michael. 1990. "Centralized Bargaining and Wage Restraint." *American Journal of Political Science* 34:982–1004.

Wallerstein, Michael, Miriam Golden, and Peter Lange. 1997. "Unions, Employers' Associations, and Wage-Setting Institutions in Northern and Central Europe, 1950–1992." *Industrial and Labor Relations Review* 50(3): 379–401.

Weiler, Paul. 1990. *Governing the Workplace: The Future of Labor and Employment Law*. Cambridge, MA: Harvard University Press.

Weiss, Manfred, and Marlene Schmidt. 2000. "Germany." In *International Encyclopaedia for Labour Law and Industrial Relations*, edited by R. Blanpain. Deventer, Neth.: Kluwer.

Weiss, Rafi. 1989. "Injunctions in the Labour Courts." Master's thesis, Tel Aviv University. [Hebrew]

World Bank. 1994. *Developing the Occupied Territories and Investment in Peace*. Washington, DC: World Bank.

Yadlin, Omry. 1999. "Good Faith in Israeli Labor Law." *Tel Aviv University Law Review (Iunei Mishpat)* 22(3): 867–98. [Hebrew]

Yizraeli, Dafna, and Orly Benjamin. 2000. *Workers Employed by Temporary Work Agencies in the Public Sector as a Gender Problem in Israel*. Jerusalem: The Women's Lobby. [Hebrew]

Yonai, Yuval. 1998. "The Law about Sexual Orientation: Between History and Sociology." *Mishpat U-Mimshal* 4:531–86. [Hebrew]

Zamir, Itzhak. 1966. "Labor and Social Security." *Scriptra Hierosolymitana* 16:298–324.

——. 1968. "Labour and National Insurance Tribunal Bill 1967." *Mishpatim* 1:228–70. [Hebrew]

——. 1970. *Labor Law—Sources, Comments, Problems* (class notes). Jerusalem: Akademon Press. [Hebrew]

——. 1974. "The Law of Labor Disputes." *Israel Law Review* 9:548–87.

——. 1978. "Labor Law in Israel: New Directions." *Israel Law Review* 13(2): 138.

Zeitlin, Jonathan, and David Trubek, eds. 2003. *Governing Work and Welfare in a New Economy: European and American Experiments*. Oxford: Oxford University Press.

Ziv, Neta. 1999. "Disability Law in Israel and the United States—A Comparative Perspective." *Israel Yearbook on Human Rights* 28:171–202.

Index